Everything I Know About Love

Everything I Know About Love

DOLLY ALDERTON

FIG TREE
an imprint of
PENGUIN BOOKS

FIG TREE

UK | USA | Canada | Ireland | Australia
India | New Zealand | South Africa

Fig Tree is part of the Penguin Random House group of companies
whose addresses can be found at global.penguinrandomhouse.com.

First published 2018
007

Copyright © Dolly Alderton, 2018

The moral right of the author has been asserted

Permissions: extract on page 42, copyright © Margaret Atwood, 1996, *Alias Grace*,
Bloomsbury Publishing, plc; lines on page 83 from 'Lovesong' taken from *Crow*
by Ted Hughes (Faber and Faber, 1972), copyright © Ted Hughes, 1970, 1972;
lines on page 163 from 'Shelter from the Storm' by Bob Dylan, copyright © 1974
by Ram's Horn Music, renewed 2002 by Ram's Horn Music, all rights reserved,
international copyright secured, reprinted by permission; and lines on page 327
from 'The More Loving One' by W. H. Auden, copyright © 1960 by W. H. Auden,
renewed, reprinted by permission of Curtis Brown, Ltd

Set in 13.5/16 pt Garamond MT Std
Typeset by Jouve (UK), Milton Keynes
Printed in Great Britain by Clays Ltd, St Ives plc

A CIP catalogue record for this book is available from the British Library

ISBN: 978–0–241–32271–0

www.greenpenguin.co.uk

For Florence Kleiner

Everything I Knew About Love as a Teenager

Romantic love is the most important and exciting thing in the entire world.

If you don't have it when you're a proper grown-up then you have failed, just like so many of my art teachers who I have noted are 'Miss' instead of 'Mrs' and have frizzy hair and ethnic jewellery.

It is important to have a lot of sex with a lot of people but probably no more than ten.

When I'm a single woman in London I will be extremely elegant and slim and wear black dresses and drink Martinis and will only meet men at book launches and at exhibition openings.

The mark of true love is when two boys get in a physical fight over you. The sweet spot is drawn blood but no one having to go to hospital. One day this will happen to me, if I'm lucky.

It is important to lose your virginity after your seventeenth birthday, but before your eighteenth birthday. Literally, even if it's just the day before, that's fine, but if you go into your eighteenth year still a virgin you will never have sex.

You can snog as many people as you like and that's fine, it doesn't mean anything, it's just practice.

The coolest boys are always tall and Jewish and have a car.

Older boys are the best kind because they're more sophisticated and worldly and also they have slightly less stringent standards.

When friends have boyfriends they become boring. A friend having a boyfriend is only ever fun if you have a boyfriend too.

If you don't ask your friend about their boyfriend *at all* they'll eventually get the hint that you find it boring and they'll stop going on about him.

It's a good idea to get married a bit later in life and after you've lived a bit. Say, twenty-seven.

Farly and I will never fancy the same boy because she likes them short and cheeky like Nigel Harman and I like them macho and mysterious like Charlie Simpson from Busted. This is why our friendship will last for ever.

No moment in my life will ever be as romantic as when me and Lauren were playing that gig on Valentine's Day at that weird pub in St Albans and I sang 'Lover, You Should've Come Over' and Joe Sawyer sat at the front and closed his eyes because earlier we'd talked about Jeff Buckley and basically he is the only boy I've ever met who fully understands me and where I'm coming from.

No moment in my life will ever be as embarrassing as when I tried to kiss Sam Leeman and he pulled away from me and I fell over.

No moment in my life will ever be as heartbreaking as when Will Young came out as gay and I had to pretend I was fine about it but I cried while I burned the leather book I was given for my confirmation, in which I had written about our life together.

Boys really like it when you say rude things to them and they find it babyish and uncool if you're too nice.

When I finally have a boyfriend, little else will matter.

Boys

For some, the sound that defined their adolescence was the joyful shrieks of their siblings playing in the garden. For others, it was the chain rattle of their much-loved bike, hobbling along hills and vales. Some will recall birdsong as they walked to school, or the sound of laughing and footballs being kicked in the playground. For me, it was the sound of AOL dial-up internet.

I can still remember it now, note for note. The tinny initial phone beeps, the reedy, half-finished squiggles of sound that signalled a half-connection, the high one note that told you some progress was being made, followed by two abrasive low thumps, some white fuzz. And then the silence indicated that you had broken through the worst of it. 'Welcome to AOL,' said a soothing voice, the upward inflection on 'O'. Followed by, 'You have email.' I would dance around the room to the sound of the AOL dial-up, to help the agonizing time pass quicker. I choreographed a routine from things I learnt in ballet: a *plié* on the beeps; a *pas de chat* on the thumps. I did it every night when I came home from school. Because that was the soundtrack of my life. Because I spent my adolescence on the internet.

A little explanation: I grew up in the suburbs. That's

it; that's the explanation. When I was eight years old, my parents made the cruel decision to move us out of a basement flat in Islington and into a larger house in Stanmore; the last stop on the Jubilee line and on the very furthest fringes of North London. It was the blank margin of the city; an observer of the fun, rather than a reveller at the party.

When you grow up in Stanmore you are neither urban nor rural. I was too far out of London to be one of those cool kids who went to the Ministry of Sound and dropped their 'g's and wore cool vintage clothes picked up in surprisingly good Oxfams in Peckham Rye. But I was too far away from the Chilterns to be one of those ruddy-cheeked, feral, country teenagers who wore old fisherman's jumpers and learnt how to drive their dad's Citroën when they were thirteen and went on walks and took acid in a forest with their cousins. The North London suburbs were a vacuum for identity. It was as beige as the plush carpets that adorned its every home. There was no art, no culture, no old buildings, no parks, no independent shops or restaurants. There were golf clubs and branches of Prezzo and private schools and driveways and roundabouts and retail parks and glass-roofed shopping centres. The women looked the same, the houses were built the same, the cars were all the same. The only form of expression was through the spending of money on homogenized assets – conservatories, kitchen extensions, cars with in-built satnav, all-inclusive holidays to Majorca. Unless you played golf, wanted your hair highlighted or to browse a Volkswagen showroom, there was absolutely nothing to do.

This was particularly true if you were a teenager at the mercy of your mother's availability to cart you around in her aforementioned Volkswagen Golf GTI. Luckily, I had my best friend, Farly, who was a three-and-a-half-mile bike ride away from my cul-de-sac.

Farly was, and still is, different to any other person in my life. We met at school when we were eleven years old. She was, and remains, the total opposite to me. She is dark; I am fair. She is a little too short; I am a little too tall. She plans and schedules everything; I leave everything to the last minute. She loves order; I'm inclined towards mess. She loves rules; I hate rules. She is without ego; I think my piece of morning toast is important enough to warrant broadcast on social media (three channels). She is very present and focused on tasks at hand; I am always half in life, half in a fantastical version of it in my head. But, somehow, we work. Nothing luckier has ever happened in my life than the day Farly sat next to me in a maths lesson in 1999.

The order of the day with Farly was always exactly the same: we'd sit in front of the television eating mountains of bagels and crisps (though only when our parents were out – another trait of the suburban middle classes is that they are particularly precious about sofas and always have a 'strictly no eating' living room) and watching American teen sitcoms on Nickelodeon. When we'd run out of episodes of *Sister, Sister* and *Two of a Kind* and

Sabrina the Teenage Witch, we'd move on to the music channels, staring slack-jawed at the TV screen while flicking
between MTV, MTV Base and VH1 every ten seconds,
looking for a particular Usher video. When we were
bored of that, we'd go back on to Nickelodeon + 1 and
watch all the episodes of the American teen sitcoms we
had watched an hour earlier, on repeat.

Morrissey once described his teenage life as 'waiting for
a bus that never came'; a feeling that's only exacerbated
when you come of age in a place that feels like an all-
beige waiting room. I was bored and sad and lonely,
restlessly wishing the hours of my childhood away. And
then, like a gallant knight in shining armour, came AOL
dial-up internet on my family's large desktop computer.
And then came MSN Instant Messenger.

When I downloaded MSN Messenger and started
adding email address contacts – friends from school,
friends of friends, friends in nearby schools who I'd
never met – it was like knocking on the wall of a prison
cell and hearing someone tap back. It was like finding
blades of grass on Mars. It was like turning the knob of
the radio on and finally hearing the crackle smooth into
a human voice. It was an escape out of my suburban dol-
drums and into an abundance of human life.

MSN was more than a way I kept in touch with my
friends as a teenager; it was a place. That's how I remember it, as a room I physically sat in for hours and hours
every evening and weekend until my eyes turned

bloodshot from staring at the screen. Even when we'd leave the suburbs and my parents would generously take my brother and me for holidays in France, it was still the room I occupied every day. The first thing I would do when we arrived at a new B&B was find out if they had a computer with internet – usually an ancient desktop in a dark basement – and I would log on to MSN Messenger and unashamedly sit chatting on it for hours while a moody French teenager sat behind me in an armchair waiting for his go. The Provençal sunshine beat down outside, where the rest of my family lay by the pool and read, but my parents knew there was no arguing with me when it came to MSN Messenger. It was the hub of all my friendships. It was my own private space. It was the only thing I could call my own. As I say, it was a place.

My first email address was munchkin_1_4@hotmail. com which I set up aged twelve in my school IT room. I chose the number 14 as I assumed I would only be emailing for two years before it became babyish; I gave myself room to enjoy this new fad and its various eccentricities until the address would expire in relevance on my fourteenth birthday. I didn't start using MSN Messenger until I was fourteen and in this space of time would also try out willyoungisyum@hotmail.com to express my new passion for the 2002 winner of *Pop Idol*. I also tried thespian_me@hotmail.com on for size, after giving a barnstorming performance as Mister Snow in the school's production of *Carousel*.

I reprised munchkin_1_4 when I downloaded MSN Instant Messenger and enjoyed the overflowing MSN Messenger contacts book of school friends I had accumulated since the address's conception. But, crucially, there was also the introduction of boys. Now, I didn't know any boys at this point. Other than my brother, little cousin, dad and one or two of my dad's cricketing friends, truly, I hadn't spent any time with a boy in my entire life. But MSN brought the email addresses and avatars of these new floating Phantom Boys; they were charitably donated by various girls at my school – the ones who would hang out with boys at the weekend and then magnanimously pass their email addresses around the student body. These boys did the MSN circuit; every girl from my school would add them as a contact and we'd all have our fifteen minutes of fame talking to them.

Where the boys were sourced from broadly fell into three categories. The first: a girl's mother's godson or some sort of family friend on the outskirts of her life who she had grown up with. He was normally a year or two older than us, very tall and lanky with a deep voice. Also lumped into this category was someone's schoolboy neighbour. The next classification were the cousins or second cousins of someone. Finally, and most exotically, a boy who someone had met when they were on a family holiday. This was the Holy Grail, really, as he could be from absolutely anywhere, as far-flung as Bromley or Maidenhead, and yet there you'd be, talking to him on MSN Messenger as if he were in the same room. What madness; what adventure.

I quickly collated a Rolodex of these waifs and strays, giving them their own separate label in my contacts list, marked 'BOYS'. Weeks would pass talking to them – about GCSE choices, about our favourite bands, about how much we smoked and drank and 'how far' we'd 'been' with the opposite sex (always a momentously laboured work of fiction). Of course, we all had little to no idea of what anyone looked like; this was before we had camera phones or social media profiles, so the only thing you'd have to go on was their tiny MSN profile photo and their description of themselves. Sometimes I'd go to the trouble of using my mum's scanner to upload a photograph of me looking nice at a family meal or on holiday, then I'd carefully cut out my aunt or my grandpa using the crop function on Paint, but mostly it was too much of a faff.

The arrival of virtual boys into the world of our school friends came with a whole set of fresh conflicts and drama. There would be an ever-turning rumour mill about who was talking to whom. Girls would pledge their faith to boys they'd never met by inserting the boy's first name into their username with stars and hearts and underscores either side. Some girls thought they were in an exclusive online dialogue with a boy, but these usernames cropping up would tell a different story. Sometimes, girls from neighbouring schools who you'd never met would add you, to ask straight out if you were talking to the same boy they were talking to. Occasionally – and this would always go down as a cautionary tale in the common room – you would accidentally expose an MSN relationship with a boy by writing a message to him in the wrong window and sending it to a friend instead. Shakespearean levels of tragedy would ensue.

There was a complicated etiquette that came with MSN; if both you and a boy you liked were logged on, but he wasn't talking to you, a failsafe way of getting his attention would be to log off then log on again, as he would be notified of your re-entry and reminded of your presence, hopefully resulting in a conversation. There was also the trick of hiding your online status if you wanted to avoid talking to anyone other than one particular contact, as you could do so furtively. It was a complex Edwardian dance of courtship and I was a giddy and willing participant.

These long correspondences rarely resulted in a real-life meet-up and when they did, they were nearly always a gut-wrenching disappointment. There was Max with the double-barrelled surname – a notorious MSN Casanova, known for sending girls Baby G watches in the post – who Farly agreed to meet outside a newsagent in Bushey one Saturday afternoon, after months of chatting online. She got there, took one look at him and freaked out, hiding behind a bin for cover. She watched him call her mobile over and over again from a phone box, but she couldn't face the reality of a meet-up in the flesh and legged it back home. They continued to speak for hours every night on MSN.

I had two. The first was a disastrous blind date in a shopping centre that lasted less than fifteen minutes. The second was a boy from a nearby boarding school who I'd spoken to for nearly a year before we finally had our first date at Pizza Express, Stanmore. For the following year, we had a sort of on-off relationship; mainly off because he was always locked up at school. But I would occasionally go to visit him, wearing lipstick and carrying a handbag full of packets of fags I'd bought for him, like Bob Hope being sent out to entertain the troops in the Second World War. He had no access to the internet in his dormitory, so MSN was out of the question, but we remedied this with weekly letters and long calls that made my father age with despair when greeted with a three-figure monthly landline phone bill.

At fifteen, I began a love affair more all-consuming than anything that had ever happened in the windows of MSN Instant Messenger when I made new friends with a wild-haired girl with freckles and kohl-rimmed hazel eyes called Lauren. We had seen each other around at the odd Hollywood Bowl birthday party since we were kids, but we finally met properly through our mutual friend Jess over dinner in one of Stanmore's many Italian chain restaurants. The connection was like everything I'd ever seen in any romantic film I'd ever watched on ITV2. We talked until our mouths were dry, we finished each other's sentences, we made tables turn round as we laughed like drains; Jess went home and we sat on a bench in the freezing cold after we got chucked out of the restaurant just so we could carry on talking.

She was a guitarist looking for a singer to start a band; I'd sung at one sparsely attended open-mic night in Hoxton and I needed a guitarist. We started rehearsing bossa nova covers of Dead Kennedys songs the following day in her mum's shed with the first draft of our band name being 'Raging Pankhurst'. We later changed it to, even more inexplicably, 'Sophie Can't Fly'. Our first gig was in a Turkish restaurant in Pinner, with just one customer in the heaving restaurant who wasn't a member of our family or a school friend. We went on to do all the big names: a theatre foyer in Rickmansworth, a pub garden's derelict outbuilding in Mill Hill, a cricket pavilion just outside of Cheltenham. We busked on any street without a policeman. We sang at the reception of any bar mitzvah that would have us.

We also shared a hobby for the pioneering method of multi-platforming our MSN content. Early on in our friendship, we discovered that since the conception of Instant Messenger, we had both been copying and pasting conversations with boys on to a Microsoft Word document, printing them out and putting the pages in a ring-binder folder to read before bed like an erotic novel. We thought ourselves to be a sort of two-person Bloomsbury Group of early noughties MSN Messenger.

But just as I formed a friendship with Lauren, I left

suburbia to live seventy-five miles north of Stanmore at a co-ed boarding school. MSN could no longer serve my curiosity around the opposite sex; I needed to know what they were like in real life. The ever-fading smell of Ralph Lauren Polo Blue on a love letter didn't satisfy me any more and neither did the pings and drums of new messages on MSN. I went to boarding school to try to acclimatize to boys.

(Aside: and thank God I did. Farly stayed on for sixth form at our all-girls school and when she arrived at university, having never spent any time around boys, she was like an uncut bull in a china shop. On the first night of freshers' week, there was a 'traffic light party', where single people were encouraged to wear something green and people in relationships wore something red. Most of us took this to mean a green T-shirt, but Farly arrived at our halls of residence bar wearing green tights, green shoes, a green dress and a giant green bow in her hair along with a mist of green hairspray. She might as well have had I WENT TO AN ALL-GIRLS SCHOOL tattooed across her forehead. I am for ever grateful that I had two years on the nursery slopes of mixed inter-action at boarding school, otherwise I fear I too would have fallen foul of the can of green hairspray come freshers' week.)

As it turns out, I discovered I had absolutely nothing in common with most boys and next to no interest in them unless I wanted to kiss them. And no boy I wanted to kiss wanted to kiss me, so I might as well have stayed in Stanmore and continued to enjoy a series of fantasy relationships played out in the fecund lands of my imagination.

I blame my high expectations for love on two things: the first is that I am the child of parents who are almost embarrassingly infatuated with each other; the second is the films I watched in my formative years. As a child, I had a rather unusual obsession with old musicals and having grown up absolutely addicted to the films of Gene Kelly and Rock Hudson, I had always expected boys to carry themselves with a similar elegance and charm. But co-ed school killed this notion pretty fast. Take, for example, my first politics lesson. I was one of just two girls in the class of twelve and had never sat with as many boys in one room in my entire life. The best-looking boy, who I had already been told was a notorious heart-throb (his older brother who had left the year before was nicknamed 'Zeus'), passed a piece of paper to me down the table while our teacher explained what Proportional Representation was. The note was folded up with a heart drawn on the front, leading me to believe it was a love letter; I opened it with a coy smile. However, when I unfolded it, there was a picture of a creature, helpfully annotated to inform me that it was an orc from *Lord of the Rings*, with 'YOU LOOK LIKE THIS' scribbled underneath it.

Farly came to visit me at the weekends and ogled at the hundreds of boys of all shapes and sizes wandering around the streets, sports bags and hockey sticks flung over their shoulders. She couldn't believe my luck, that I got to sit in pews every morning in chapel within reaching distance of them. But I found the reality of boys to be slightly disappointing. Not as funny as the girls I had met there, not nearly as interesting or kind. And, for some reason, I could never quite relax around any of them.

By the time I left school, I had stopped using MSN Messenger as religiously as I once had. My first term at Exeter University swung round and, with it, the advent of Facebook. Facebook was a treasure trove for boys online – and this time, even better, you had all their vital information collated together on one page. I regularly browsed through my uni friends' photos and added anyone who I liked the look of; this would quickly accelerate into messages back and forth and planned meet-ups at one of the many Vodka Shark club nights or foam parties happening that week. I was at a campus university at a cathedral city in Devon; locating each other was no hard task. If MSN had been a blank canvas on which I could splatter vivid fantasies, Facebook messaging was a purely functional meet-up tool. It was how students identified their next conquest; lined up their next Thursday night.

By the time I left university and returned to London, I had firmly given up my habit of cold-calling potential love interests on Facebook with the persuasive aggression of an Avon representative, but a new pattern was forming. I would meet a man through a friend or at a party or on a night out, get his name and number and then form an epistolary relationship with him over text or email for weeks and weeks before I would confirm a second real-life meet-up. Perhaps it was because this was the only way I had learnt to get to know someone, with a distance in between us, with enough space for me to curate and filter the best version of myself possible – all the good jokes, all the best sentences, all the songs I knew he'd be impressed by, normally sent to me by Lauren. In return, I'd send songs to her to pass on to her pen pal. She once commented that we sent good new music to each other at a wholesale price, then passed it on to love interests as our own, with an 'emotional mark-up'.

This form of correspondence nearly always ended in disappointment. I slowly began to realize that it's best for those first dates to happen in real life rather than in written form, otherwise the disparity between who you imagine the other person to be and who they actually are grows wider and wider. Many times, I would invent a person in my head and create our chemistry as if writing a screenplay and by the time we'd meet again in real life, I'd be crushingly let down. It was as if, when things didn't go as I imagined, I'd assumed he would have been given a copy of the script I'd written and I'd feel frustrated that his agent obviously forgot to courier it to him to memorize.

Any woman who spent her formative years surrounded only by other girls will tell you the same thing: you never really shake off the idea that boys are the most fascinating, beguiling, repulsive, bizarre creatures to roam the earth; as dangerous and mythological as a Sasquatch. More often than not, it also means you are a confirmed fantasist for life. Because how could you not be? For years on end, all I did was sit on walls with Farly, kicking the bricks with my thick rubber soles, staring up at the sky, trying to dream up enough to keep us distracted from the endless sight of hundreds of girls walking around us in matching uniform. Your imagination has the daily workout of an Olympic athlete when you attend an all-girls school. It's amazing how habituated you become to the intense heat of fantasy when you escape to it so often.

I always thought my fascination and obsession with the opposite sex would cool down when I left school and life began, but little did I know I would be just as clueless about how to be with them in my late twenties as I was when I first logged on to MSN Messenger.

Boys were a problem. One that would take me fifteen years to fix.

The Bad Date Diaries:
Twelve Minutes

The year is 2002. I am fourteen years old. I wear a kilt skirt from Miss Selfridge, a pair of black Dr Martens and a neon-orange crop top.

The boy is Betzalel, an acquaintance of my school friend Natalie. They met on Jewish holiday camp and have been speaking on MSN and giving each other 'relationship and life advice' ever since. Natalie is in the market for new friends, having just lost hers by spreading a rumour that a girl in our year self-harms when actually it's just bad eczema, and I am one of her targets.

She knows I want a boyfriend so suggests she sets Betz and I up on MSN Messenger. I am more than happy with the unspoken agreement that Natalie gifts me a new boy to speak to and in return I occasionally eat lunch with her.

Betz and I are basically going out after a month of speaking with each other every day after school on MSN. He thinks everyone his age is immature, as do I, and he's also tall for his age, as am I. We chew the fat of these shared experiences constantly.

We agree to meet in Costa, Brent Cross shopping centre. I ask Farly to come, so I am not on my own.

Betz arrives and he looks nothing like the photo he's

sent me – he's shaved all his curly hair off and has put on stacks of weight since camp. We wave at each other across the table. Betz orders nothing.

Farly does all the talking, while Betz and I stare at the floor, embarrassed, silent. Betz has a shopping bag – he tells us he's just bought *Toy Story 2* on video. I tell him that's babyish. He says my skirt makes me look like a Scottish man.

I tell him we have to leave because we need to catch the 142 back to Stanmore. The date lasts twelve minutes.

When I get home and log on to MSN, Betz immediately sends me a long message I know he's already written on Microsoft Word and copied and pasted into the chat window in his trademark italic purple Comic Sans. He says he thinks I'm a nice girl but he doesn't have feelings for me. I tell him it's out of order of him to write a speech and sit at home waiting for me to log on, when he lives so near Brent Cross and my bus is twenty-five minutes from home, just because he knows I fancied him less than he fancied me and he didn't want me to say it first.

Betz blocks me for a month but he eventually forgives me. We never have a second meeting, but we become relationship confidants until I am seventeen.

Free from my contractual obligation, Natalie and I never eat lunch together again.

The Bad Party Chronicles: UCL Halls, New Year's Eve, 2006

It is my first holiday home after my first term at university. Lauren, also home for Christmas, suggests we go to a New Year's Eve party in the UCL halls of residence. She's been invited by Hayley, a girl she went to school with and hasn't seen since prize-giving.

We arrive at the large communal flat in a dilapidated building on a backstreet in between Euston and Warren Street. The party attendees are an even mix of UCL stoners, Lauren's school friends and opportunistic passers-by who see the door open and hear R. Kelly's 'Ignition' on repeat for the best part of an evening. Lauren and I have a bottle of red wine each (Jacob's Creek Shiraz, because it's a special occasion), which we drink from two plastic glasses (not the bottle, because it's a special occasion).

I scan the room for boys with working limbs and a detectable pulse. I am, at this point, eighteen, six months into my sexually active life and at a uniquely heightened stage of sexuality; an ephemeral period where sex was my biggest adventure and discovery; a time when shagging was like potatoes and tobacco, and I, Sir Walter Raleigh. I couldn't understand why everyone wasn't doing it all the time. All the books and films and songs that had been written about it were not enough to cover all corners of how great it was; how did anyone see the opportunity in any evening for anything other than having sex or finding someone to have sex with? (This feeling had insidiously evaporated by my nineteenth birthday.)

I spot a familiar, friendly face on a tall body with broad shoulders and quickly identify him as a boy who was the runner on a sitcom I did work experience on after my GCSEs. We'd flirt and bitch about the diva cast members during furtive cigarettes behind the studio. We approach each other now with outstretched arms for a hug and almost immediately start snogging. This is how I operated when my hormones were pumping through my bloodstream so thick and fast; a handshake became a snog, a hug became a dry hump. The social markers of intimacy all climbed up a few steps.

After a couple of hours of sharing Shiraz and rubbing up against each other, we lock ourselves in the bathroom to seal the deal. We begin fumbling around each other's respective jeans and skirt, drunken teenagers trying to fix a broken fuse box, when there is a knock at the door.

'THE LOO ISN'T WORKING!' I shout, The Runner gnawing at my neck.

'Doll,' Lauren hisses. 'It's me, let me in.' I button up my skirt, move to the door and open it a crack.

'What?' I say, poking my head round. She shuffles in through the gap.

'So I've been getting off with Finn –' She notices my friend in the corner of the bathroom, now sheepishly zipping up his jeans. 'Oh, hello,' she says to him breezily.

'So I'm getting off with Finn but I'm worried he's going to feel my knickers.'

'So?'

'They're control pants,' she says, lifting up her dress to show me a flesh-coloured girdle. 'To hold your stomach and back fat in.'

'Well, just take them off. Pretend you weren't wearing any,' I say, pushing her towards the door.

'Where do I put them? Everyone is in every room, I've been into every room and there are groups in every single one.'

'Put them there,' I say, pointing behind the loo's grubby cistern. 'No one will find them.' I help Lauren pull them down her legs, we stuff them behind the loo and I shove her out.

Sadly, due to the vast vats of alcohol we have consumed and the shared spliff, The Runner can't perform. We make several attempts to remedy the situation, one of which is so frenetic we accidentally unhinge the shower unit from the wall, but all are futile. So we cut our losses and amicably go our separate ways – he leaves for another party and we hug goodbye. It has just gone midnight.

Lauren and I reunite in the room where the most marijuana is being smoked to catch up on our respective venery. Finn has also departed for the promise of a better party in the inky-black first hours of a new year. We toast the proficiency of friendship and endless disappointment of boys, before spotting and swiftly befriending an emo band we've met on the Whetstone open-mic circuit. She takes the singer with Robert Smith hair, I take the bassist with Cabbage Patch Doll cheeks. We all slouch against a wardrobe, passing Silk Cuts and spliffs up and down our factory line of four and taking turns to put our iPods into the speaker dock to play an even mix of John Mayer and Panic! At The Disco. The music suddenly stops.

'Someone has broken the shower,' Hayley announces imperiously. 'We need to find the person who broke the shower because they need to pay for it, otherwise we'll get into huge trouble with the warden.'

'Yeah, we need to find them,' I chime in with a slur. 'I think it was that short guy with the long hair.'

'Which guy?'

'He was here a moment ago,' I say. 'It was definitely him, he came out of the bathroom with a girl and they were laughing. He's gone outside to have a cigarette, I think.'

I lead a witch-hunt of the halls' residents out into the street to find the made-up man, but quickly lose interest in the decoy when I see Joel, who is looking for the party. Joel is a famous North London heart-throb; a Jewish Warren Beatty with gelled spikes and acne scars; Danny Zuko of the suburbs. I offer him a cigarette and immediately we are snogging like we're making small talk about TFL. We migrate back into the flat where I enjoy publicly snogging Joel, a fair few kudos points higher than The Runner of yore. I am only sad that I can't colonize the bathroom once more, now crowded with Hayley and her half-baked *Silent Witness* team of party-pooper forensics, trying to deduce who broke the shower and how. I am looking for a new hiding place when Christine, a beautiful blonde (the Sandy to Joel's Danny), asks if she can have a word with him. I graciously leave them to it because, as the old adage goes, if you want to shag something, let it go.

Lauren and I reconvene for a fag – on to the Mayfairs now.

'They used to go out when we were at school,' she tells me. 'Very up and down, very intense.'

'Oh,' I say.

I look across the room to see Christine and Joel holding hands and leaving the flat. He waves at me apologetically on his way out.

'Bye,' he mouths.

Lauren is preoccupied with the emo singer and they're talking about chord progressions; a sure sign she's committed to the idea of sex. It is nearly four a.m. and I need to wake up in two hours to get to my job as a sales assistant at an upmarket Bond Street shoe shop where I am on one per cent commission that I cannot afford to lose. I go in search of a piece of carpet in a darkened room to sleep on and, to my delight, find a vacant single bed and set my alarm for six.

Two hours later I wake up with the worst hangover of my life; my brain feels like it's been turned inside out, my eyes are glued together with mascara and my breath smells like a Sauvignon-swilling rat has crawled into my mouth during the night, died and decayed. I look down at my brown Topshop miniskirt, bare legs and pirate boots, remembering that I haven't brought my work uniform with me.

'Hayley,' I hiss, prodding her body with my big toe as she sleeps on a pile of jumpers on the floor next to me. 'Hayley. I need to borrow a dress. Just a plain black dress. I'll bring it back later today.'

'You're in my bed,' she says flatly. 'You wouldn't get out of it last night.'

'Sorry,' I reply.

'And Lauren told me it was you who broke the shower,' she mutters into the jumpers. I say nothing, leave quietly and regret the altruism I displayed only a few hours earlier in finding a notebook of Hayley's sad little poems under her pillow and not reading it cover to cover.

'You look like a homeless person,' my witchy-faced boss Mary snarls at me as I walk into work. 'You smell like one too. Get down to the stockroom,' she says, waving her hand at me dismissively as if batting away a fly. 'You can't be near customers today.'

When I get home that night, after the longest day's work of my life, I log on to Facebook to survey the photographic damage from the night before. There, at the top of my homepage, is a close-up photo of Lauren's enormous knickers loaded by Hayley into an album called 'Lost Property'. Everyone from the party is tagged. The caption reads only: 'WHOSE PANTS ARE THESE?'

A Hellraiser Heads
to Leamington Spa

The first time I got drunk, I was ten. I was a guest at Natasha Bratt's bat mitzvah along with four other lucky chosen girls from our year. In the sun-flooded marquee in their Mill Hill back garden, the wine was flowing and the smoked salmon was circling; the women's hair was blow-dried into aggressively undulating trajectories, their lips a uniform frosted beige. And for reasons I will never understand, all of us girls – clearly prepubescent in our Tammy Girl strapless dresses and butterfly clips in our hair – were given glass after glass of champagne by the catering staff.

At first, it just felt like a wave of warmth flushing through my body, my blood sprinting, my epidermis humming. Then like all the screws in all my joints had been loosened, leaving me as springy and light as just-proved dough. And then came the chatting – the funny stories, the dramatic impressions of teachers and parents, the rude jokes, the best swear words. (To this day, this three-step progression is still how I experience initial drunkenness.)

The father–daughter dance to Van Morrison's 'Brown Eyed Girl' was brought to an abrupt and premature finish when one of the girls, slightly further along than the rest of us, threw herself belly-first on to the dance floor and wiggled manically underneath the legs of both parties, like a flapping fish out of water. I quickly followed suit before we were both removed and told off by an aggrieved uncle. But the night had only just begun.

Flooded with newfound confidence, I decided it was time for my first kiss, followed by my second (his best friend), followed by my third (the first's brother). Everyone got stuck in, swapping and trying out kissing partners as if they were shared puddings at a table. Eventually, this suburban child orgy was broken up and we were all taken to the front room and given black coffee; the door was locked and our parents were called to come pick us up. So unprecedented was the bad behaviour, we were reprimanded a second time by our headmistress on Monday and scolded for 'representing the school in a bad light' (this was often an accusation thrown at me during my scholastic years and it always struck me as a slightly weak takedown, particularly when I had never chosen to represent the school; rather my parents had chosen the school to represent me).

I was never the same after that night, the contents of which provided enough material to fill the pages of my diaries well into my teens. I had, at far too young an age, got the taste for alcohol. I begged for small, diluted glasses of wine at any family event. I'd slurp the sweet, throat-catching syrup from the bellies of liqueur chocolates at Christmas in the hope of a hit. At fourteen, I finally found out where my mum and dad hid the key to their drinks cabinet, and would knock back capfuls of cheap French brandy when they were out of the house, enjoying the warm, woozy haze it pulled over the task of homework. Sometimes I'd rope Farly into my furtive, suburban binging – we'd swig at their Beefeater gin and refill it with water, then sit cross-legged on the plush carpet and watch *Who Wants to Be a Millionaire?*, drunkenly fighting over the correct answer.

I have never hated anything as much as I hated being a teenager. I could not have been more ill-suited to the state of adolescence. I was desperate to be an adult; desperate to be taken seriously. I hated relying on anyone for anything. I'd have sooner cleaned floors than be given pocket money or walked three miles in the rain at night than be given a lift home by a parent. I was looking up the price of one-bedroom flats in Camden when I was fifteen, so I could get a head start on saving up with my babysitting money. I was using my mum's recipes and dining table to host 'dinner parties' at the same age, forcing my friends round for rosemary roast chicken tagliatelle and raspberry pavlovas with a Frank Sinatra soundtrack, when all they wanted to do was eat burgers and go bowling. I wanted my own friends, my own schedule, my own home, my own money and my own life. I found being a teenager one big, frustrating, mortifying, exposing, co-dependent embarrassment that couldn't end fast enough.

Alcohol, I think, was my small act of independence. It was the one way I could feel like an adult. All the

EVERYTHING I KNOW ABOUT LOVE

by-products of drinking that my friends were hooked on – the snogging, the squealing, the secret-swapping, smoking and dancing – were fun, but it was the pertinent adultness of alcohol that I loved the most. I would live out make-believe vignettes of mundane adult life. I would confidently wander into local off-licences and browse the backs of bottles while having pretend conversations into my Nokia 3310 about 'a casual drinks party this Saturday' or 'a nightmare day in the office' or 'where I left the car'. While holding my dog-eared copy of *The Female Eunuch* (ironically, mainly decorative), I would place myself in the middle of the corridor within earshot of teachers in the four o'clock rush out of school on a Friday and shout, 'WE'RE STILL ON FOR DINNER, YEAH?' at Farly, 'I FANCY A FULL-BODIED BOTTLE OF RED!' and enjoy the slightly quizzical look on their faces as they passed me. *Well, screw you*, I would think. *I'm doing something you do too. I'm drinking. I'm an adult. Take me fucking seriously.*

It was only when I went to boarding school at sixteen that I really cultivated a habit for hard drinking. My co-ed school was the last of the English boarding schools to have a bar on-campus for sixth formers. On Thursdays and Saturdays, through a token system, hundreds of sixteen to eighteen-year-olds descended on a small basement, claimed their two cans of beer and rubbed up against each other on a dark, sweaty dance floor to the sound of 'Beenie Man and Other Dance Hall Legends'. My boarding house was, luckily, right opposite the bar, which allowed a swift stumble home come eleven o'clock, where our matron would lay out boxes of pizza for us to drunkenly gobble together. It also meant that our house garden was used as a hedonistic, after-hours playground, and half an hour after curfew, my house-mistress would strap a pit helmet to her head and go out into the bushes foraging for semi-clothed, fumbling pupils. After sending any girl found in the garden up to bed with no pizza and sending the boy back to his house, there was always a wonderful moment when we'd over-hear her calling the boy's housemaster from her study.

'I found your James behind my rhododendron bush with my Emily with his trousers down,' she'd say in her broad Yorkshire accent. 'I've sent him on his way, he should be with you in ten minutes.'

All the teachers knew we drank before we got to the bar. We'd smuggle bottles of vodka in our suitcases hid-den in empty, washed-out shampoo bottles; we had a never-ending supply of Marlboro Lights under our mat-tresses. We covered the scent of our tracks with cheap perfume and menthol gum; when I smoked a spliff and had bloodshot eyes, I'd wet my hair as if I'd just got out of the shower and blame it on the shampoo. The general unspoken rule was: we're trusting you to know your limits, so don't be a dick about it. Drink and smoke, but don't behave badly and don't make it obvious. On the whole, the system worked. There was always the odd kid who took it too far and smashed a chair or tried to hump a young maths teacher on duty, but the rest of us managed to hold it together. The teachers were, on the whole, very respectful of the pupils; they treated us like young adults rather than children. The only years of my adolescence that I enjoyed were the last two spent at boarding school.

University is never going to be an ideal place for someone with an unhealthy relationship with booze, but my God I chose the worst one imaginable the day I submitted a UCAS application to Exeter. Nestled in the green, rolling hills of Devon, Exeter has long been known as a university for half-soaked, semi-literate Hooray Henrys. If you ever meet a middle-aged man who still plays lacrosse, knows every rule to every drinking game and sings better Latin than English when he's drunk, the chances are he went to Exeter University – or 'The Green Welly Uni' as it was known in the 1980s. I only applied because Farly applied. Farly only applied because it was good for Classics and she liked the seaside. I only went because I didn't get on to the one course I really wanted at Bristol, and my parents told me I had to go to university.

To this day, I am convinced that the three years I spent at Exeter left me more stupid than when I arrived. I did little to no work; I went from being a voracious bookworm to not reading a single page of a book that wasn't a set text (and I don't think I even finished one of those). From September 2006 to July 2009, all I did was drink and shag. All anyone did was drink and shag, pausing only briefly to eat a kebab, watch an episode of *Eggheads* or shop for a fancy-dress outfit for a 'Lashed of the Summer Wine' themed pub crawl. Far from being the hub of radical thinking and passionate activism I had hoped for, it was the most politically apathetic place I had ever been. During my entire time there, there were only two protests I was aware of: the first, a student-body stand against the removal of curly fries from the Student Union Pub's menu; the second, one young woman's petition to have a bridleway built on campus so she could travel to and from her lectures on a pony.

I would deeply resent the years of my life wasted at Exeter were it not for the one thing that made the whole sorry experience worthwhile: the women I met. Within the first week, Farly and I found a gang of girls who would become our closest friends. There was Lacey, a gobby and gorgeous golden-haired drama student; AJ, a luminous brunette from a strict all-girls school who sang hymns when she got drunk; Sabrina, the charming blonde, full of life and wide-eyed enthusiasm. There was South London girl Sophie, red-headed, funny and boy-ish, always coming round to fix things in our flats. And then there was Hicks.

Hicks was our ringleader – a Suffolk-born Stig of the Dump with a bleach-blonde bob, wild eyes in a cape of shimmery turquoise shadow, long, coltish, teenage legs and tits I could identity in a line-up, because she had them out so much. I had never met anyone like her; she was bold and dangerous, quick-witted and daring. Nothing seemed to ever have a consequence when you were with Hicks. It was as if she operated as an empress in her own kingdom with its own rules where the night finished at one p.m. and the next night began the following afternoon, where an old man you met in a pub would end up as a temporary lodger in your house. She was entirely, wholly, completely present; impossibly glamorous and enviably rock 'n' roll. Her reckless, limitless appetite for a good time set the tone for the following three years.

The atmosphere at Exeter was so aggressively laddish and male, I often wonder if it is an explanation for why we behaved the way we did when we were students; whether my all-female group of friends was trying to match that energy with our behaviour. It was a perpetuation of American frat-boy culture from the films we had grown up watching, intersecting with the boorish hierarchical system of public school. We enjoyed group-crouching urination behind skips (Farly and I were once caught out and reprimanded for doing this on the outskirts of a graveyard, bare bottoms on show for passing traffic – unfortunately one of them happened to be a police car). We stole traffic cones which piled up in our living room. We picked each other up and threw each other around on club dance floors. We talked about sex like it was a team sport. We were puffed up on bravado and rodomontade; and we operated with ruthless honesty and zero competition with each other, often boring each other's prospective conquests senseless with long, drunk lectures about how amazing our friend was.

In the ramshackle house with the red door in which I lived with AJ, Farly and Lacey, we had a 'visitors' book' for 'overnight guests' to sign on their way out the next morning. There was a defunct 1980s television in the back garden that sat there, come rain or shine. Slugs that covered our hallway, that I'd save one by one after a night out by taking them outside and putting them in a special corner of grass (Lacey later admitted they put pellets down for them but never told me). It was a time of heightened, eccentric debauchery. A world where two of my friends stayed up all night dancing before heading to Exeter cathedral for a Sunday service and warbling hymns while wearing gold Lycra; a world where Farly once got up for a nine a.m. lecture to find me and Hicks still downstairs drinking Baileys with a middle-aged cab driver we'd invited in the night before. We were the worst type of students imaginable. We were reckless and self-absorbed and childish and violently carefree. We were Broken Britain – in fact, we used to shout it as we walked to pubs. Now, I cross roads and get off tubes a stop early to avoid being in the direct vicinity of the exact type of noisy, silly, self-satisfied exhibitionists that we were.

If I ever wanted to gauge the extent of the binge-drinking culture in my group of friends at my university, I only had to see it in the eyes of the people who visited. My little brother, Ben, came to stay for a couple of days when he was seventeen and was 'appalled' at the half-clothed, barely conscious apparitions he met in the clubs

I took him to, taking particular umbrage at an area of one bar nicknamed 'Legend's Corner' because only members of the rugby team were allowed to sit there. He later told my parents that his three-day visit to Exeter was one of the main reasons he refused to apply to university and chose to go to drama school instead.

Lauren went to read English at Oxford and a few times we did a sort of university exchange programme. She'd get the Megabus down to Exeter and knock some brain cells out of her head for a few days with me; I'd return to Oxford with her and wander round the Magdalen deer park, imagining an alternate life where I read books and wrote bi-weekly essays and lived in a spire-topped house with no television(s).

On Lauren's first ever visit, it was as if I was teaching her how to be a student. On a night out, I ordered a bottle of five-quid rosé from the bar.

'OK,' she said. 'Is that just for the two of us?'

'No, that's just for me,' I replied as Lauren looked round at my various friends all carrying separate bottles of wine and one plastic glass from the bar. 'We get one each.' The following day, lying around on the sofa eating overpriced, sweet, doughy pizza, she watched her first episode of *America's Next Top Model*. That afternoon she met the lacrosse player on campus who famously began writing his Human Geography dissertation in the pub at two p.m. on the day it was due in. Lauren said she always went back to Oxford feeling relaxed and refreshed after a much-needed break from her exhausting university experience of intellectual peacocking. After a few days in Oxford, I always returned to Exeter feeling a bit low and ready to leave.

When illustrating the bubble of unanswered bad behaviour with no punishment that was my university experience, I often return to a particular anecdote involving Sophie – now a successful and respected journalist covering crucial LGBTQ and women's issues – to remember how far we've come. One night, having left a Thai full moon party at a quayside club – dressed as a Thai fisherman – she lay by the water next to a pissing male friend, thinking she was about to vomit on account of the eight-shot bucket of Vodka Shark she had just purchased and consumed. To her side was a half-comatose friend of a friend who was lying on her back like a starfish. Sophie spotted an opportunity both to take a young woman back to safety and to potentially get lucky. But once she got to the girl's halls of residence, it was clear this wasn't on the cards, so she got another cab back to the club where she ordered another bucket of Vodka Shark. She then met a boy who said he was heading to a local late-hours curry house for a takeaway. Sophie went with him, chanting 'PASANDA, PASANDA' while banging on the shop counter. They ordered their food, went to his house and ate a mountain of curry. Sophie was sick into a perspex bowl in the boy's bedroom and left it on the side. She passed out in his bed, woke up the next morning in her fisherman's costume, glanced at the vomit bowl but did nothing about it and then took the boy's micro scooter and glee-fully scooted all the way home.

'We were just trying to collect stories for each other,' she tells me now, whenever I question how we could all have had such an infantile appetite for recklessness and such little self-awareness. 'That's what we traded in. It wasn't to show off to anyone else but each other.'

It was obvious that while everyone loved drinking, I really loved drinking. I'd down booze at breakneck speed. A lot of it was simply that I loved the taste and sensation of booze, but I also drank as a student for the same reason I drank on my own at fourteen: pouring alcohol into my brain was like pouring water into squash. Everything diluted and mellowed. The girl who was sober was riddled with anxieties, convinced everyone she loved was going to die, fretting about what everyone thought of her. The girl who was drunk smoked a cigar-ette with her toes 'for a laugh' and cartwheeled on dance floors.

I graduated from Exeter a month before my twenty-first birthday and come September I was a student in London, studying for a Masters in Journalism. This was, believe it or not, the year in which my partying peaked; I had been unceremoniously and brutally dumped and I threw myself into weight loss to sidetrack myself from heartbreak, and I drank and smoked for the distraction.

I still hadn't lost the taste for it. It was just as exciting at twenty-one as it had been at Natasha Bratt's bat mitzvah eleven years earlier. I remember sitting on the tube on one of many Saturday nights that year, looking out on the glittering city as I journeyed from the suburbs to central London on the Metropolitan line that rode like a cantering horse on the tracks. *All of London is mine*, I thought. *Anything is possible.*

My hedonism this year came to a head in a particularly un-rock 'n' roll way: a long journey in a minicab. In my defence, Hicks started it. In our third year of university, she became a household name amongst the student body of Exeter when she left a night out at a bar on the High Street, got into a taxi and asked the driver to take her to Brighton. She spent every penny she had getting there and stayed on the floor of a hotel suite with her married friends who were there on a romantic getaway. She returned to Exeter the following week to tell the tale.

The night began when me and my new curly-haired clever friend from my Journalism MA course, Helen, went to our friend Moya's house for a glass of wine and to talk through our revision for a big exam we had coming up. Helen and I proceeded to drink bottle after bottle of wine in the sun, getting steaming drunk, leaving Moya's at midnight.

I decided the night wasn't over and that I wanted a party, so we got on a bus from West Hampstead to Oxford Circus. However, I became suddenly much drunker the minute the bus journey began – which also took an unfeasibly long time due to a road accident – so at some point while in transit I managed to convince myself that we weren't on a bus to Oxford Circus, but were in fact on a coach to Oxford city centre. Helen, rendered similarly to me, went along with my persuasive theory. Lauren had graduated from Oxford at this point so I didn't call her; instead, I texted a few of her friends who I had met on my visits there who I knew were in their final year. The messages were barely comprehensible, but they went along the lines of: 'Me and my friend Helen have accidentally got on a coach to Oxford. We're nearly there – where is good for a night out and would you like to join us?'

We alighted near the flagship Topshop, which I noted was larger than I had remembered the last time I visited Oxford. We stood outside the shop while I incessantly rang anyone I had ever met from Oxford University – *still* not taking in that I was in London – but no cigar. Helen and I agreed the night out was a lost cause, but it was too late for me to get the last tube back to my parents' house in the suburbs. So we got another bus back to the Finsbury Park flat that Helen shared with her boyfriend and she said I could sleep on their sofa.

Refusing to let go of my inebriated hallucination, when stepping into the flat I concluded that we were in Oxford University Halls; that a friend of Helen's was still a student here, perhaps. Helen went to bed and I scrolled through my phonebook to see if anyone I knew would be up for a party. I rang my friend Will – he was a tall, wild, wiry Canadian with long curly hair and eyes as pale as opals. I had always had a gigantic crush on him.

'Hello, darling,' he slurred in his vodka-soaked voice.

'I want a party,' I said.

'Come here then.'

'Where are you?' I asked. 'Aren't you still at uni in Birmingham?'

'Warwick. I'm living in Leamington Spa,' he said. 'I'll text you the address.'

I wandered out of Helen's flat and went looking for a cab firm. After ten minutes of roaming the streets – the alcohol slowly leaving my system as I finally just about grasped I was in London and not Oxford – I found a small, wooden-fronted minicab company. I announced that I wanted a car to take me to Leamington Spa and money was absolutely no object – except it had to be £100 or less as that's all I had in my account and I was at the limit of my overdraft. One of the three bemused men went behind the glass partition to take a dusty map of England out from his drawer. He unfolded the map and theatrically spread it across two tables pushed together, much to the amusement of his colleagues. They all huddled around it as one planned the journey with dashes marked with a red pen as if he were the captain of a ship plotting an attack on pirates. Even in my drunken state, I thought it to be a touch over the top.

'£250,' he finally declared.

'That's RIDICULOUS,' I said with pearl-clutching, middle-class customer-rights outrage; as if *he* were the one posing the most absurd request out of the two of us.

'Lady – you wanna go somewhere three counties

away at three o'clock in the morning. £250 is a very reasonable price.'

I got him down to £200. Will said he'd pay for the other £100.

I started sobering up on the M1 at around four a.m. (there's a sentence I hope none of the rest of you ever have to say or write down in all your remaining days). But it was too late to turn back – how I often felt in the middle of these small-hour adventures, convincing myself that this was just getting my money's worth out of my youth. A Margaret Atwood quote hung over this period of my life like a lampshade from the ceiling.

> When you are in the middle of a story it isn't a story at all, but only a confusion; a dark roaring, a blindness, a wreckage of shattered glass and splintered wood; like a house in a whirlwind, or else a boat crushed by the icebergs or swept over the rapids, and all aboard powerless to stop it. It's only afterwards that it becomes anything like a story at all. When you are telling it, to yourself or to someone else.

It would pay off in the end, I thought while I stuck my head out of the window on the motorway, the sky turning to dawn. *The anecdotal mileage in this will be inexhaustible.*

I arrived at half five in the morning. Will greeted me at the door with five twenty-pound notes. I felt triumphant that I'd managed to get there. The journey and the destination were the story; what unfolded was almost irrelevant. We stayed up drinking, talking, and lay in bed half-clothed smoking weed and listening to Smiths albums, stopping only briefly for some half-arsed snogging. We fell asleep at eleven a.m.

I woke up at three p.m. with a terrible headache and a terrible sense that the punchline to the joke wasn't as funny as I thought it had been the night before. I checked my bank account: zero. I checked my phone: dozens of worried messages from friends. I had forgotten I had sent Farly a photo of me gleefully smiling in the back of the cab at four in the morning while hurtling down the motorway with the message: 'QUICK TRIP TO THE WEST MIDLANDS!!'

I made a plan. My teenage boyfriend who I had retained a vague friendship with was training to be a doctor at Warwick Uni. I could stay with him for a few days until some overdue money came through from my weekend job as a promo girl and get a train home in time for my Journalism MA exam on Tuesday. But when I texted him, he told me he was away on holiday.

My phone rang – it was Sophie.

'Is it true you're in Leamington Spa?' she asked when I picked up.

'Yes.'

'Why?'

'Because I wanted an after-party and my friend Will was having one and he lives in Leamington Spa.' Will, still half asleep, gave a closed-eye smile and a guilty-as-charged thumbs-up.

'OK, that doesn't make any sense,' she said. 'How are you going to get home?'

'I don't know. I was going to stay with an old boyfriend, but he's not here and I don't have any money for the train.' There was a long pause and I could hear Sophie's concern for me morph into irritation.

'Right, well I'll book you a bus home then,' she said. 'Is your phone charged?'

'Yes.'

'I'll send you the details once it's done.'

'Thank you thank you thank you,' I said. 'I'll pay you back.'

Sophie booked me a seat on the longest coach journey she could find – her plan being that I needed some sobering time with just my thoughts so I could contemplate the consequences of my actions. Much to her annoyance, I ended up on a coach with a raucous London-bound hen party. We all did shots of tequila on the journey and they gave me a sombrero to wear. The next day, when I phoned to thank Sophie for saving the day, I asked her if she was annoyed with me.

'Dolly,' she said, 'I'm not annoyed with you, I'm worried about you.'

'Why?' I asked.

'Because you were so drunk you thought you were in Oxford city centre when you were outside the Oxford Circus Topshop. Do you know how vulnerable that makes a person? Wandering around London that drunk?'

'I'm sorry,' I said petulantly. 'I was just having fun.'

'How many of our friends need to bankrupt themselves getting taxis across Britain before this madness
stops?'

(It would take just one more – Farly, a few months
later, from South West London to Exeter. She was in a
cab going home from a club when she got a text from a
boy she fancied who was still at university and she asked
the driver if he could turn around and go, instead, to
Devon. To this day, she shrugs off accusations of extrava-
gance and says the entire journey cost '£90 and a packet
of fags'. The figure has incrementally climbed in value
the more we probe her on it.)

But they were all good stories, and that's what mattered. It was the raison d'être of my early twenties. I was
a six-foot human metal detector for fragments of potential anecdotes, crawling along the earth of existence, my
nose pressed to the grass in hopes of finding something
to dig at.

Another night, with £20 between us, Hicks and I went
to a posh London hotel as she had promised that it was a
hotbed for 'bored millionaires with buckets of booze
who want the company of fun, young people'. Sure
enough, we found two middle-aged men from Dubai
who respectively owned a curry house on Edgware Road
and one of those English Language 'universities' above a
mobile phone shop on Tottenham Court Road. Hicks
and I did our old routine of flamboyantly telling the well-
rehearsed made-up story of how we had met on a cruise.
I was singing with the band, her husband had thrown

himself overboard and we'd started talking one day when we were both sitting alone on the top deck, smoking and looking out to sea.

They asked if we fancied heading to their friend Rodney's house, who they assured us was 'a party boy' – the universal euphemism for 'generous with his alcohol and drugs'. We all piled into their car waiting outside and their driver took us to a tower block on Edgware Road, which was far from the Studio 54 promise of excess and glamour we had been sold. Hicks and I held hands as we walked to the entrance, and in the lift I sent Farly a text with the address of where we were in case anything happened to me that night, a rather morbid ritual she had got quite used to.

A Cypriot man in his mid-seventies wearing stripy pyjamas opened the door.

'My God!' he shouted as he looked us over. 'Ees too late!' He threw his hands in the air in despair. 'I am too old for thees!'

Our two new friends promised it wouldn't be too long a party and that we just wanted a few drinks. Rodney graciously invited us in and asked what we wanted to drink. He said cocktails were his speciality, while gesturing at his well-stocked 1970s drinks cabinet. I asked for a dry Martini.

I was quite fascinated by Rodney; particularly by the dozens of framed photographs of grandchildren that were scattered on every available surface. We walked around with our Martinis, him still in his pyjamas, and he gave me the names, ages and character description of all of them. Meanwhile, Hicks was doing what she always did on nights like this – earnestly talking about philosophy with one of the Dubai millionaires, gesticulating dramatically while monologuing about French existentialists, her eyes popping out of her head like forget-me-nots springing from cracks in the pavement.

Rodney and I sat on his sofa and he told me the mythology of his past: the failed business ventures, the bar he owned that was now a Waitrose, the models who broke his heart. He paused from his storytelling at one point, rolling up a five-pound note for the coke he had lined up on his coffee table, and sat back to look at me.

'You know, ees funny, you remind me so much of a woman I met a few times in the seventies. Long blonde hair; she had eyes just like yours. She was dating a friend of mine for a while.'

'Oh yeah?' I asked, sparking up a cigarette. 'Who was she?'

'Barby. I think her name was Barby.' I swallowed, remembering a story my mum once told me of the fun-but-loathsome nickname she was given in her early twenties.

'Barbara,' I replied. 'Barbara Levey.'

'Yes!' he yelped. 'You know this woman?'

'That's my mum,' I replied. I thought of her, in bed in the suburbs, and imagined what she'd make of her daughter getting high with a seventy-five-year-old Cypriot man she'd met in the seventies. I went into the other room, broke up Hicks's one-woman literary salon with her simultaneously enamoured and indifferent audience and told her we needed to leave immediately. She said there would be a great 'after-party' at the curry house one of the men owned on Edgware Road. I told her we were already at the after-party. I wondered if perhaps I had accidentally fallen into the murky hinterland of after the after-party and now I was just stuck there all the time. I wondered if I needed a ladder out.

But I can't say it was all tragic, because it wasn't. My friends and I continued to believe what we were doing was a great act of empowerment and emancipation. My mum often told me this was a misguided act of feminism; that emulating the most yobbish behaviour of men was not a mark of equality ('She was so detrimental to the cause, that Zoë Ball,' she once commented). But I still think there were moments when those years of partying were a defiant, celebratory, powerful act; a refusal to use my body in a way that was expected of me. A lot of it was just a really good time on our own terms – many of the memories revolve around me and one of the girls leaving a situation we were bored of or didn't like, just to spend time with each other. I was starving hungry for experience and I satisfied those cravings with like-minded ramblers. And it created a gang mentality that none of us have ever shaken off.

Some of the memories I have are joyful, some of them are sad, and that was the reality. Sometimes I danced with a grin on my face until dawn in a circle of my

closest friends, sometimes I fell over on the street running for the night bus in the rain and lay on the wet
pavement for far longer than I should have. Sometimes
I knocked myself out walking into a lamp post, left with
a purple chin for days. But sometimes I woke up in a
loving tangle of hung-over girls, filled with nothing but
comfort and joy. Occasionally, I now meet people from
those slightly hazy years who say they spent an evening
with me drinking in the corner of a house party and I'm
immediately filled with panic because I can't remember
it. A year or so ago, I shuddered with embarrassment
when a black cab driver asked if my name was 'Donny'
as he was pretty sure he'd picked me up in 'a right state'
walking down a London street with no shoes on in 2009.

But a lot of it was magnificent, carefree fun. A lot of
it was an adventure, through cities, counties, stories and
people, with a gang of explorers in neon tights and too
much black eyeliner by my side.

And at least, I thought, I had finally proven to everyone that I was a grown-up. At least I could finally be
taken seriously.

Recipe: Hangover Mac and Cheese

(*serves four*)

For the full immersive experience, eat this in your pyjamas in front of *Maid in Manhattan* or a documentary about a serial killer.

- 350g pasta – macaroni or penne works well
- 35g butter
- 35g plain flour
- 500ml whole milk
- 200g grated Cheddar cheese
- 100g grated Red Leicester cheese
- 100g grated Parmesan cheese
- 1 tbsp English mustard
- Bunch of spring onions, chopped
- Dash of Worcestershire sauce
- 1 small ball of mozzarella cheese, torn into pieces
- Salt and black pepper, to season
- Olive oil, to drizzle

In a large pan of boiling water, cook the pasta for eight minutes, so it is slightly undercooked – it will continue to cook when you bake it. Drain and set aside, stirring olive oil through it so it doesn't stick together.

In a separate large pan, melt the butter. Mix in the flour and keep cooking for a few minutes, stirring all the time until the mixture forms a roux paste. Whisk in the milk little by little, and cook over a low heat for ten to fifteen minutes. Keep stirring all the time and cook until you have a smooth and glossy sauce that gradually thickens.

Off the heat, add around three-quarters of the Cheddar, Red Leicester and Parmesan into the sauce, along with the mustard, some salt and pepper, the chopped onions and a dash of Worcestershire sauce, and keep stirring until it is all melted.

Preheat the grill as high as it will go. Pour the pasta into the sauce and mix everything together in a baking dish, stir in the mozzarella, then sprinkle over the remaining Cheddar, Red Leicester and Parmesan. Grill (or place into a hot oven at 200°C for fifteen minutes), until the mixture is golden and bubbling with a crisp top.

The Bad Date Diaries: A Hotel
on a Main Road in Ealing

It is my first Christmas back from university and I have a full-time job as a sales girl at L.K. Bennett in Bond Street. Debbie, the glamorous fashion student who always makes the highest commission, paints my lips Vivien Leigh red in the changing room ready for a big date.

The man is called Graysen and I met him at York Uni when visiting a school friend there a month previously. I was waiting at the student union bar to buy two vodka Diet Cokes, when someone grabbed my hand. Graysen – lanky, pale, interesting, Elvis eyes smudged in a cloud of eyeliner – turned my palm over.

'Three children. You'll die at ninety.' He looked at me. 'You've been here before,' he whispered dramatically.

He is the first person of my age I have ever met who chooses not to be on Facebook. I think he is Sartre.

We meet under a giant Christmas tree and he takes me to a Martini bar because he remembers I said it was my favourite drink (at this point I am still in the 'training myself to like Martinis' phase, so worry he'll see my first-sip wince, but I manage to hold it together). We then move on to the oldest pub in London where I drink strawberry beer. He shows me a set of keys – his boss has given him a hotel room for the night. He never explains why.

Three buses later, in the time it takes for him to explain to me why 'London has been more of a parent to me than my parents have', we arrive at a dingy hotel in a converted suburban home on a main road in Ealing.

I don't want to sleep with him because I want to get to know him better, so we spend all night lying in the bed, staring at the off-white ceiling, and talk about our eighteen years so far. He is the son of a very old, very elegant, very rich man who was 'the last of the colonizers' and discovered a rare type of fish on his travels, wrote a book about it and has lived off the money ever since. I am agog with wonder. We fall asleep at five.

Early the next morning, Graysen has to go to work. He kisses me, says goodbye and leaves a peach pastry on the bedside table. That's the last time we ever see each other.

I will spend the following five years constantly wondering if Graysen was just an actor looking for a gullible audience and an escape from himself for a night. If it was all made up: the palm reading, the hotel, the fish, the eyeliner.

Then years and years later, I will fall for a biology PhD student who will become the great love of my life. One Sunday night I will be lying on his bed in his jumper and he will get out a book to read before we sleep about a man who discovered a fish. I will grab it off him and look at the inside cover to see a photograph of a man with the same face and surname as Graysen. The boyfriend will ask why I am laughing. 'Because it was all real,' I will say. 'And it was so ridiculous.'

The Bad Party Chronicles:
Cobham, New Year's Eve, 2007

'There must be *something* happening,' I say to Farly as we watch our thirteenth episode of *Friends* while slumped across the sofa at my mum's house at five p.m. on New Year's Eve. 'We're nineteen years old, we have to be able to find a party somewhere.' I send a seemingly personal message out to everyone in my phone book. Our friend Dan suggests a warehouse rave in Hackney, but Farly is scared of groups of people taking drugs and has never been further east than Liverpool Street.

Just as we're losing hope, someone bites. Felix – a friend from school who was in the year below me, who I've always had a gigantic crush on. He speaks of a 'massive rave in Cobham' and tells me it's not one I want to miss. He asks me to bring female friends. Farly agrees to go as it's our only option and she knows how much I fancy Felix. She's taking one for the team, being my wing woman – going to the party for the greater good of my vagina. It's a mutual, fair and successful system of turn-taking which we've long used, having always both been single – I sacrifice my night to help her pursue a boy, I bank this act of goodwill and can cash it in at any point to have her do the same for me. It's shagging democracy. It's swings and roundabouts.

We arrive at the large detached house in Surrey, the *Footballers' Wives* belt, to find very much not a rave, but instead a sort of sedentary oven-pizza party made up of ten intertwined couples and one burly bloke in a rugby shirt who is playing with the family Labrador.

'Hello!' I say tentatively. 'Is Felix here?'

'He's gone to the shop to get vodka,' the monotone rugby player replies, not looking up from the dog.

'Weren't you in the year above us at school?' a horsey-faced girl with corkscrew curls asks.

'Yeah,' I say, gingerly helping myself to a square of pepperoni.

'Were none of your friends free tonight?'

Felix appears with a clanking carrier bag.

'Hey!' he shouts, outstretching his arms for a hug.

'Hi!' I say, giving him a hug. 'This is Farly. Everyone here is in a couple?' I mutter out of the side of my mouth.

'Yeah,' Felix says. 'We were expecting a more diverse crowd, but loads of people who said they were going to come haven't come.'

'Right.'

'We'll have fun, though!' he says, putting his arms round both of us. 'Three musketeers.'

The next few hours pass with a chummy, drunken ease; enough to make me think that the long road to Cobham may have been worth it. Felix, Farly and I go to the conservatory and play drinking games and we chat and laugh; at one point he puts his arms round me and Farly and I exchange the briefest half-smile and flicker of eye contact with her. Enough to make her go take a fake phone call upstairs to leave us alone. I couldn't have loved her more.

'Can I talk to you somewhere quiet?' he asks.

'Sure,' I say, smiling. He takes my hand in his and walks me out to the garden.

'This is awkward,' he says as I sit on a plastic chair and he hops from foot to foot.

'Why? Just say it.'

'I really fancy your mate Farly,' he says. 'Is she single?' In a nanosecond, I weigh up how much of a good person I am.

'No,' I reply, deciding I've got plenty of time left in life for personal growth. 'No, she's not single.'

'Fuck,' he says. 'Is she in a relationship?'

'Yes, a very serious one,' I say gravely, nodding. 'With a boy called Dave.'

'But she was making out in conversation like she was single?'

'Well, they're not together any more *officially*,' I ad-lib. 'But they're still kind of a thing. It's very full-on. She's on the phone to him right now, in fact. You know how it can be at New Year. Thinking of all your regrets and the things left unsaid and so on and so forth. Anyway, she's definitely not ready to move on with anyone.'

Farly returns to the table bouncily, bottle of wine in hand. A deflated Felix excuses himself to go to the loo.

'Did you snog him?' she asks excitedly. 'Was I interrupting?'

'No, he fancies you and he's asked if you're single and I've said no because I'm a bad person and I don't want you to get off with him so I've said you're in a complicated on-off relationship with a boy called Dave and it's all very upsetting and you're not ready to move on with anyone.'

'OK,' she replies.

'Is that OK?'

'Of course it's OK,' she says. 'He's not my type anyway.' We hear the footsteps of Felix.

'I said you were just on the phone to Dave,' I garble in a whisper.

'Yeah,' she speaks up as Felix sits back down. 'So anyway, yeah, that was Dave on the phone just now,' she says robotically, with all the nuanced subtlety of a character in *Acorn Antiques*. 'Again!'

'What did he say?'

'Oh, same old, same old. Wants me back, thinks we can make it work. And I'm like, "Dave, we've been here before." I did feel something though, even though we aren't together. It just makes it all the more obvious to me that I'm definitely not ready to move on with anyone,' she parrots.

Felix chews his lip aggressively then downs the rest of his wine in one. 'Nearly midnight,' he says and leaves the table to head into the house.

As we chant the countdown, I stand in the heavy, dull, cream suburban living room belonging to the family of this boy I have never met and I swear to never,

ever plan an evening around a potential conquest again. We stare at the flatscreen television, playing out the BBC coverage of red-cheeked, drunk people in scarves cheering on the South Bank and I yearn to be there. Big Ben strikes at midnight. 'Auld Lang Syne' plays. Then, for some reason I don't think I will ever be able to fathom, everyone in the room starts slow dancing like it's the last song at the disco. Apart from Felix, who is at the other side of the room sulkily playing a game on his phone. I turn the brass handle of the mahogany antique drinks cabinet and help myself to a bottle of whisky. I look over at Farly, who has the family's black Labrador on its hind legs to make it stand up, its paws in her hands. They too slow dance to the funereal sway of 'Auld Lang Syne'.

We've missed the last train back to London, so I stand outside the house and ring some local taxi companies for a quote to get home but they're all too expensive. We are trapped in Surrey for at least eight hours in a house full of couples and a crush who doesn't fancy me – all from the year below me at school. I re-enter the seventh circle of suburbia and see Farly and the miscellaneous rugby player necking up against the fridge before sneaking into the airing cupboard. I go to the garden to chain-smoke the rest of my cigarettes on my own.

'Where's Farly?' Felix asks, who's had the same idea as me. I can't be bothered with the charade any more.

'She's in the airing cupboard with that rugby player guy,' I say expressionlessly, before taking a glug from the whisky bottle.

'What? What about Dave?'

'I dunno,' I say, lighting my cigarette and exhaling smoke into the cold, still night air. 'She and Dave are very complicated, Felix, and the sooner you realize that the better. It's up, it's down, it's on, it's off.'

'But she said it was *on* an hour ago,' he replies in outrage.

'Yeah, well I think he probably rang again and they probably had another fight and she probably realized she was over it, actually.'

'Great,' he says, sitting down on the garden furniture next to me and taking a cigarette. 'This is the worst New Year's Eve ever.'

'Yeah,' I say. We watch the last of Surrey's fireworks in silence. 'It is.'

10th November

Dear anyone I've ever met and a few people I've never met,
Forgive the group email I feel absolutely no repentance for.
Sorry for the shameless self-promotion I feel absolutely no
shame about. I am emailing you because there's a vanity
project I have been working on for all of a fortnight and I
feel all of you owe it your time, money and attention.

I am hosting an evening of music, spoken word and film
in an event called Lana's Literary Salon, taking place in an
abandoned car park in Leytonstone. The idea is that the
evening will evoke the mind-expanding conversational
traditions of the Oxford Union with the atmosphere of
Noel's House Party.

To begin, there will be some spoken-word poetry written
by India Towler-Baggs on the subjects of her recent life-
changing haircut, the difficult choice of selecting her
default web browser setting and finding her way back to
herself through a mix of ayahuasca ceremonies and Zumba
classes. She will perform all her work with a slight Jamaican
accent despite attending Cheltenham Ladies' College.

As most of you already know from a steady stream of
spam on Facebook, Ollie has started his own political party,
Young Clueless Liberals, so he'll be reading his manifesto
aloud followed by a discussion on stage with journalist
Foxy James (*T4*, *MTV News*) about his three principal aims
for the party: first-time buyers, student fees and the
reopening of Fabric nightclub. You'll be able to sign up for
the party at the 'venue'.

Then, the headline act: my short film. *No One Minds That Ulrika Jonsson is an Immigrant* explores the themes of cultural identity, citizenship and sovereignty in a future dystopian setting. After the three-minute film ends, Foxy will interview me on stage about it for two hours – we will reference the film and its crew (mainly my family) as if it is a universally recognized piece of work and speak with showbizzy, eye-rolly, in-jokey camaraderie about behind-the-scenes stories as if I were Martin Scorsese giving a director's commentary on *GoodFellas*.

There will be craft beer, brewed by my flatmate on the balcony of our Penge new-build. The Death of Hackney tastes like a sort of fizzy Marmite and smells like a urinary tract infection and is yours for £13 a bottle. Enjoy.

There will also be a bucket circulating in which you can charitably donate as little or as much as you want to a really worthwhile cause: me. The sequel to *Ulrika* is currently in pre-production and I want to get it made as soon as possible, but I don't want to get a boring job like everyone else (much like Kerouac, I'm just not a morning person).

Thank you so, so much for your support with this. I will literally love every single one of you who turns up – except for people I don't know that well, who I will greet in a cursory way then say, 'Oh my God why is he here I literally haven't even seen him since primary school? I think he's obsessed with me,' to my friends.

May art be with you –

Lana xxx

Being a Bit Fat, Being a Bit Thin

'Do you love me any more?' I asked.

'No,' he said. 'No, I don't think I do love you any more.'

'Do you at least fancy me?' I asked. There was a silence.

'I don't think so.'

I hung up.

(I've since advised people that it's best to lie about this if they're dumping someone. The 'falling out of love' stuff is pretty bad. The 'I don't fancy you' stuff is killer.)

I was just twenty-one, I was a month out of university. And my first proper boyfriend had just dumped me over the phone.

Harry and I had been together for a little over a year despite being completely and utterly wrong for each other. He was conservative, obsessed with sport, did a hundred press-ups before bed every night, was the social secretary of the Exeter University Lacrosse Club and owned a non-ironic T-shirt that said 'Lash Gordon' on the front. He hated excessive displays of emotion, tall women wearing heels or being too loud. So basically everything that made up my personality at the time. He thought I was a disaster, I thought he was a square.

Our entire relationship was spent arguing, not least

because we never had any time apart. He had practically lived at the flat I shared with Lacey, AJ and Farly in our final year at university and had moved into my parents' house for the summer while he did an internship.

One of our lowest moments came at the end of that long, hot, agitated August with no space from each other, when we got a train to Oxford for Lacey's twenty-first birthday party. I went rogue from my table after the main course and happened upon a swimming pool, which looked appealing. So I took all my clothes off and went for a dip, and, when a few friends came looking for me, encouraged everyone else to do the same. The night descended into a mass pool party and I became a sort of naked, poolside Master of Ceremonies. Harry went ballistic. The next morning, Farly and AJ hid behind a tree with uncontrollable giggles as they watched him shout 'YOU WILL NEVER SHOW ME UP LIKE THAT AGAIN!' at me, my head-hanging shame made even more apparent by the fact the pool had been overchlorinated and my bleached hair had turned a vibrant bottle green.

We had absolutely nothing in common. But he wanted to be my first proper boyfriend, and when I was nineteen that was a good enough reason to go out with someone.

I was living in an East London flat the night he called me, staying with a friend indefinitely while I began my journalism course to avoid the long commute from Stanmore. Farly turned up an hour later at one a.m., having driven from her mum's house, and told me she was taking me home.

I was inconsolable on the journey back, trying to recount our conversation to Farly, but barely remembering any of the detail. My phone rang – it was him. I told her I couldn't speak to him. She pulled over, picked up and pressed it to her ear.

'Harry, why have you done this?' she barked. I couldn't make out what he was saying on the other end of the line. 'Fine, but why do it to her over the phone? Why couldn't you have come see her and do it in the flesh?' she barked again. There was more indecipherable talking on his side. Farly listened. 'YEAH? WELL YOU CAN GO FUCK YOURSELF,' she shouted, hanging up and throwing the mobile on to the seat behind her.

'What did he say?'

'Nothing, really,' she said.

Farly slept in my bed that night. And the night after that. She ended up staying for a fortnight; I didn't move back to the flat. It was the first time I had experienced heartbreak and I'd never thought the overwhelming feeling would be such acute confusion; as if I had no reason to trust anyone ever again. I didn't have an exact idea of what had happened or why. All I knew was that I hadn't been good enough.

I also couldn't eat. I had heard about this upshot of a break-up before, but I had never imagined it would affect me. I was, and always had been, a very hungry girl. Perhaps the hungriest of all. I hadn't managed a diet that had ever lasted longer than two days. My family all loved food, Farly and I had loved food. My mum, a natural cook who grew up with Italian grandparents, started teaching me to cook when I was five, standing me next to her on a chair so I could help knead dough or whisk eggs at the kitchen counter. I cooked for myself through-out my teens and I cooked for everyone at university. My first ever diary entry, when I was six, was an enthusi-astic record of what I had eaten that day. I recalled phases of my life by what was on a plate: the crispy baked pota-toes on seaside holidays in Devon, the lurid, sticky jam tarts of my tenth birthday, the roast chicken of every Sunday night, bathing the dread of the school week in gravy. No matter how terrible life became, no matter how blistering the pain, I was always sure I'd still have room for seconds.

I never felt overweight, but my body type was often muddily described as 'a big girl'. I come from a long, tall line of giants. My brother, God love him, was a six-foot-seven teenager who had to buy clothes in shops called things like 'Magnus' and 'High and Mighty'. By the time I was fourteen, I was five foot ten. By the time I was six-teen, I was six foot. But I wasn't one of those adorably tall, lanky teenage part-foal-part-human girls – I was broad, with big boobs and hips. I was the opposite of the girls photographed in the pages of *Bliss* and described in *The Baby-Sitters Club* book series. Just as I was never mentally built of the right stuff to be a teenager, neither was my physical being well-suited to it.

I found being so tall as a teenager difficult – I never knew how much I was supposed to weigh, because every girl was half my height and talked about their 'fat weight' as being a weight I hadn't been since childhood, which engendered a great sense of shame. That, partnered with boredom eating and puppy fat, meant I was shopping for size 16s when I was not yet sixteen. I was aware I was bigger than my friends and was sometimes called fat, but I always had faith that my shape would make more sense when I wasn't a kid. The only truly mortifying moment came when, at a barbecue aged fifteen, my parents' extremely drunk and spectacularly overweight friend Tilly grabbed my love handles like she was steering the wheel of a ship before announcing to the garden that 'us chunky girls have got to stick together' and telling me in no uncertain terms that 'men like a bit of meat on a girl', before I received a conspiratorial wink from her husband who was, incidentally, also the width of a Vauxhall Zafira.

Some weight slowly peeled off when I went to boarding school and by the time I got to university I was a comfortable size 14 – but I didn't really mind that I wasn't very slim. I still kissed the boys I wanted to kiss. I could wear Topshop. And I loved food and cooking. I understood that that was the trade-off.

And yet, here I was. Finally unable to eat anything. From head to toe, I was flooded with a sickly yellow feeling and my appetite – my most resplendent asset – had vanished. My intestines felt kinetic. There was a constant lump in my throat. Mum would give me bowls of soup in the evening, telling me it was easy to swallow, but I'd only manage a few spoonfuls and put the rest down the sink when she wasn't there.

After a fortnight, I got on the scales. I had lost a stone. I stood in front of the mirror naked and saw, for the first time in my life, the very beginnings of what I had been led to believe were the true qualifications of femininity. A smaller waist, hip bones, collarbones and shoulder blades. In this new landscape that I didn't understand – where the boy I'd shared a home and life with for over a year was suddenly repulsed by me – I felt a flicker of something finally making sense. I had stopped eating, therefore my body was changing. It worked. Here, in the mess, I found a simple formula of which I was the master. Here was something I could control that would lead me somewhere new, somewhere I could be someone different. The answer was in my reflection: don't eat any more.

I made a project of my new mission; I weighed myself every day, I counted my steps, I counted my calories, I did sit-ups in my bedroom every morning and night, I wrote down my measurements every week. I lived off Diet Coke and carrot sticks. If I wanted to eat something, I'd go to bed or have a hot bath. More weight dropped away. I shed it day by day, pound by pound; it never seemed to plateau. This filled me with an energy that initially acted as a substitute for food; I felt like a high-speed train that was magically running on empty.

Another month passed, another stone dropped. My period didn't arrive, which simultaneously frightened and encouraged me. At least it meant something was changing inside and outside too; at least I was closer to being someone new.

During this time, when I wasn't at lectures, I was hunkered down at home. I still felt fragile from the break-up and I didn't want to socialize. The first person who noticed something was wrong was Alex, Harry's sister, who I had become very close to during our relationship and who, thankfully, stuck by me through our break-up. She had just moved to New York and we were skyping every day. One day, in the middle of one of our chats, I stood up while we were speaking and she saw my body in full length for the first time in months.

'Where are your tits?' she asked me, her eyes widening as she scanned me up and down, leaning into her camera.

'They're there.'

'No they're not. And your stomach is like an ironing board. Dolls, what's happened?'

'Nothing, I've just lost some weight.'

'Oh my darling,' she said, frowning. 'You're not eating, are you?'

Others were less perceptive. I started going out more and seeing friends from university. People told me they'd heard about Harry and how sorry they were. People told me he had a new girlfriend. People told me how great I looked, over and over and over again. Every compliment fed me like lunch.

I went out and drank constantly to try and distract from the pain of hunger. My mum, progressively more concerned, would leave plates of food out for me on the kitchen table for when I'd get home from a night out. She thought that, rightly, I'd be more likely to eat then. I learnt to go straight up to bed when I got home.

By December, I'd lost three stone. Three stone in three months. I found it harder to summon the thoughts and strict rituals that had kept me away from food until that point. I was exhausted, my hair was thin and I was constantly, bone-searingly freezing. I sat in the shower to try and warm myself up with the water turned on so hot it burnt my back and left marks. I lied constantly to my worried parents about how much I'd eaten that day or when I was going to eat next. I would dream that I had consumed mountains and mountains of food and would wake up in tears of frustration that I had stupidly broken the spell I had cast.

Hicks was at Exeter for an extra year after the rest of us graduated. One weekend, Sophie, Farly and I decided to drive down to spend the weekend with her and go to all our old haunts. It also meant I could see Harry, who was in his final year there, which I thought might feel like something had come full-circle and bring me a semblance of closure. I told him we needed to give each other our stuff back; he agreed to see me.

The girls drove me to his house early on the Saturday evening and parked outside.

'WE'LL WAIT RIGHT HERE, MATE,' Hicks

bellowed out of the car window, her feet and a fag dangling out of it. I went to Harry's front door and rang the bell.

'Oh my God,' he said when he opened the door. 'You look –'

'Hi, Harry,' I said and walked past him and went upstairs. He followed after me. We stood at opposite ends of his bedroom, staring at each other.

'You look amazing.'

'Thanks,' I said. 'Can I have my stuff?'

'Yeah, yeah, sure,' he said in a daze. He handed me a plastic bag of my clothes and books. I took his rolled-up jumpers out of my handbag and threw them on his bed.

'That's all your stuff I found at my house.'

'OK, thanks,' he said. 'How long are you here for?'

'The weekend. Me and Farly and Soph are staying with Hicks.'

'Oh, great,' he said. He was speaking uncharacteristically diminutively. 'Well, do send them my love. Although, they probably don't want to hear from me.' There was a brief silence as we continued to stare at each other. 'I'm sorry for –'

'Don't be,' I snapped.

'I am,' he said. 'I'm sorry for how I handled it.'

'Honestly, don't be, you did me the biggest favour,' I babbled. 'Look, I've even grown my nails, I don't bite them any more, I've had my first ever manicure, would you believe it, and it only cost five quid,' I said,

aggressively sticking my hands out towards him. I heard
the car honking outside. Sophie and Hicks were drinking tinnies and both beeping the horn, while Farly
flapped about trying to stop them.

'I've got to go,' I said.

'Sure,' he replied. We walked in silence down the
stairs and he opened his front door.

'Are you OK?' he asked. 'You look really –'

'Thin?' I asked.

'Yeah.'

'I'm fine, Harry,' I said, before giving him a cursory
hug. 'Goodbye.'

The girls took me out for a curry to celebrate what
they saw as the big finale of the whole sorry mess; I
picked at rice and drank pint after pint of beer. I felt
more agitated, more humiliated, more angry and more
out of control than ever. Whatever it was I wanted to
achieve by seeing him hadn't worked. I hadn't got it.

I threw myself into weight loss harder and faster. My
anger fuelled me. The weight began to plateau – a sign
that the cogs of my metabolism were confused and
slowing down – so I ate even less. Friends started confronting me about it – Farly told me she thought I was
gripped by an obsession. She tried to help me open up,
but I brushed off her questions with humour. Generally,
I realized a good tactic to get people off my back was to
constantly make jokes about how little I was eating. I

would bring it up before anyone else did, so they knew it wasn't a problem, just a diet. And besides, as I kept pointing out, I was still only a size 10. I wasn't underweight, I just started out big.

I carried on because it was the only thing I could control. I carried on because I just wanted to be happy and everyone knows when you're thinner, you're happier. I carried on because, at every turn, society was rewarding me for my self-inflicted torture. I received compliments, I received propositions, I felt more accepted by people I didn't know, nearly all clothes looked great on me. I felt like I had finally earnt the right to be taken seriously as a woman; that everything before that had been redundant. That I had been foolish to think I had ever been worthy of affection. I had equated love with thinness and, to my horror, reinforcement of this belief was everywhere. My health was plummeting, my stocks were up.

And a woman can never really be thin enough, that's the problem. It is not seen as too high a price to pay to be hungry all the time or to restrict an entire food group or to spend four nights a week in a Fitness First gym. To be an empirically attractive young man, you just have to have a nice smile, an average body type (give or take a stone) a bit of hair and be wearing an all-right jumper. To be a desirable woman – the sky's the limit. Have every surface of your body waxed. Have manicures every week. Wear heels every day. Look like a Victoria's Secret Angel even though you work in an office. It's not enough to be an average-sized woman with a bit of hair and an all-right jumper. That doesn't cut it. We're told we have to look like the women who are paid to look like that as their profession.

And the more perfect I strived to be, the more imperfections I noticed. I had been more body confident as a size 14 than I was over three stone lighter. When I got naked with a new partner, I wanted to apologize for what I had to offer and list a series of things I'd change, like a middle-class hostess who says, 'Oh, don't look at the carpet, the carpet's just dreadful, I promise it's all going to change,' when she has guests round.

Some of my friends' concerns began to merge with irritation. I arrived at parties basically half dressed, having not eaten anything for days, and would wander around in a trance, barely able to say anything. Sabrina and AJ went travelling together and I turned up to their leaving party late, felt too faint to talk to anyone, made an excuse and left after half an hour. I could feel myself pushing my life away and became more and more absorbed in a completely false sense of control.

And then I fell in love for the first time.

I was wandering around a grimy house party in Elephant and Castle when I first met Leo. I had never seen a man more perfect. Tall and lean with dark floppy hair, a strong jaw, sparkling eyes, a retroussé nose, a seventies tache; a face that was half Josh Brolin and half James Taylor with – and here's the best part – absolutely no idea of his own beauty. He was a hippie PhD student; a monomaniac with a monobrow.

We started seeing each other soon after that night. I knew it was serious because I didn't go to bed with him for two whole months, wanting desperately to get it right, to savour every moment of time with him – not to speed through anything. He lived in Camden and at the end of one of our nights together, normally around four a.m., he'd walk me to the bus stop outside Chalk Farm station and I'd wait for the N5 to take me ten miles north to Edgware. From there, I'd do the forty-five-minute westerly walk to Stanmore, winding through the deserted streets lined with Volkswagens, watching the sun rise over the semi-detached red-brick houses, and I was happier than I'd ever imagined I could be.

One night, as we did this familiar walk through Camden, he stopped to kiss me and ran his hands through my hair, feeling the bumps of my clip-in hair extensions. He picked the heavy hair off my face and held it back behind my head.

'You'd look really good with short hair,' he said.

'No way,' I replied. 'I had a bob when I was a teenager and I looked like a friar.'

'No, I'm talking really short. You should do it.'

'Nah,' I said. 'I don't have the face for it.'

'You do!' he said. 'Don't be a scaredy cat. It's just hair.'

Little did he know that 'just hair' was all I thought I was good for. Just hair, just collarbones, just sit-ups.

'Just' was all I had expended my energy on for the best part of a year and it's all I thought I was worth.

A month later I took a photo of Twiggy to the hairdresser, did a shot of vodka and cut fifteen inches off my hair. With it went some of my obsession with how I looked. It snipped off and fell to the floor.

Leo hadn't realized my secret, because I didn't want him to think I was a nutcase, but after a few months of dating, he added a few things up. I managed to avoid any situation where there would be food; I always told him I would eat breakfast later when we left each other in the morning. Finally, a friend had told him she thought that I was ill.

'Is this a problem?' he asked me.

'It's fine,' I said, feeling both mortified and frightened that I was about to lose the best person I had ever met.

'Because I can do this with you. I can help you. But I can't fall in love with you if you can't talk to me.'

'OK, it's been a problem,' I told him. 'But it will change. I promise.'

I would have done anything to keep this man in my life. The love I felt was aggressive and fraught – I loved him with panic and passion. I didn't fall in love; love fell on me. Like a ton of bricks from a great height. I didn't have a choice but to let go of an obsession that was on its way to destroying everything.

So I did. I read all the right books; I went to the doctor. Slowly a stone crept back on me. Slowly I got used to eating normally. My health returned. I even tried group support meetings in community centres where, would you believe, the first thing they do is put a plate of biscuits in the middle of the room and fuss over whose turn it is on the rota to bring the snacks the following week, which seemed to me to be as useful as putting a bottle of Jack Daniel's in the middle of an AA meeting.

I fell back in love with cooking. I fell back in love with eating. I spent every weekend doing both with Leo. My mum and I watched old Fanny Cradock and Nigella episodes together. Everyone kept telling me I looked 'healthy' every time they saw me and I tried to ignore the thought that this meant I was fat again. The war was over; the recovery began. I got my life back.

My hippie liberated me from my enslavement to perfection. We'd get drunk and cut my hair even shorter. He'd snip huge chunks out with kitchen scissors while I sat at the table squeezing limes into beers. I eventually shaved both sides, leaving me with a tufty Mohawk. I lived in plimsolls and his jumpers and I'd spend days with him without touching a make-up bag or a razor – a total first. We'd go for weekends on the coast and wash our faces and bodies and dishes in the sea. We set up a tent in his bedroom on Sunday nights when we were bored. It was pure and free and perfect.

But I knew deep down that I was still morphing myself at the behest of a man's gaze; I had just gone to the opposite end of the spectrum. Leo hated me wearing too much make-up, so I'd wipe it off on the bus on the way home to him after a party. I'd change out of my heels into high-tops.

The weight I put back on was not anything I wanted to do for myself. Had I not met Leo, I think I would have carried on getting thinner, but with a stroke of luck, he helped lead me to total recovery. As I got older and mercifully more aware of what a precious gift a healthy working body is, I felt ashamed and bewildered that I could have treated mine so badly. But it would be a lie to say I think I will ever be entirely free of what happened in that time, which is something no one ever tells you. You can restore your physical being to health; you can develop a rational, balanced, caring attitude to weight as well as good daily habits. But you can't forget how many calories are in a boiled egg or how many steps burn how many calories. You can't forget what exact weight you were every week of every month that made up that time. You can try as hard as you can to block it out, but sometimes, on very difficult days, it feels like you'll never be as euphoric as that ten-year-old licking lurid jam off her fingertips, not ever again.

Everything I Knew About Love at Twenty-one

Men love a wild, filthy woman. Have sex on the first date, keep them up all night, smoke hash in their bed in the morning, never call them back, tell them you hate them, turn up on their doorstep in an Ann Summers nurse's outfit, be anything but conventional. That's how you keep them interested.

If you ignore the boyfriends of your best friends for long enough, they'll eventually go away. Treat them a bit like how you would the common cold or a mild case of thrush.

A break-up will never be as hard as the first one. You'll float around aimlessly in the months afterwards, feeling as lost and confused as a child, questioning all the things you knew to be true and contemplating all the things you have to relearn.

Always stay at a man's house, then you can leave whenever you want in the morning.

The perfect man is olive-skinned with brown or green eyes, a big, strong nose, a thick beard and curly dark hair. He has tattoos that aren't embarrassing and five pairs of vintage Levis.

When you're not having sex, have a bush like a wild, climbing shrub. There's no point wasting all that time, money and fumes on hair-removal cream unless some-one's going to see the results.

When you are thin enough, you'll be happy with who you are and then you'll be worthy of love.

Don't go out with someone who won't let you get drunk and flirt with other people. If that's part of your identity, they should take you for who you are.

Orgasms are easy to fake and make both parties feel better. Do a good deed today.

You'll feel settled, centred and calm when you fall in love with the right man.

The worst feeling in the world is being dumped.

Men, on the whole, are not to be trusted.

The best bit of a relationship is the first three months.

A good friend will always put you before a man.

When you can't fall asleep, dream of all the love affairs with olive-skinned, curly-haired men that lie ahead of you.

Gooseberry Fool:
My Life as a Third Wheel

It began with a train journey. I always thought something brilliant might happen to me on a train. The transitional state of a long journey has always seemed to me the most romantic and magical of places to find yourself in; marooned in a cosy pod of your own thoughts, suspended in mid-air, travelling through a wodge of silent, blank pages between two chapters. A place where phones dip in and out of consciousness and you're forced to spend time with your thoughts, working out what needs to be reshaped and reordered. I have done big dreaming while sitting on trains. The clearest moments of epiphany or gratitude have hit me when zooming through unidentifiable English countryside, staring out at a golden rapeseed field, considering what I am leaving behind or about to approach.

In 2008, I got on a train at Paddington that changed my life for ever, but not in the way I anticipated. It wasn't at all like *Before Sunrise* or *Some Like It Hot* or *Murder on the Orient Express*. I didn't fall in love or do a raunchy, boozy performance of 'Runnin' Wild' on the ukulele or get entangled in a murder mystery; instead I began a chain of events that would unfurl slowly over the next five years until finally the story was so frustratingly far away,

I couldn't touch it, let alone undo what I had begun. The story of the train journey that changed my life, actually, hardly involves me at all.

It was the coldest winter that I could remember (probably due to my fondness at the time for the form-fitting bodycon dress) and while I was on the last Sunday-night train from London back to Exeter University, it started to snow. The train broke down just outside Bristol and while other passengers moaned and sighed and stomped about in frustration, I couldn't have found the whole thing more romantic. I bought a bottle of cheap red wine from the First Great Western buffet carriage and returned to my seat to stare out into the inky, silent countryside being neatly frosted with thick snow like icing on a Christmas cake.

On the seat across from me, there was a boy about my age with the prettiest face I had ever seen. He had been trying to catch my gaze while I had been staring out of the window, dreaming of a man on this broken-down train trying to catch my gaze. Finally he caught my eye, introduced himself as Hector and asked if he could join me for a drink.

He had the sort of peculiar, unshakeable confidence that had so obviously been cultivated at a public school. It's a confidence that comes from being handed an ancient blazer of identity aged thirteen – a set of house colours, a crass nickname and a motto that can be recalled in song even after five pints. It's the brash confidence that comes from being in a debating society aged thirteen, then ultimately elbows its way to the top of government; the type that makes you believe it has a right to be here and things to say. Fortunately, Hector could offset such arrogance because he had the features of a cherub: sparkly blue eyes with irises like cornflowers and an upturned nose like a boy in a 1950s soap advert. He had the curly, floppy hair of a young Hugh Grant along with the rich, plummy, playful voice. We talked for two hours as the train sat still, laughing and drinking and eating the mince pies my mum had packed me off with.

Now, I know what you're thinking: if *only* this encounter could have been more twee. Well, that went through my nineteen-year-old brain too. So, inspired by the many romcoms shown on terrestrial television on a Sunday night, I decided it would be a serendipitous act if we didn't swap numbers and hoped to be reunited again by chance. And off he went, into the cold night at Bristol station, leaving me with enough material to write about on my rambling, anonymous 'single girl's adventures' blog for at least three entries.

Two years later to the month, a few months after Harry and I had broken up, I was standing at the bar in a pub on Portobello Road when he walked in. Even with just two years of aging, his cherubic face had become ironic and sexy when paired with a grown-up suit and coat and a slightly less floppy haircut.

'Of all the pubs in all the world,' he said as he approached me and kissed me on both cheeks. As history dictated, we passed the night drinking cheap red wine while the snow fell heavily outside and, come last orders, we were trapped again. The snow was too heavy for me to get a bus home and I was too drunk to muster the energy to play hard to get. Unable to tackle the snow in a wobbly, cheap pair of heels, he flung me over his shoulder like a Persian rug and we went back to his flat.

Come four a.m., we were still awake, lying naked on his floor, chain-smoking American Spirits and flicking ash into a cup balanced on my stomach. He took my eyeliner out from my handbag and wrote a line from a Ted Hughes poem on his wall (*'Her eyes wanted nothing to get away / Her looks nailed down his hands his wrists his elbows'*). The words hung, slurred and smeared in kohl, next to numerous charcoal drawings of a naked woman. ('I did them. They're my ex,' he boasted, as I lay naked as his current project, staring up at his wall of artefacts of shags gone by. 'Sweet girl, shame she was married.') Next to his bed there was a black leather address book with three words embossed in gold on the front: BLONDES, BRUNETTES, REDHEADS. You had to hand it to him – he may have been a shagger, but he was certainly an imaginative shagger.

Hector was waggish, impish, boyish, caddish, rakish, roguish; all the ishes you would use to describe a man in a Noel Coward play. I had never met anyone like him before. Everything about him was antiquated: his family had titles, he wore a floor-length wolf fur coat from Russia that belonged to his grandfather and his shirts had labels in them from boarding school. Everything in his room was overused or borrowed. Even his career was borrowed; his boss was the ex-toy-boy lover of his ex-socialite mother, who had given this disastrous graduate a job in the City out of adoration for her. I used to leave Hector in the morning and wonder what on earth he would do at work in between flouncing around in my underwear which he put on under his (unpressed) trousers and sending dirty emails to me all day from his work account.

Our relationship was entirely nocturnal because he was entirely nocturnal, like a mythical beast of the night, like the wandering wolf that was skinned for his coat. We went out and got drunk in dark bars, we had dates that began at midnight. I once actually turned up at his house naked under a trench coat. I was twenty-one and living out a Jackie Collins novel, starring opposite an overgrown, randy Just William.

He never met my friends and I never met his – which suited us just fine. I didn't even know he had housemates until I drunkenly stumbled into the kitchen one morning at six a.m., entirely naked, to be confronted by a man called Scott. I slammed open the door and switched on the light to find him sitting in his suit, eating cereal and reading the paper before work. Hector thought it was funny – more than funny, he found the idea of his housemate seeing me full-frontal naked hot. We had our first row.

A few days later, I was making scrambled eggs in his

kitchen when Scott reappeared in his dressing gown. He smiled at me apologetically.

'Hello,' he said with an awkward wave.

'Hello,' I replied. 'I'm so, so sorry about the other morning. Hector told me no one was in. I was so angry with him.'

'It's fine. Honestly, it's fine.'

'It's not fine, it's awful, I'm so sorry,' I babbled. 'The last thing you want to see before work.'

'It was . . . er . . . a nice surprise,' he said. I offered him some eggs and toast as an olive branch.

We sat and made polite conversation that eased us on to the subject of dating. Was he seeing anyone? No. Did I have any nice single friends he could date? Yes, I had the perfect girl. My best friend, Farly.

'But she definitely isn't looking for a relationship at the moment, she's happy being single, so it would be more of a casual thing,' I warned.

'That sounds perfect.'

'Great! I'll give you her number. It's the least I can do,' I said. I tapped her number into his phone. Why not? He seemed like a nice guy – attractive, courteous. She probably fancied a fling. I mentioned it to her in passing and thought nothing of it again.

I think it's important that I pause here to do a bit of explaining, so you are aware of why I single-white-female my way through the rest of this story.

My friendship with Farly was not instantaneous – she

spent her first year at school tightly bound to a group of Power Princesses. They were a brand of North London suburban girl who ruled school. They had blonde highlights, Tiffany jewellery and anecdotes from Brady, a social and sports club in Edgware for Jewish teenagers; the Chinawhite of the suburbs. I, on the other hand, wore a lot of black at the weekends and spent time at school devising plays in the drama department, trying to depict the trauma of a plane crash using only a wooden block. But we were put in the same classes for French and maths and we soon discovered we had a shared sense of humour and a passion for *The Sound of Music* and watermelon lip balms.

Our out-of-hours friendship started tentatively, after a few months of sitting next to each other in lessons. I invited her round to my house first and my mum made roast chicken. My dad did that thing he does with all my friends when he holds on to one fact about them in a panic to find a common language and brings it up in every other sentence. With Farly this is anything pertaining to Jews or Judaism, which he has continued to do for around ten years, saying things like 'Have you seen Sir Alan Sugar has had to downsize Amstrad? Great shame' or 'I saw an advert recently for reduced flights to Tel Aviv. Must be lovely, hot weather there at the moment.' But after a slow start, we were inseparable. We spent every moment we could together at school and when we got home we wolfed down our dinners then called each other to go through any other business we forgot to cover at our various meetings throughout the day. So ingrained was this ritual that even now I can recall Farly's mum's landline number between the years of 2000–2006 quicker than I can remember my credit card PIN.

I hated school and was often getting into trouble. Aged twelve, after a suspension, bust-up with my deputy head and a detention, I returned to lessons for geography with a teacher who particularly disliked me. We were asked to get out our exercise books, which I had forgotten to bring, as I did with everything when I was a kid. I was a disaster. Every year at the Christmas party a bin bag was awarded as 'The Dolly Alderton Prize for Disorganization'. The chosen pupil had to go round the school and pick up all her belongings she'd left lying around. I hated it.

'Where is your exercise book?' the teacher asked, peering down at my desk, her sour breath curdled with Nescafé and cigarettes.

'I forgot it,' I muttered.

'Oh, there's a surprise,' she said, raising her voice to the volume of a public announcement and pacing around the classroom. 'She forgot it. Has there been a day in your life when you *haven't* forgotten something? It's a book, *one* book, it's not difficult.' She slammed her board rubber down on her desk.

My face reddened and I felt the rising nausea of holding hot tears at the back of my throat. Farly squeezed my hand underneath the table twice, fast and hard. I knew what it meant. A universal, silent Morse code for *I'm here, I love you*. At that moment I realized that everything had changed: we had transitioned. We had chosen each other. We were family.

Farly and I had always been each other's plus ones for every day of each other's lives. We were each other's sidekicks at every family dinner, every holiday, every party. We have never properly rowed unless steaming drunk on a night out. We have never lied to each other. In over fifteen years, I have never gone more than a few hours without thinking about her. I only make sense with her there to act as my foil and vice versa. Without the love of Farly, I am just a heap of frayed and half-finished thoughts; of blood and muscle and skin and bone and unachievable dreams and a stack of shit teenage poetry under my bed. My mess only takes a proper shape with that familiar and favourite piece of my life standing next to me.

We know the names of all our grandparents and our childhood toys and we know the exact words that, when put in a certain order, will make each other laugh or cry or shout. There isn't a pebble on the beach of my history that she has left unturned. She knows where to find everything in me and I know where all her stuff is too. She is, in short, my best friend.

Valentine's Day, 2010. That's the day Scott and Farly chose to have their first date. I mean – who does that? I don't even know why they bothered with a date, I was under the impression that the drink was just a formality; what they were really doing was meeting up for a one-night stand.

'I know it sounds weird,' she explained. 'But we've been texting back and forth for a bit and it's the only day we can both do.'

'Where are you going?'

'I don't know. He's going to pick me up from work and he's said there's a nice place in Notting Hill for dinner.'

'DINNER?' I bellowed. 'Why are you going out for bloody DINNER? I thought this was just going to be a shag?'

'Well, I can't just go round to his house, Doll, I have to at least talk to him first.'

'Yeah but why dinner, it's not like we're ... forty. What a waste of money. Also, why Valentine's Day?'

'I've told you, otherwise we'd have to wait for ages, we're both very busy.'

'"We're both very busy,"' I mimicked. 'You're acting like you're married.'

'Oh, shut up.'

'Don't you think it's going to be weird when he – a man you've NEVER met – meets you at work then takes you to have DINNER on VALENTINE'S DAY around LOADS OF COUPLES? Don't you think it's going to distort your judgement of whether you actually like him or not?'

'No. It's going to be very casual.'

The dinner went well. The dinner wasn't very casual at all. Scott picked Farly up from Harrods where she was working on a jewellery counter, in the rain (in the rain – *Christ*, talk about gilding the lily); they got in a cab to Notting Hill, went to the restaurant and had the best date of Farly's life. I knew it was the best date of Farly's life because she didn't do her usual thing of wittering on and on about how it was the best date of her life. When I asked her about Scott, she was coy. Measured. She even sounded a bit like an adult.

It was the infuriating adultness of Farly and Scott's courtship that made me realize what a joke my relationship with Hector had become. The 'ishes' of Hector went off like milk – selfish, oafish, nightmarish. He was too disastrous and the shtick wasn't fun any more; I didn't want to drink a bottle of white wine for breakfast or hit him round the head with a loafer in a play fight or pretend to be a naughty pixie as a part of his whimsical, overcomplicated narrative in his sexual fantasies. Twice in the space of a week he got drunk, passed out and locked me out of his house in the rain for the best part of a night. The enviable head-boy confidence came with something else – the need for a matron. And that was not the job for me.

'Please, Dolly,' Farly begged on a Friday night out. 'Please just see him for one more night, please.'

'No,' I said firmly. 'I don't fancy him any more.'

'Oh, but me and Scott aren't at a point where I can just go round to his flat, I'll look like a stalker.'

'It's never bothered you before.' (Farly once gave a man £20 for phone credit and made him promise he would text her – he never did.)

'Yes but I want to be normal with him,' she said earnestly. 'I *am* being normal with him, it's really nice. Please text Hector. We can go round together, it won't be awkward.' I thought about it. 'Come on, I've done this for you.'

Damn her to hell, she had.

I texted Hector and said I was bringing Farly. We got on a night bus to Notting Hill.

Predictably, after the four of us had a drink together in their living room, Hector wanging on about the history of nipple clamps in his annoying, drunk Nigel Havers voice while Farly did her best hair-twirling and shy smiling at Scott, the pair of them went off. Hector led me up to his bedroom because he wanted to 'show me something'. He was being uncharacteristically affectionate and needy, the way men like him are when they sense you've grown distant (I hadn't answered his pornographic limerick emails in over two weeks). I sat on his bed and drank warm white wine straight from the bottle.

'What is it?' I asked flatly. He picked up a guitar. Oh no. Not this – *anything* but this. The bedroom I had spent months dreaming of, wishing I were in, had quickly become a cave of my own personal nightmares. I suddenly saw the bohemian mess for what it was: dirty socks all over the floor, a faint smell of mould and must like an old cricket pavilion on a wet day, a duvet with holes burned from comatose chain-smoking. The beautiful charcoals of naked women had morphed into ugly, knowing gargoyles staring down at me. *We had to go through this, now you do too*, they hissed.

'There'shomething I want you to hear,' he slurred and struck two violent chords, in between an attempt at tuning his guitar.

'Oh God – no, it's fine, you don't have to.'

'Dolly Alderton,' he announced, as if he were at an open-mic night. 'I am vey shmitten. I wrote thishong for you.' He started playing the pattern of three chords he had already played me over and over again before.

'I saw her on a train,' he sang in an Americana croak. 'Life would never be the same. After the first night we –'

'Hector,' I said sullenly as I felt the wine hit me with full force. 'I think we should stop seeing each other.'

I left with Farly early the next morning and that was it; I never saw him again. I was assured by Farly and Scott that I really *did* break his heart and apparently the Mulberry Bayswater handbag of an overnight guest didn't appear on the kitchen table for at least three weeks after that night.

(Footnote: Hector is now a very successful entrepreneur and married to a Hollywood actress. I found out through an article in the Mail Online while sitting in my pyjamas eating a whole chocolate yule log to myself: go figure.)

Things I Am Scared Of

- Dying
- People I love dying
- People I hate dying so I feel guilty about all the times I said bad things about them
- Drunk men on the street telling me I'm tall
- Drunk men on the street telling me I'm fat
- Drunk men on the street telling me I'm sexy
- Drunk men on the street telling me I'm ugly
- Drunk men on the street telling me to cheer up
- Drunk men on the street telling me they want to shag me
- Drunk men on the street telling me they'd never shag me
- Drunk people 'trying on' (stealing) my hat at parties
- Losing jewellery
- Falling out of a window
- Accidentally killing a baby
- Parlour games
- Talking about the history of American politics
- Starting fires everywhere
- Not understanding the washing machine
- Cancer

- STDs
- Biting down on wooden lolly sticks
- Plane crashes
- Plane food
- Working in an office
- Being asked if I believe in God (a bit)
- Being asked if I believe in horoscopes (a bit)
- Being asked why I believe in the above
- Going into an unarranged overdraft
- Never owning a dog

Being Björn Again

After I stopped seeing Hector, I assumed it would be only a matter of time before Farly and Scott fizzled out. I had been the glue that bonded them and when I left that grimy block of flats in Notting Hill, I assumed they'd have little left in common. But, within a few weeks, Farly dropped into conversation that they were going on a mini-break to Cambridge. Jealousy pumped through my blood system and my whole body stung like it was vinegar. *I* was the one who had always had a boy on the scene and yet now she was the one with an actual proper, older boyfriend. Not one who wore her knickers into work, not one who made her wear a fishnet body stocking or didn't know her surname or only texted her once a week. Farly had a boyfriend who spent more time with her sober than not sober, who took her on mini-breaks and rang her instead of texting and wanted to have actual conversations with her.

'What's even *in* Cambridge?' I ranted bitterly to AJ. 'What, like, a Bella Italia? Well good luck. Have fun.'

'What's he like?' AJ asked. The truth is, I barely knew.

'Bad news,' I said gravely. 'Too old, too serious for her.'

And then, three months in, almost to the day, he told her he loved her. She announced it at a dinner with

EVERYTHING I KNOW ABOUT LOVE

mates. We all toasted it and shrieked with joy – I wrote a sad soliloquy about it on my iPhone notes on the night bus home.

Although I had hated watching Farly be treated so badly by stupid teenage boys over the years – being led on, ignored, dumped – I realized there had been a safety in it. As long as boys weren't taking any serious notice of her, I still had her all to myself. The minute a grown-up man with a brain stopped and took interest in her, I was utterly fucked. How could he not fall in love with her? She was beautiful, funny. The kindest person I knew – she had spent years lending me money to get out of trouble and picking me up at three a.m. in her car when my bus home had stopped running. She was made of the stuff that would make the perfect partner: she thought of others first; she listened; she remembered things. She left notes in my packed lunch box before I went to work and sent cards just to say how proud she was of me.

The way I had always made boys like me was with smoke and mirrors, exaggeration and bravado; heavy make-up and heavy drinking. There was no performance or lies with Farly – if a boy ended up loving her, he loved every cell of her from date one, whether he knew it or not. She was my best-kept secret, and now it was out.

We had our first row since adolescence at a Christmas party at our friend Diana's house the following year. I was there with Leo. She arrived late with Scott and it was the first time I had seen her in a month. I made no visible effort to say hi to her but watched them out of the corner of my eye. I made a point of laughing very loudly at very unfunny things so she knew I was there and having demonstrative levels of fun without her.

When she came over, the conversation was stilted and curt.

'Why have you been ignoring me tonight?' she finally asked.

'Why have you been ignoring me for a year?' I replied.

'What are you talking about, I texted you yesterday.'

'Oh yes, texting. Texting, you're great at. Texting is your "get out of jail free" card that means you don't have to see me for months on end and go to Scott's flat every night and when anyone asks you about it you can say, "Oh, but I text her. I text her every day."'

'Can we do this upstairs?' she hissed.

I refilled my plastic cup with Glen's vodka and a splash of Coke and stomped up to Diana's bedroom. For two hours, we shouted at each other. We started very loud, then got quieter, until finally we were too pissed and tired to carry on and we made up. I told her she had abandoned me; I created a complicated metaphor about how I'd realized she'd always viewed me as Björn Again.

'WHAT DOES THAT EVEN MEAN?' she shouted.

'Björn Again. They were the warm-up band for that Spice Girls gig we both went to. They were shit and we couldn't wait for it to be over. I've realized I've just been your warm-up act for eleven years until your headliner came along. Well, you've NEVER been my warm-up act, you've ALWAYS been my Spice Girls and I wish I'd known sooner so then I could have put you down the bill and MADE YOU BJÖRN AGAIN.'

She told me I was being melodramatic, that she was allowed to have her first boyfriend. I told her she was allowed to have her first boyfriend, I just hadn't realized she would prioritize him above everyone else. We emerged with our faces smeared like canvases splattered by Jackson Pollock with a bucket of mascara. Scott and Leo stood sheepishly at the bottom of the stairs in silence, having obviously run out of football and gentle current affairs chat. We grabbed them and our coats and left separately. Years later, Diana told me they'd turned down the music downstairs so the entire party could listen to the argument.

'He's her boyfriend,' my infuriatingly rational academic boyfriend said as we did the long walk back to his Stockwell flat while drinking tinnies. 'They're in love, she's changed. That's fine, it's part of growing up.'

'You're *my* boyfriend,' I snapped. '*I'm* in love. I haven't changed. She's still the most important person in my life. She's still the person I want to see the most. *I* don't prioritize my relationship.'

He took a swig from his can of beer.

'Well, maybe that's not normal,' he replied.

After two years together, Leo and I split up. I had tried with all my might to make it work, but so much had changed since we had met as students wandering around a house party in Elephant and Castle. We'd both grown up and turned into very different people.

For nine long months after I finished journalism training, I had drifted from magazine to newspaper as an unpaid chair-filler under the guise of a work experience placement. I had been turned down as an intern at *Tatler*, an editorial assistant at *Weight Watchers* magazine and a waitress at a local Pizza Express. I reprised my old job as a promo girl to support myself, walking down Old Brompton Road with a bunch of out-of-work West End dancers and air hostesses, handing out flyers for a rib restaurant. I quit the day they made me dress up as a pig and was attacked by anti-fur demonstrators outside Harrods.

I was desperate for a job. It was all I thought about from the moment I woke up until the moment I went to sleep in my childhood bedroom. I yearned for a job in my early twenties with the same hunger as I did for my first boyfriend in my early teens – obsessing over who I knew who had one; grilling them on the details of how they acquired one. Lying in bed night after night, wondering how many more years this could go on for.

Finally, one early evening, I was standing on a train platform when I got a call from an unknown number. It was Tim, a story producer for E4's new structured reality show *Made in Chelsea*. I had written a series of online reviews of the first series (again, paid in the post-grad currency of 'exposure' – this time it actually worked) that the production company had read and found funny.

He asked me to come into their East London office to talk about a potential creative job on the show.

I was interviewed by Tim and Dilly, the thirty-something, teeny-tiny, fresh-faced BAFTA-winning executive producer. They explained that they had read my review of the final episode which had included some tongue-in-cheek advice to the producers of the show on how to make the following series better. The owner of the company, Dan – who had found fame in the 1990s as the producer and co-host of a hugely successful late-night chat show – had scoured every review on the internet. When he found mine, he printed copies off for all the producers who read it on the way to a meeting with the channel – surprisingly, they agreed with all of it.

I left my first half-hour interview with Dilly and Tim relaxed about the fact it was very possible I would never hear from them again. I couldn't grasp at all what they were after and we spent the majority of the interview dissecting the habits of posh people and psychoanalysing the cast. We didn't really talk about my qualifications or work history or the job requirements at all. Little did I know then that accurate psychoanalysis is 90 per cent of making successful reality television. And my years of observing the habits of posh people while feeling on the outside of their club – standing in boarding school tuck shops and in the smoking areas of King's Road nightclubs – would, for once, over-qualify me for a job.

I got the second call from the series producer three days later while I was at a music festival with Leo. We had become the Official Glitter Appliers of our camping party; a role we took to with aplomb. A boy coming up on acid heard repetitive ringing coming from my tent and thought it was Kraftwerk doing a surprise set. It was, in fact, Dilly. She told me I'd got the job as the show's story producer and to come in for my first meeting the next day.

I arrived at the office straight from the festival, having not showered for four days, my nose sunburnt, my white-blonde pixie hair matted into a Mohawk. Leo waited in reception with our backpacks and tent while I went to my first ever story meeting. I had run out of clean clothes, so wore Leo's oversized T-shirt as a dress with his denim jacket, laddered tights and a pair of ballet pumps. The outfit was a fitting send-off: it marked my last day as a kid and my first day as a grown-up.

I fell in love with the creativity, fun and relentlessness of my new job, my new colleagues and my new bosses nearly as ferociously as I had fallen in love with Leo. When I wasn't in the office or on location, I began picking up freelance journalism work so I would write in the evenings and weekends, leaving me with little to no time for anything else, much to Leo's frustration. He felt a little cheated. He had fallen in love with a rootless girl who wanted nothing but to pack a bag of plimsolls and jeans and go on any adventure he took her on; who embroidered his initials into jumpers and spent the entirety of a party locked in a bathroom with him, sitting in the empty bath, staring at his face with eyes like saucers. He ended up with a woman with her own adult identity and a preoccupation with her work.

I felt our relationship had been one of the most enriching experiences of my life and I knew he would always be a huge part of the person I had become, but we had outgrown each other. I knew I had to let him go so he could be with someone who really wanted to be in a relationship with all the love and commitment he deserved.

Farly, AJ and I were finally moved out of our parents' suburban homes and into our first London home. AJ, too, had newly become single. Farly was still with Scott.

A part of me hoped that by living with two single women, Farly would realize what she'd been missing throughout her twenties and she'd break up with Scott. But if anything, living with AJ and me only made her treasure him more. She once watched me rush around getting ready for a first date, trim some new fake eyelashes, apply them, then scream in agony as I realized I had used the kitchen scissors that I chopped chillies with over a pizza the night before. She found a bag of frozen potato smiley-face shapes and held them on my eyes as I texted the bloke to cancel. 'God, I don't miss this,' she sighed.

One night, when Scott was away on a work trip, Farly, AJ and I had been out dancing in our favourite Camden dive bar. We came home and opened a bottle of out-of-date Tia Maria, and things got confessional in the way they so often do in the afterglow of a night out.

'I miss Scott,' Farly announced after knocking back the last of her Tia Maria.

'Why?' I yelped. AJ stared at me. 'I mean . . . he's only away for a few days.'

'I know, but I still miss him when he's gone. And I get excited to see him, every time. Even if he just goes to the corner shop and comes back, I look forward to hearing the front door open again.' She saw my frown. 'I know it sounds cheesy, but it's true.'

'I think she really loves him,' I said the next day.

'Of course she loves him,' AJ said, while lying on the sofa and gnawing through a bacon sandwich. 'Why do you think they've been together for three years?'

'I don't know. I thought maybe she just wanted to see what having a boyfriend was like.'

AJ shook her head in disbelief. 'Come on, mate.'

After I realized this, I finally started noticing small signs everywhere. Scott's parents met Farly's parents. Farly spent more and more weekends with his grown-up friends, doing grown-up things like 'thirtieth birthday weekends in the Cotswolds' and wine tasting on a weeknight. Scott was round quite a lot, which I hated. And I also hated it when he wasn't there. He couldn't win. I didn't want him to win.

The Most Annoying
Things People Say

- 'I'm not going to have a starter, are you?'
- 'I'm more of a boys' girl'
- 'I'm a natural salesperson'
- 'I'm engaged!'
- 'You're always late'
- 'You were quite drunk last night'
- 'You've told me this story before'
- 'He says it like it is'
- 'She's very handsome'
- 'I think you need a glass of water'
- 'I'm quite OCD'
- 'We've got a very complicated relationship'
- 'Would you like to sign Alison's birthday card?'
- 'Let's go en masse'
- 'Let's have a catch-up'
- 'Are you across this?'
- 'Marilyn Monroe was a size 16'
- 'You are due your next dental appointment'
- 'When was the last time you backed up?'
- 'How do you find the time to do all those tweets?'
- 'Sorry, it's been mental'
- 'Holibobs'

The Uncool Girls of
Uncool Camden

When I was twenty-four, in the first year of living in London with Farly and AJ, I went out for a drink with a friend on a Tuesday night after work. Despite my attempts to keep her out until last orders, she had to call it a night at half eight due to an early meeting the next morning. I texted anyone in my phonebook who I knew might be around and want to carry on the night with me, but everyone was busy or in bed or tired. I sulkily got on the 24 bus home – my trusty steed that took me from the centre point of London to right outside my door in twenty minutes – and felt restless and disappointed that I couldn't stay out for just one more hour and one more glass of wine. It is a feeling I grew very used to – panicked and throaty; a sense that everyone in London was having a good time other than me; that there were pots of experiential gold hidden on every street corner and I wasn't finding them; that one day I was going to be dead so why bring any potentially perfect and glorious day to a premature end with an early night.

I snapped out of my sulk when the 24 pulled up at a pub at the end of my road. It was an NW5 hovel, a once-famous music venue turned grim boozer for the nine a.m.

drinkers of Camden. I got off the bus and went in. It was the first time I'd been since the day we moved in when we were told Farly had made history by being the first patron in forty years to order a coffee. The landlord went across the road to the corner shop to buy some Nescafé Gold Blend and milk and charged her 26p.

I ordered a beer and made small talk with the barman, who seemed completely unsurprised to be serving yet another solo drinker. A man next to me in his late sixties and sporting a grey yeti beard asked how my day had been and I lamented the lack of a drinking buddy to see the night through with me. He said he was the man for the job. As we drank, he told me all about his life spent growing up in the area: the school he'd truanted from, how things had changed, the watering holes that had closed; the John Martyn gig he'd been to at the Camden Palace before I was born, the live recordings of which I had listened to obsessively. I left at midnight, scrawling the man's number on the back of a beer mat with the mutual promise that we'd spend an afternoon together listening to records, but knowing I'd never be in touch with him again. He was just 'a night', of which I wanted many. An experience, an anecdote, a new face, a memory. He was a piece of advice, a gossipy story and an interesting fact that lodged in my inebriated, unconscious mind, only to be pulled out and regurgitated as my own one day. *Where did you hear that?* someone would ask. *I haven't the foggiest*, I'd reply.

The next evening, when I came home from work with

an unmoveable hangover to find Farly and AJ curled up on the sofa, I told them how I'd ended up in a dingy pub down the road the night before.

'Why on earth did you do that?' AJ asked bemusedly.

'Because it was Tuesday night,' I replied. 'And I could.'

I am so grateful that I fetishized the measured-out-in-coffee-spoons minutiae of adulthood so vividly as a teenager because the relief of finally getting there meant I have found very little of it to be a burden. I've loved paying my own rent. I've adored cooking for myself every day. I even used to get a thrill sitting in the GP's waiting room, knowing I registered and got myself there without the help of anyone else. In my first year of bill-paying, I'd practically go weak-kneed over a letter from Thames Water addressed to me. I would happily take on the administrative weight of responsibility that comes with being an adult in exchange for the knowledge that I always have the freedom to go to the pub on my own and make friends with an old man any day of the week.

To this day, I have never, ever been able to get over the fact I don't need to drink gin from shampoo bottles any more; that there is no lights-out; that I can stay up watching films or writing until four a.m. on a weeknight if I want to. I am relieved, energized, invigorated that I can eat breakfast foods for dinner, play records really loud and have a cigarette out of my window. I still can't quite believe my luck. My entire life as a young twenty-something adult was lived like Macaulay Culkin in *Home*

Alone 2: Lost in New York when he finds himself booked in at The Plaza and orders mountains and mountains of ice cream from room service and watches gangster movies. I blame this entirely on a strict upbringing. Nearly every adult I've met who went to boarding school cannot believe they now live a life where they can go to a Kentish Town old man's pub on a Tuesday night and not be given a detention or a suspension or a rustication, whatever that means. If university had been a playground in which to live out my adult fantasies, my own house and salary in London was a veritable nirvana.

We searched for three months before we found our first adult London home. Our budget was small and flats with three double bedrooms were hard to find. There was the house in Finsbury Park that cunningly photographed like a Notting Hill mews house and, on arrival, we realized was more like a wing of Pentonville Prison ('All we'd do here is stay in watching *The X Factor* while eating Sainsbury's Basics penne,' AJ commented). There was the disastrous viewing of the flat on the estate in Brixton that Farly and AJ attended alongside a large group of millennial hopefuls all queuing up outside like it was Madame Tussauds. The estate agent forgot to bring the keys, so kept everyone waiting for half an hour, then after they'd finally done a three-minute tour of the dump and left, they all had to get down to the ground as there was a gunman on the loose being chased by police outside the property. Finally, just as we were about to lose hope, Farly found a three-bed within our budget through a private landlord on Gumtree.

It was just off a notoriously dodgy crescent that joined the Chalk Farm end of Camden Town with the Kentish Town end. It had a proper old-fashioned market twice a week that sold pairs of five-pound slippers and cartoon bed sheets; it had a daily fruit and veg stall and a cash-only independent supermarket that sold weed from under the sandwich counter. It was graceless and garish and gorgeous.

The house was a beautiful mess. One in a row of 1970s ex-council maisonettes made of Lego-yellow bricks and bizarre placement and proportions of windows and doors that made it look like it was built in a rush by a teenager playing a game of *The Sims*. The front garden had two overgrown bushes that meant, in the summer, you couldn't make your way through the rotting wooden front gate without vigorous arm-swiping. The tiles in the kitchen had English countryside scenes painted on them. The back garden was a forest of weeds. There were these odd liquid streak stains down the hallway wall which, after much examination, we could only assume to be piss. Everything smelt quite damp. The flat above us was occupied by squatters.

The landlord, Gordon, was a good-looking man in his forties with a boxy midlife-crisis leather jacket and suspiciously dark, floppy hair. He was also a BBC news presenter and liked everyone to know about it: his voice was loud and posh, his manner bizarrely brusque and informal.

'So, this is the hallway,' Gordon bellowed. 'As you can see, lots of storage space.' We opened one of the large dusty white doors. A black box lay in the middle of the empty shelves with 'RAT ATTACK!' emblazoned on it in a bold yellow font. 'Oh, ignore that,' he said, scooping it up in his hand. 'All sorted now.' There was a brief exchange of glances between us. 'Do you know what?' he said, crinkling his nose slightly. 'I think the best thing is – I'm just going to get out of your way and let you have a look around the place yourselves. Tell me when you've seen everything.'

It was wonky and wobbly and eccentric, but we knew it was the perfect first home not only for us but for our extended family of friends who we planned to have round every weekend. We went back downstairs to tell Gordon we wanted it – he was in the middle of a call.

'Ya . . . ya . . . well. That's the worst-case scenario,' he said, flapping his hand at us dismissively. 'Ya. Well, for the moment let's just try and keep it out of court. Don't want to be back there AGAIN.' He looked at us and rolled his eyes. 'Great, well I'll be round tomorrow at ten to see this roof. OK. Yap. OK. Yes, yes. OK. Bye.' He put his phone in his jeans back pocket. 'Bloody tenants,' he said. 'So do you want it or not?'

We scrimped and saved to cover our deposits so the first month was spent living in exciting, frantic, frenetic frugality. We had barely anything for the house so Farly

bought a pack of Post-its to stick on various surfaces and
state things like: 'TV WILL BE HERE' or 'TOASTER
WILL BE HERE'. We ate Marmite and cucumber
sandwiches every night for dinner. On the second night
in our new home, I returned to find both the girls running around the living room in their wellies as they'd
spotted the first mouse and didn't want it to run over
their bare feet as they tried to catch it. Farly bought a
block of Pilgrims Choice Cheddar from the Nisa Local,
put it in her emptied vanity case and waggled it along the
carpet, trying to entice the mouse to a safe rescue.

We also quickly made acquaintances with the manager
of the local corner shop, a middle-aged bloke called Ivan
who was built like a marine. On our first visit, he omi-
nously told us that if we 'fell into any trouble with any
gangs' to come to him immediately as it would be 'dealt
with'. Farly was wearing a string of pearls at the time. But
I felt strangely safer knowing Ivan was always ten seconds' walk from our front door and when the mouse
thing became a recurring problem, he always came to the
rescue. I would often run straight out of the house barefoot in pyjamas and into the shop shouting 'IT'S BACK,
IVAN! IT'S BACK!' with a sort of Blanche DuBois
hysteria.

'All right, dahlin', all right,' he would say. 'I'll come
now. Do you want me to bring my gun?' I'd decline, ask
him to bring his torch instead, and he'd crouch under
every bed, fridge and sofa to try and find it.

(Eventually, Gordon organized for an exterminator

to come in. An East End geezer with, ironically, the surname 'Mouser'. When he laid down some traps, I asked him if there was a more humane way of dealing with the problem.

'No,' he said, his arms folded in dismay.

'OK,' I replied. 'It's just that I'm vegetarian.'

'Well you don't have to eat it,' he replied.)

Camden felt like the right place for us to be: it was central, it was near all the nicest parks and, best of all, it was perilously, hopelessly uncool. None of our friends lived there; in fact no one our age lived there. When we went out on Camden High Street, we were confronted with swarms of Spanish teenagers on a school trip or forty-something men with Paul Weller haircuts and winkle-picker shoes who were still waiting for Camden's glory years of Britpop to return. 'Goon Watch', AJ used to call it. We'd walk down the High Street on a Saturday night and she'd slur 'Goon, goon, goon' in my ear, pointing at passers-by. For the first few months I lived there I had a glamorous but ultimately ruinously self-obsessed musician boyfriend who lived in East London and refused to ever come visit me, because it was 'too 2007' to go to Camden.

Occasionally, during the years we were there, we'd go for a party or a night out in East London and be surrounded by young, cool, gorgeous people and we'd wonder if this was really where we were supposed to be at our age. But, as we left, we would always feel rather exhausted by the experience and grateful that we lived somewhere where we never had to pretend we were cooler than we were; which was not very at all. We could go to the shops in our leggings and hoodies and no bra and not bump into anyone we knew. We could take over a dance floor doing a drunken, comic cancan in a line and comfortably still be the coolest people in the entire bar. We could go out and spend the whole evening absorbed in each other, not trying to impress anyone. There was simply no one left in Camden to impress.

One of the first things I bought for the house was an industrial-sized cooking pot fit for a soup kitchen. Our friends had always been great eaters and I was thrilled to have a stove and a kitchen table to call my own. In those first years living together, we had people round for dinner three times a week. I worked out the cheaper things to make – pot after pot of dhal, tray after tray of Parmigiana. We'd have candlelit dinners in our hideously overgrown garden in the summer; at one point so overgrown that a tree caught fire in a strangely biblical way and we all drunkenly threw saucepans of water and glasses of Ivan's dodgy five-pound Sauvignon Blanc over it.

There was a freedom in the feeling that our house was fundamentally too broken to fix. Gordon was relaxed about it too – he let us paint all the walls bright colours and never commented when the paint just stopped with a wobbly line on the staircase wall where we had got to the bottom of the Dulux tin. It meant it was a house we could really live in; a house we weren't precious about.

We could trash it on a Saturday night and all it would take was a ten-minute tidy the next morning to make it look passable again. We could have our record player on its loudest volume and stay up until six a.m. without the neighbours complaining – I swear those 1970s houses were built to be disco-proof, because in the years we lived there we never received one noise complaint. In fact, the neighbour told me she'd never heard us. And for this reason, our house was also the place where everyone could come to get high.

I got the majority of drug experimentation completely out of my system in my first couple of years living in London. First, I created a familial rapport with a friendly drug dealer called Fergus. Fergus wasn't a sit-in-the-car-moodily-and-pass-you-a-baggie-under-the-dashboard dealer, but rather would join me late on a Friday night when I had friends round for dinner, rolling spliffs at the table and telling long-winded jokes while digging into the leftovers, before I'd finally send him packing with a Tupperware box of spaghetti carbonara. Farly, who had always been much more sensible than me and was always in bed by midnight when we had people round for dinner, never had the pleasure of meeting Fergus, but was always baffled by the way that I spoke about him as if he were 'a cousin or a family friend'. One night, she was woken up at four a.m. by the sound of me giving Fergus an estate agent's walking tour of the house as he advised me on the feng shui of each room.

The next day, she came into my room to find me huffing and puffing while moving my bed to the opposite wall.

'What are you doing?' she asked.

'I'm moving my bed. Fergus says it's not in a good position at the moment.'

'Why?'

'Because the headboard is too close to the radiator. He says it's not good for your head to be near heat – especially for your sinuses.'

'Yeah, the man sells you Class A drugs, Dolly,' Farly said. 'He's in no position to be handing out health advice.'

Fergus dropped out of contact rather suddenly, as I was told they often do, so I was then pointed in the direction of CJ – who was a steadfast disaster. CJ was known to be the worst drug dealer in London. His time-keeping was appalling, he would regularly give the 'wrong order' to the 'wrong customer' and turn up at your doorstep half an hour later asking for the 'product' back. His phone was never charged. His satnav was always conking out. It got to a point where he'd kept me waiting for an hour and a half and I found myself telling him on the phone that he was 'his own worst enemy', like a frustrated teacher. The last straw came on the Thursday before I left London to go to a festival and I rang him to ask if he could sell me some MDMA.

'What's that?' he asked.

'MDMA,' I replied. 'Mandy.'

'Who's she?'

'Ecstasy. Come on. MDMA.'

'I've never heard of it,' he said.

No matter how I got them or who I got them from, it was the acquisition of drugs that was nearly always more exciting than the drug itself. Talking about whether to get any, calling the number, getting the cash out; someone waiting in the flat while someone else went to go find the car, coming back with a tiny plastic pocket of herbs or powder; the promise of what was to come – that was the bit that got my heart beating fastest. Farly once witnessed the effort that it took to buy, divide up and take cocaine and she couldn't quite believe how tediously time-consuming it was; 'Like making a shepherd's pie,' she observed. But the time-consuming faff of lining up powder and rolling up spliffs is the very joy of it for someone who never wants a night to end – it's a distraction, a guaranteed night extension. It's the muting of your rational mind that says *Go to bed at eleven, we've talked about everything we could possibly want to talk about now* and in its place brings an artificial desire for the party to continue endlessly. For me, cocaine was only ever a vehicle to carry on drinking and staying awake long after I was tired; I was never that wild about any sensation it offered.

I thought that, to be a writer, I had to be a collector of experiences. And I thought every experience worth having, every person worth meeting, only existed after dark. I always remembered something Hicks told me as we lay in bed under the fairy lights of her student room twink-ling around her window.

'One day we will sit in a nursing home, Dolly, bored out of our minds and staring at the quilt on our laps,' she said. 'And all we will have to make us smile are these memories.'

But the increasing regularity of these nights meant I felt myself being defined by these stories, rather than a specialist collector of them. Staying out until dawn stopped being a one-off; instead I began equating any evening out with a hedonistic all-nighter. And, worst of all, everyone else expected it of me too. A night with me meant a night that ruined you for the next day and friends awaited that constant level of debauchery from me, even when we'd meet up for a quick pad thai on a Thursday evening. My energy, bank balance and mental state couldn't keep up with it. And I didn't want to self-mythologize and inflate myself into this sort of tragic Village Drunk figure that everyone would dread plan-ning a coffee with, knowing that it would probably end the following morning in some all-night casino in Leicester Square.

'I do love those stories,' Helen once said the morning after we'd been at a party and I had gathered a group of people to bore them with my best folkloric tales of nights out. 'But there are quite a lot of them, Doll.'

Another thing that no one tells you about drinking as you get older is that it isn't the hangovers that become crippling, but rather the acute paranoia and dread in the sober hours of the following day that became a common feature of my mid-twenties. The gap between who you were on a Saturday night, commandeering an entire pub garden by shouting obnoxiously about how you've always felt you had at least three prime-time sitcom scripts in you, and who you are on a Sunday afternoon, thinking about death and worrying if the postman likes you or not, becomes too capacious. Growing up engenders self-awareness. And self-awareness kills a self-titled party girl stone-cold dead.

I also ended up having two entirely separate jobs, working in TV and being a freelance writer. They demanded more and more of my time and focus, and regular blackout boozing and hangovers were not conducive to productivity and creativity. 'You're trying to lead two lives,' a friend once said to me when I was on the brink of exhaustion. 'You have to choose which you'd rather be: the woman who parties harder than anyone else or the woman who works harder than anyone else.'

I decided to strive for the latter. Life grew fuller in the daylight hours and there was less need to escape at night. But it would still take me some time to realize that the route to adventure doesn't just involve late nights and hot bars and cold wine and strangers' flats and parked cars with lights on and little bags of powder. I always saw alcohol as the transportation to experience, but as I went through my twenties I understood it had the same power to stunt experience as it did to exacerbate it. Sure, there were the juicy confessionals you'd get out of people with dilated pupils in a loo cubicle; the old men with good stories who you'd otherwise never meet; the places you'd go; the people you'd kiss. But there was also all the work that wouldn't get done when you were hung-over. All the bad impressions you would make to potential friends because you were so drunk you could barely speak. All those lost conversations, in which someone tells you something really, really important, which are rendered meaningless because neither of you can remember it the next morning. All those hours spent lying in sweat and panic in your bed at five a.m., your heart beating as you stare at the ceiling, desperately willing yourself to sleep. All the hours lost in the cul-de-sac of your head torturing yourself with all the stupid things you said and did, hating yourself for the following few days.

Years later, I would discover that constantly behaving in a way that makes you feel shameful means you simply will not be able to take yourself seriously and your self-esteem will plummet lower and lower. Ironically, my teenage one-woman mission to be a grown-up through excessive drinking left me feeling more like a child than any other of my actions in my life. For years of my twenties, I wandered around feeling like I was about to be accused of something terrible, like someone could very easily march up to me and say, 'YOU'RE the dick who drank Jo Malone Pear and Freesia bath oil in a pint glass at my house party for a dare – you owe me £42!'; or 'OI! TOSS POT! I *still* can't believe you got off with my boyfriend outside the Mornington Crescent Sainbury's!' – and I would have to nod reverently and say, 'Yes, I can't recall that specifically, but I shall take your word for it and I'm sorry.' Imagine walking around in a world where you think someone is ALWAYS about to tell you you're an arsehole, and you're ready to agree with them whole-heartedly. What sort of fun is that?

Wherever I am on a Tuesday night, from now until the day I die, you can be sure that I would prefer to be in a grim pub in Camden drinking beer while talking to a stranger. But I eventually grew out of those clockwork-regular blackout benders that wiped out the next day like a tsunami, just like I eventually grew out of the yellow-bricked maisonette that was crumbling down. For a short while, though, sitting in my overgrown garden of Eden, drinking sour Sauvignon with the women I loved, the record player turned up loud and the empty plates piled high by the sink, I thought I lived in the best house in the world. I still think I did.

Recipe: The Seducer's Sole Meunière

(*serves two*)

I made this for the aforementioned musician I dated when I was twenty-four in the early stages of our court-ship to try and make him love me. It worked for about a week. I've since made it for other boys worth my time and brown butter and the effects have been successful and more long-lasting.

- 4 tbsp plain flour
- 2 fillets of lemon sole
- 1 tbsp rapeseed oil (or sunflower will do)
- 50g butter
- 2 tbsp pre-cooked brown shrimps
- juice of ½ a lemon
- 1 tbsp capers
- A fistful of flat-leaf parsley, chopped finely
- Salt and black pepper, to season

Mix the flour and seasoning on a plate then dip the fillets in the mixture so they are evenly coated. Shake off excess.

Heat the oil on high until it is very hot. Cook the fillets for two minutes on each side. They should be crisp and golden.

Set fish aside and cover with foil to keep warm.

Lower the heat of the pan, add the butter and melt until it is lightly brown. Take off the heat, toss the shrimps through the butter, add the lemon juice.

Place the sole on the plates, pour the butter and lemon mixture over each fillet, finish with a sprinkling of capers and parsley. Season.

Serve with a side of green salad or green beans and roast new potatoes (don't serve with your big open heart).

3rd February

Dear friends who I normally only ever get completely leathered with,

I'd love to have you round to witness my attempt at behaving like an adult. Some call this a dinner party, but I think that sounds a bit stuffy, so I'm going to call it something vague enough to seem relaxed but nothing that hints at a knees-up, like: 'a get-together' or 'some food and drinks' or 'a casual, chilled-out dinner'.

The important thing is, this definitely won't be a knees-up.

Please arrive at my flat at seven o'clock. By which I mean, please plan to arrive at seven o'clock until you get a very panicked message from me at six o'clock asking you to come at eight o'clock because I couldn't find kohlrabi anywhere for Jamie Oliver's Asian slaw, so had to get a £25 Uber to Waitrose and back and it put me behind an hour. As I said, it's all very casual and chilled.

The guest list is as follows:

1 x Outrageous gay friend (Ed) who is happy sharing colourful stories from his varied sex life. He will be the sort of truth-telling court jester of the evening – think Julian Clary meets the Gravediggers in *Hamlet*.

1 x Benevolent new boyfriend belonging to Ed (name TBC) who everyone will make a huge effort with until just after the main course when he will be largely ignored until he books an early Uber home but no one will realize he's left until two hours later.

1 x Northern feminist friend (Anna) who will make Ed feel more comfortable because of her liberal outlook and left-leaning politics and vice versa.

1 x Single man I don't know that well from work (Matthew) who will flirt with everyone. Matthew isn't generically attractive, but he's tall and has a loud voice. The plan is that everyone will fancy him as they get drunker and realize he's the best of a bad bunch. A bit like how we all felt about Nick Clegg in the 2010 election.

1 x Posh engaged couple (Max and Cordelia) to add a touch of grown-up homeyness to the evening. They will happily talk about every detail of their upcoming wedding to keep things ticking over in moments of conversational sparseness. NB Keep Max and Anna apart from each other when talk turns to the welfare state or climate change.

1 x Slaggy friend who drinks too much (Leslie) who will make us feel like we are still in the white heat of youth while simultaneously making us feel better about our lives (thanks for this, Leslie). She will also take the lead in documenting the evening on Instagram with a hashtag such as '#asianslawgivememore' or '#sinnershavingdinner' or something else to this effect.

Please bring a bottle of wine. I will assume you'll bring Oyster Bay as it's the only one we all know that isn't rubbish-tasting but also only costs a tenner. Jacob's Creek will do. Echo Falls is of course welcomed but its price point will be noted.

After throwing all your coats on a bed and giving you a glass of warm white wine, of which I will have already consumed half the bottle before you arrive out of sheer anxiety induced by the earlier *Challenge Anneka* chase for kohlrabi, I will present you with four bags of Kettle Chips. This will be your starter.

Having set myself the challenge of making eight separate dishes to follow the trend of what everyone calls 'Mega Relaxed Ottolenghi-style Dining', I will be absent for the first two hours of the evening. Safe suggested topics of conversation for the semi-sober are as follows:

- The efficiency of the Victoria line
- Comparing respective rent costs
- Recent celebrity deaths
- Hairdresser recommendations
- Who will be the next Bond
- The dollar/pound exchange rate on a recent trip to New York
- How much water we should actually all be drinking
- Any play currently in production featuring a recognizable TV actor
- Budgeting apps
- Bedding

Dinner will be at ten p.m. By this point everyone will be drunk enough to make sexual innuendos relating to the meal – 'Have you got hummus up your end?', 'Let's toss the salad', etc. – but not quite drunk enough to all get their phones out and watch mildly amusing videos on

YouTube. This will happen after the main course and before pudding.

Suggested videos:

- News reporter bloopers
- Cats getting stuck in things
- Children getting upset about missing chocolate
- Dogs falling asleep in odd places
- Any Louis C. K. routine
- Anything with Céline Dion

Leslie – it would be great if you could incorporate drugs into the evening after this. Either by sharing some old weed you have in your handbag or texting your dealer for some cocaine. If you plump for the latter, everyone will put up a bit of a fight, citing being 'so skint this month' or having not done it 'since two birthdays ago' but, rest assured, they still want it and will cough up when Candy Man arrives.

If you do go for the second option, Cordelia and Max will have an argument as Max will offer to pay for an extra gram. Cordelia will be confused – they're apparently too broke to have a string quartet play 'Signed, Sealed, Delivered' as she walks down the aisle, but he's willing to drop £60 on Class A drugs for a room of people he barely knows?

Past midnight, it's time to get on to what I will call the 'Pointless and Trite Debating' portion of the evening. This House Believes in Something Obvious I Read in a *Guardian* Column vs This House Believes in Something Slightly Less

Obvious I Read on a Vice Blog. All topics and opinions will be broad, non-committal and predictable with made-up statistics and exaggerated personal anecdotes to support flimsy arguments. Suggested subjects:

— Is there such a thing as left wing or right wing any more?
— If women want genders to be equal, why is it called feminism and not equalism?
— Is it art if I could make it?
— Why do we eat pigs but not dogs?
— What is the legacy of Tony Blair according to all of our parents that we will pass off as our own opinions?
— How late is too late to have children?
— Was Margaret Thatcher a feminist?
— Will soaring London property prices mean people will actually move to Margate?
— Is it OK for Matthew to be wearing a Ramones T-shirt despite not being able to name one of the Ramones or any of their songs?

When things get too heated between Max and Ed during 'Homosexuality: nature or nurture?', it's time for Leslie's Drunk Overshare, in which she reveals a secret about herself in a long and winding monologue to a silent audience.

Suggested confessions for Leslie:

— You don't like any Welsh people
— Recent chlamydia contraction

- Your uncle groping you as a teenager
- Affair with a married man
- You think you can communicate with the dead
- You think voting is pointless and boring
- Fear of infertility

Scheduled times of departure:

Ed – four a.m., after he's proved he knows the original dance routine to Hear'Say's 'Pure and Simple' and every word of Lil' Kim's rap for 'Lady Marmalade'.

Cordelia – two a.m., because of a made-up brunch the next morning.

Max – two thirty a.m., after getting an angry text from Cordelia to come home.

Matthew and Anna – four fifteen a.m., in the same Uber.

Leslie – four p.m. the following day.

Really looking forward to it, guys! Will be so good to have a chilled one!! Xxx

Recipe: Apple Pizza With Can't Be Arsed Ice Cream

(*serves four*)

A recipe given to me by my mum, to impress people when they came round to my crap house for crap dinner parties, requiring zero skill or effort.

For the ice cream
- 4 egg yolks (must be very fresh)
- 100g icing sugar
- 340g mascarpone cream
- vanilla essence

Whisk egg yolks and sugar until pale and creamy.

Beat in mascarpone cheese and vanilla essence. Put in a Tupperware box.

Freeze overnight or for at least 3–4 hours.

For the apple pizza
- Pack of puff pastry
- Pack of marzipan
- 500g apples, peeled and sliced
- Jar of apricot jam

Roll out the puff pastry.

Cover with a circle of marzipan.

Lay the sliced apples on top.

Bake in the oven at 200°C till golden and meanwhile heat apricot jam on the hob.

When the apple pizza comes out, pour the warm apricot jam over the pizza and leave it to rest.

Serve with the ice cream.

'Nothing Will Change'

One of the things I hated most about Farly meeting Scott is that I never saw her family any more. I missed her mum and dad and stepmum and brother and sister. For years, I spent every other weekend and holiday with her family and they were like my own. But after Scott came on to the scene, I didn't get the call-up from Farly any more, so I only saw them once or twice a year. Scott now occupied the seat I had been in at the dining-room table for birthdays and Sunday roasts; he was the one who joined them on cool, cosy autumnal half-terms in Cornwall while I looked at the photos on Instagram.

After a few months of living in our new London house, Farly invited me out on a walk with her family one Saturday afternoon. We stopped at a pub for lunch and I basked in the warm familiarity of their rituals: the nicknames, the in-jokes, the stories about Farly and me when we were teenagers. I felt smug; whatever space Scott had been occupying for the last few years was a different shape to mine, because nothing had changed at all.

On our last leg of the walk, we lagged behind the rest of the group and the dog, like we'd always done as teenagers, due to competitive over-eating at lunch.

'Scott's asked me to move in with him.'

'What have you said?' I asked.

'I'm going to do it,' she said almost apologetically, her tentative words floating in the cold air. 'It felt right when he asked me.'

'When?'

'After I've done a year with you guys in Camden,' she answered. I resented the phrase 'done a year' like I was a gap-year ski season or a TEFL course in Japan; a thing you do once for an interesting anecdote.

'OK,' I replied.

'I'm so sorry, I know it's so hard.'

'No, no, I'm happy for you,' I said. We did the rest of the walk in silence.

'Do you want to bake chocolate chip cookies?' Farly said when we got back to our house.

'Yeah.'

'Great. Make a list of what we need and I'll go get the ingredients. And why don't we watch that Joni Mitchell documentary that's been sitting on the shelf for ages?'

'Sure,' I said. It reminded me of the time my mum took me to McDonald's when I was eight after my gold-fish died.

We sat on the sofa eating cookies, our legs inter-twined, our tummies poking out from pyjamas. Graham Nash was talking about the soul-baring lyrics of *Blue*.

'I know every single word of that album,' I said. It was the only album we'd taken on a three-week summer road trip when Farly passed her driving test aged seventeen.

'Me too. "Carey" is my favourite.'

'"All I Want" is mine.' I paused to eat the last of my cookie and wipe the crumbs from my mouth. 'We'll probably never do a road trip like that again.'

'Why?'

'Because you're moving in with your boyfriend, you'll do all your road trips with him now.'

'Don't be stupid,' she said. 'Nothing will change.'

I would like to pause the story a moment to talk about 'nothing will change'. I've heard it said to me repeatedly by women I love during my twenties when they move in with boyfriends, get engaged, move abroad, get married, get pregnant. 'Nothing will change.' It drives me bananas. Everything will change. *Everything will change.* The love we have for each other stays the same, but the format, the tone, the regularity and the intimacy of our friendship will change for ever.

You know when you were a teenager and you'd see your mum with her best friends and they'd seem close, but they weren't like how you were with your friends? There'd be a strange formality between them – a slight awkwardness when they first met. Your mum would clean the house before they came and they would talk about their children's coughs and plans for their hair. When we were kids, Farly once said to me: 'Promise we'll never get like that. Promise when we're fifty we'll be exactly the same with each other. I want us to sit on the sofa, stuffing our faces with crisps and talking about thrush. I don't want to become women who meet up once every couple of months for a craft fair at the NEC.' I promised. But little did I know how much work it takes to sustain that kind of intimacy with a friend as you get older – it doesn't just stick around coincidentally.

I've watched it time and time again – a woman always slots into a man's life better than he slots into hers. She will be the one who spends the most time at his flat, she will be the one who makes friends with all his friends and their girlfriends. She will be the one who sends his mother a bunch of flowers on her birthday. Women don't like this rigmarole any more than men do, but they're better at it – they just get on with it.

This means that when a woman my age falls in love with a man, the list of priorities go from this:

1. Family
2. Friends

To this:

1. Family
2. Boyfriend
3. Boyfriend's family
4. Boyfriend's friends
5. Girlfriends of the boyfriend's friends
6. Friends

Which means, on average, you go from seeing your friend every weekend to once every six weekends. She becomes a baton and you're the one at the very end of the track. You get your go for, say, your birthday or a brunch, then you have to pass her back round to the boyfriend to start the long, boring rotation again.

These gaps in each other's lives slowly but surely form a gap in the middle of your friendship. The love is still there, but the familiarity is not. Before you know it, you're not living life together any more. You're living life separately with respective boyfriends then meeting up for dinner every six weekends to tell each other what living is like. I now understand why our mums cleaned the house before their best friend came round and asked them 'What's the news, then?' in a jolly, stilted way. I get how that happens.

So don't tell me when you move in with your boyfriend that nothing will change. There will be no road trip, the cycle works when it comes to holidays as well – I'll get my buddy back for every sixth summer, unless she has a baby in which case I'll get my road trip in eighteen years' time. It never stops happening. Everything will change.

Farly moved out on my twenty-fifth birthday. She and Scott found a one-bed with a roof terrace to rent in Kilburn. It was opposite a gym, which they said was good because they liked to play badminton, apparently. She made a fuss of showing me there was a direct bus from Camden to Kilburn High Road. I took it in a sulk on the way to their house-warming drinks.

I spent the party chain-smoking on the roof terrace with Farly's teenage sister, Florence, on my lap, showing me her yearbook. Later, when I was drunk, I told her I secretly hoped one of them was unfaithful or Scott was gay so Farly would have to move back to our house. She laughed and gave me a hug.

'I hate that,' Farly said, pointing at a framed Manchester United shirt covered in the team's signatures and hanging in the hall, sensing I needed something to pour my misery into.

'Yeah, it's horrible,' I replied.

'Rank,' she said. 'Living with a boy. Urgh.'

'Girls are so much better to live with.'

'The best.' She smiled. 'Do you like the flat?'

'I love it. I think you're going to be really happy here.' And, annoyingly, I finally believed it.

Our university friend Belle, who came with a guitar and a desire to go out dancing all weekend, moved into Farly's room and life carried on as normal. The fridge still leaked. The downstairs loo carried on being broken. Gordon still barged his way into our house uninvited most Saturday mornings trying to dump hideous pieces of furniture on us as a 'treat' because he couldn't be bothered to take them to the skip. We still did something called 'ladies' choice' when one of us went to the shop, which means you get whatever chocolate bar they come back with. At first, I saw Farly more than I had done when we lived together, simply because she was hyper-aware of making me feel like 'nothing's changed'. But eventually I started seeing less of her. Everything changed.

*

Three months after they moved in together, I was sitting at my desk at work when I saw on my phone that I had been invited by Scott to join a WhatsApp group titled 'Exciting News'.

I knew what it was so I didn't open it. I had been waiting for this moment since the day Farly told me they were moving in together. I wasn't ready to know, so I carried on working, as if it was all just a pending dream; an unsent message in the ether's outbox. My phone sat on my desk for an hour, the notification staring at me.

Finally, I got a call from AJ – who had also been invited to the group – and she told me to open it. It said he was proposing. Valentine's Day. Four years after their first date. He asked if we could get a group of her friends together and surprise her at a bar after he'd done it. I said I'd love to. I said I couldn't wait. I said I was over the moon.

I cried, knowing I had lost whatever battle I was fighting with whoever I was trying to fight against.

Dilly walked past.

'Dollbird,' she said. 'What's going on?'

'Nothing,' I muttered.

'Come on.' She grabbed my hand and took me to the boardroom. 'Tell me what's going on.' I told her about the proposal. She was up to speed with the saga, having already met Farly a few times and been fascinated by the Scott–Farly–Dolly love triangle for years, citing it as 'the perfect structured reality plot'.

'And I know it sounds like I'm being melodramatic,' I said in between sobs. 'I know people grow up and things change but *Christ* I never thought everything would change when we were only twenty-five.' She looked at me and sighed, shaking her head solemnly.

'What?' I asked.

'I always knew we should have rigged the place with cameras when you guys moved into that house,' she said, rolling her eyes. 'I knew it – I said it to Dave at the time. I know you say you don't want to be on camera, but this whole thing would have been such a nice series arc.'

I rounded up our friends and told them Scott's plan. We organized a time and place where we would be waiting with a present. I bought them a framed print off Etsy with the lyrics of 'There Is A Light That Never Goes Out', their favourite Smiths song. AJ said she'd buy me the 'Heaven Knows I'm Miserable Now' one.

I had never wanted any of this. I never wanted her to spend every weekend with Scott's friends and their wives at barbecues in bloody Balham. I didn't want to see her for catch-up dinners. I didn't want her to move out after a year. I didn't want her to get married. And the worst thing was, it was all my fucking fault. If only I could've gone back in time and never set them up. Never dated Hector. Never gone back to Hector's on that snowy night in Notting Hill. I wished I could go back and ignore him when he'd started talking to me on the train. I wished I'd never got on that fucking train in the first place.

The problem with having a Farly in your life is that their story feels like your story. She wasn't living the life

I had planned for us and I was in mourning for the future I now knew we'd never have. Up until Scott, we were on track with the plan: we went to the same university where we chose to be in the same halls, then lived in the same house for two years. When we graduated I thought we'd have 'The London Years' – not 'The London Year'. I thought there would be many houses, not *a* house. I thought we'd have hundreds of nights out together that ended at sunrise. I thought there'd be gigs and double dates and trips to European cities and weeks spent stretched out, side by side, on the beach. I thought we had claim over each other's twenties before we'd inevitably have to give the other one up. I felt like Scott had robbed me of our story. He'd taken ten years that were mine.

A month before Scott proposed, a group of us went out for drinks one Saturday night with Farly.

'Scott said something weird to me this week,' she announced. We secretly looked at each other – knowing we'd already chipped in for the Smiths print and had cleared Valentine's Day – with blinking, bug-wide eyes.

'Go on,' I said sombrely.

'He said he has a surprise for me for Valentine's Day and it's small but it's also very big. And – I know this sounds crazy – but a part of me thought maybe it might be an engagement ring?'

'I don't think it's that,' Lacey said suddenly, sure to avoid all of our intense gazes – the nanosecond meeting of which would surely give the game away.

'No, I know. You're right, it won't be,' Farly said quickly, with a self-effacing laugh.

'Yeah,' AJ said. 'I think you're reading into it too much, dude.'

'What could be small but big, though? I can't work out what it is,' Farly said.

'Ooh, I don't know,' Lacey said. 'Maybe plane tickets for a holiday or something?'

'Maybe it's a dog collar,' I said flatly.

'What?' she asked.

'That's a small thing but very big. Maybe he's decided to become a man of the cloth and he wants to tell you on your anniversary.'

'Oh, stop it, Dolly,' Farly sighed.

'Or maybe . . . maybe,' I said, my mouth catching up with the litre of white wine I had drunk. 'Maybe he's decided to get a Manchester United tattoo on his face. Seems small but actually it's huge really, isn't it? It might change the way you feel about him.' AJ signalled at me to stop with a discreet throat-slitty motion. 'Or maybe it's the keys to a boat, maybe he's bought a speedboat for the Thames. Quite a massive lifestyle change, particularly if he wants to take it out at the weekends. I imagine it's quite expensive to maintain. Maybe that's it. He's a sea-faring man but he's never found the moment to tell you.'

'I don't want to guess what it is any more,' Farly snapped.

I couldn't sleep the night before the engagement, thinking about how Farly's life was about to change and she had no idea. I sent Scott a text the next morning: 'Good luck tonight. I know you'll ace it. I hope she says yes. If not, it's been nice knowing you x.'

'Thanks for the vote of confidence, Dolls x,' he replied.

A group of us sat in the bar, waiting for the text from Scott.

'What if she says no?' AJ asked. 'Do we just go home?'

'She's not going to say no,' I said. 'But if she does I've already looked up what else is on and there's a disco night at KOKO, so we just go there for a dance – it's ten quid on the door.'

At ten, I got a text from Scott telling us they were engaged. He'd told her they were going to go for one final celebratory drink before they went home. We ordered a bottle of champagne, poured them two glasses and stared out of the window, waiting for their taxi to arrive. Finally, we saw them walk into the bar and AJ squeezed my sweaty palm twice, the silent universal Morse code.

'CONGRATULATIONS!' we all shouted as Farly walked through the door. She looked at us in utter shock, then at Scott. He smiled at her and she came running towards me for a hug.

'Congratulations,' I said, handing Scott his glass of champagne. 'You've made my best friend very happy.'

'I'm so glad you dated that idiot Hector,' he said, laughing. 'I love you, Dolly.'

His eyes filled with tears and he gave me a hug.

I wondered if he knew how I was feeling. I wondered

if he'd always known. Maybe that's why he'd tried to include me on the night they got engaged; gave me my own project; somehow involved me.

Two hours later, Farly had asked me to be her maid of honour, I had drunk the lion's share of their celebratory champagne and I was feeling vocal.

'I wannamakea speech,' I slurred at AJ and picked up a fork to tap against my glass.

'No, darling,' AJ said, taking the fork away from me and signalling at the other girls who swiftly removed all the cutlery from the table and gave it to the waiter. 'No speeches.'

'But I'm her fuckin' maid of honour.'

'I know, babe, but there will be plenty of time for speeches.' When AJ went to the loo, I crawled under the table and found her car keys in her handbag. I clinked them to the glass with a *ding ding ding*.

'When I first found out that Scott and Farly were engaged – yeah, sure, I was pissed off about it,' I announced.

'Oh God,' Belle groaned.

'Because I've known this little weirdo for over twennyfiveyears.'

'Over twenty-five years?' Lacey asked Hicks.

'SHUDUP!' I shouted, pointing at Lacey, my wine spilling on to the table.

'THIS IS SHIT, YOU'RE NOT MAID OF HON-OUR ANY MORE!' Farly drunkenly heckled across the table.

'But when I look around, I see that the world –' I paused for dramatic effect – 'is . . . juss as it should be. For my best friend has won the best man.'

'Awww,' everyone said, with a collective out-breath of relief.

'To Scott and Farly,' I bellowed through tears and sat down. Everyone gave a weak round of applause.

'Beautiful,' Belle whispered to me. 'Even though I know you took that from Julia Roberts's speech in *My Best Friend's Wedding*.'

'Oh, she won't know,' I hissed and flapped my hand dismissively.

The rest of that evening, I'll be honest, is a bit of a blur to this day. I invited Dilly and her husband, who were in the area celebrating Valentine's Day, along for the celebrations. I did the cancan in the dining area of the bar while singing 'One' from *A Chorus Line* and high-kicked a tray of plates clean out of a waiter's hands, smashing them to pieces on the floor. I said goodbye to Scott and Farly, then went back to my flat in Camden and made everyone carry on drinking until six a.m. I woke up next to a semi-clothed Hicks who had *happy valtine day* written on her breasts in liquid eyeliner.

I spent the next day watching Farly's 'engagement weekend' (I don't want to seem too precious about this particular detail, but I had assumed one evening was sufficient) unfold on social media. There was a family barbecue, lunch at the Wolseley, Scott's friends and their wives showering her with gifts like Smythson wedding planner notebooks and magnums of champagne, making my framed print look a bit measly. I began to feel like the fourth, forgotten Wise Man (who had brought a piece of tat off Etsy).

'I think you found Friday night quite overwhelming,' Farly said on the phone. 'Are you OK?'

'I'm fine! I don't know what you mean, "overwhelming". I mean, I'm not the one who got engaged. You're the one who seemed overwhelmed. I saw on Facebook Michelle bought you that Smythson wedding planner book – that's nice, isn't it?'

'Do you want to go to dinner next week, just us two?'

'Sure.'

I emailed Hector – the first time in four years.

Remember me? Scott and Farly are getting married. Thank God you sent me down to your kitchen with no clothes on.

He replied. He'd said he'd seen the news on Facebook. He told me he'd quit the City for travel PR and he had an enormous expense account and asked if he could take me for a boozy lunch, to toast our skills as matchmakers. I thought we were the thin end of the wedge of 'matchmakers' but I said yes because I was feeling low. I searched my inbox for all his old dirty poems in a flush of forced nostalgia. I cancelled lunch the day before it happened.

'Why do you think you emailed him?' Farly asked in between bites of her burger at dinner a few days later.

'I don't know. I think I just want a boyfriend.'

'Really?' she asked, wiping her mouth with her napkin. 'You always say you don't want one.'

'Yeah, but I've been feeling differently lately.'

'What's triggered it?'

What had triggered it? I was jealous. Not of Scott this time; I was jealous of Farly.

'You getting engaged.'

'Why?' she asked.

'Because I hate that your life is so different to mine now. I hate that we have always done stuff at the same time and now we don't,' I sighed. 'I hate that our children could be so far apart in age. I hate that you're about to buy a flat with a man and I had to beg my landlord to let me pay my rent three weeks late this month. I hate that you drive around in Scott's Audi he got given from work and I still can't drive. I hate that his friends are so different to me and I'm scared they'll take you away because their lives resemble your new life and mine doesn't. I know it sounds mad and it's not about me and I'm ruining your special moment and I should just be happy for you. But I feel so far behind you and I'm worried you'll run out of sight.'

'If you had met your husband when you were twenty-two, I would have found it really, really hard,' she said.

'Really?'

'Of course! I would have hated it.'

'Because sometimes I feel like I'm going mad.'

'You're not going mad. I would have felt exactly the

same. But I never chose to meet Scott when I was twenty-two. I wasn't looking for a husband.'

'Yeah,' I said half-heartedly.

'And I will be there to celebrate and experience all the milestones in your life, whether they're next month or in twenty years.'

'More like forty years,' I mumbled. 'I still don't live in a flat with curtains.'

'We're not at school any more. Stuff will happen at different times. You'll be doing some things ahead of me too.'

'Like what? Meth?'

So, I finally made my peace with Scott. I realized he wasn't going anywhere. I spent time with both of them and I reprised my familiar and well-received role as Official Third Wheel. It is an irritating typecasting, but one I do very well. Out of all my years on this earth, only a handful have been spent in a relationship. I am well-versed and rehearsed in third-wheeling; I am The Threewheelin' Dolly Alderton.

My entire adolescence was spent hanging about with my friends and their boyfriends. Smiling along as they play-fought on the sofa or pretending to play snake on my phone while they snogged in a corner of the room. I smile and pretend with couples very well, it's how I've spent most weekday evenings around a table in my twenties. I let them have fake arguments in front of me about whose turn it is to load or unload the dishwasher. I laugh along when they tell long stories about each other's sleeping habits. I am silent as they discuss details of people's lives I have never heard of in an overly animated way ('No WAY?! Priya didn't end up buying those tiles! I don't BELIEVE it! After all that! Oh God, sorry, explain to Dolly who Priya is and the whole story of the loft conversion from start to finish') to prove they have a wildly interesting life that doesn't involve me. And all the while I pretend I don't know why I am third wheel; why I am doing all the laughing and the listening. But of course I know I am merely an aphrodisiac in their game of Domestic Bliss — I know when I leave they'll rip each other's clothes off, having got all revved up on an extended joint discourse about their holiday in the Philippines, particularly when they both said the same island when I asked them what their favourite bit was. I am just a reluctant audience member.

But I sit and watch all these shows anyway because the alternative — losing my friends — is not an option.

And when Farly and Scott weren't doing Their Bit on me, I discovered, to my utter shock, that Scott and I got on rather well. In fact, I resented that I hadn't realized this sooner as I would have enjoyed his company when he was round when Farly and I lived together, instead of just grunting at him. He was funny and smart. He read the paper and had opinions on things. Scott turned out to be a pretty great guy and it seemed so obvious to me in retrospect that Farly would have chosen to marry someone cool. It was something I got very wrong.

When I wasn't excitedly helping Farly plan her wedding, I also made more of an effort with his friends. Whenever I had met them in the past, I had made a huge, embarrassing performance of proving I was different to them. I got excessively drunk at a Sunday lunch at our house once and lectured them all on the 'meat is murder' doctrine as they ate their roast lamb. Once, in a pub, I had accused one of his friends of being a misogynist because he made a comment about my height. But after Farly and Scott got engaged, I tried my hardest to relax, be polite and get to know them. They were, after all, the people she was spending most of her time with now. They had to be half interesting.

And then suddenly, one Friday evening in August, we all stopped thinking about the wedding. Florence, Farly's eighteen-year-old sister, was diagnosed with leukaemia. 'Life is on hold' was Farly's dad's refrain over the months that followed. Life was on hold. The wedding was put back a year. Florence was a bridesmaid and they wanted to make sure she was well enough by the time it came round. I had spent months obsessing over the wedding, and now I couldn't care less about it.

The month after the diagnosis, it was Farly's twenty-seventh birthday. We wanted to celebrate with her to take her mind off Florence's illness, but she was drained of energy, having spent every hour she could in the hospital. She didn't want to drink, she didn't want to be in a big crowd, she didn't want to have to talk to a load of people about how she was doing. Her family couldn't come as they were camping out at the hospital. It was decided by Scott: AJ and I would go over to their new flat and he would cook the four of us dinner.

The first birthday I had celebrated with Farly was her twelfth. She had blown out more birthday candles with me than without me. I remember the first one like it was yesterday – when she was still just a friend who I sat next to in maths. She wore a pink Miss Selfridge dress and we danced the Macarena in Bushey church hall.

But this birthday was unlike any birthday we had celebrated together. Farly was tinier than I had ever seen her, as diminutive and fragile as a baby bird. There was no boisterous hugging, no binge drinking. We were quiet and gentle, no one more so than Scott.

He had got up early to go to the fishmonger, as AJ and I had both stopped eating meat. He made the most beautiful sea bass stuffed with fennel and oranges with roast new potatoes and laid it out with the bitten-tongue concentration of a *MasterChef* contestant. He kissed Farly's head every time he walked past her. He held Farly's hand under the table. I saw the man she had fallen in love with.

I texted Scott in the kitchen to tell him I had a tray of birthday cupcakes hidden behind the sofa. We waited for Farly to go to the loo and AJ barricaded her in with a chair while I manically scattered the cakes across a platter and Scott searched for a box of matches.

'WHAT'S GOING ON?!' Farly yelped.

'ONE MINUTE!' I shouted as Scott and I lit all the candles.

We sang her 'Happy Birthday', and presented her with her gifts and card. She blew out the candles and laughed while the three of us enveloped her in a big group hug.

'Why did it take ages?' she asked. 'Did you bake them while I was having a piss? I was in there so fucking long I started doing my thigh exercises.'

'What thigh exercises?' AJ asked.

'Oh, these new lunges I've read about.' She started leaning up and down, some of her old, vibrant colour trickling through her face. 'I try and do them every morning. I don't think it's making any difference. My legs still look like giant gammon joints.' AJ started emulating her, bobbing up and down stiffly, being instructed by Farly like a Rosemary Conley video.

Scott looked across the room and caught my eye. He smiled at me. 'Thanks,' he mouthed. I smiled back at him and all at once realized the world that now lay between us. The invisible dimension created from the history and love and future we shared for this one person. It was then I knew everything had changed: we had transitioned. We hadn't chosen each other. But we were family.

The Bad Date Diaries:
A £300 Restaurant Bill

It is December 2013 and I am on my third date with a handsome entrepreneur I met on Tinder. He is the first rich man I've ever dated and I feel deeply conflicted about him spending money on me. Sometimes, when he politely picks up the bill, I feel flattered – like this is how adult courtship is meant to work. In other moments, I feel frustrated with myself for getting so predictably weak-kneed about an older bloke with a fast car and a drinking problem buying me champagne. This manifests itself in incontrollable anger at him.

'You can't own me!' I shout for no reason in the Mayfair restaurant he has chosen, three bottles of wine to the good. 'I'm not a possession for you to own – I won't guilt myself into getting all dressed up just so you'll buy me lobster! I can buy it myself!'

'Fine, darling, buy it yourself,' he slurs.

'I will!' I squawk. 'And not going Dutch – the WHOLE thing.'

The waitress comes over with the bill for £300.

I go to the loo to text my flatmate AJ, asking her to lend me £200 and to transfer it into my account immediately.

The Bad Party Chronicles: My House in Camden, Christmas, 2014

I have been pushing for a Rod Stewart-themed party since we moved into our Camden house two and a half years ago. My thinking is that Rod Stewart, as a concept, bridges the gap of the extreme campness of Christmas and the careless joie de vivre of a twenty-something house party.

My flatmates, Belle and AJ, reluctantly agree that our Christmas drinks party be Rod Stewart themed, but stress that they want no accountability for it.

In the run-up to the party, I both prematurely age and bankrupt myself by tracking down Rod Stewart-themed memorabilia. We have plastic cups with his face on, Rod Stewart ashtrays, mince pies customized with sugar paper Rod Stewart faces, a life-size Rod Stewart cardboard cut-out, a Rod Stewart sign signalling where the loo is and a Rod Stewart banner with MERRY CHRISTMAS, BABY!! on it. Sabrina, India, Farly, Lauren and Lacey come early to help deck the house out with Rod decorations, and all of them agree with Belle and AJ that it was a complete waste of money.

'Oh God,' I say, pinning the banner to the wall while Sabrina holds the chair I stand on. 'I've just realized the Faces posters I ordered haven't arrived on time. Do you think anyone will mind?'

'No,' she sighs. 'No one will mind about any of this other than you.'

The first guests to arrive at seven o'clock on the dot are my charming, rather loud new American friend who I have only met once previously and her bearded boyfriend. It is clear they have been drinking all day. They have also brought their Cavalier King Charles spaniel, dressed in a tiny Christmas jumper.

The other guests don't start trickling in until nine o'clock, so we try to catch up with our first two guests but, alas, the boyfriend passes out on the sofa with his spaniel on top of him for the rest of the evening, so he is in plain sight of anyone who enters the party. Friends trickle in slowly, one by one. Things are stilted. The man continues to be passed out with the dog on him, which creates an arresting eyesore on entry to the party. One guest – a friend of a friend; a music video director from the cool Peckham contingent – walks in, takes one look at the tableau, makes up that he has another event to go to that he forgot about and leaves.

Halfway through the evening, I go to the bathroom to take a break from the crowd, made up of completely disparate social groups who have nothing to say to each other, 'You Wear It Well' playing on repeat in the background while people complain about the Rod-only playlist. AJ and Belle are in there, AJ sitting on the loo, Belle on the side of the bathtub. We talk about how bad the party is. We think of ways we can get people to leave and make it end. AJ says she needs to have a lie-down for ten minutes because she feels tired and miserable. There is a knock on the bathroom door and my brother comes in.

'Quite a weird crowd down there, guys,' he says.

When I reappear downstairs the guest mass has dwindled in size even further. There is a very tall skinhead bloke in a leather bomber jacket raiding the fridge.

'Um. Hi. Who are you?' I ask.

'I was told to come here,' the man says in a thick Romanian accent, sipping from a can of beer he has helped himself to. 'For delivery.'

'Delivery?'

'Yes,' he says, looking at me conspiratorially. 'Delivery.'

'OK, would you mind just –' I guide him to the front door – 'just waiting here.' I walk past the American, who is slow-dancing with her be-jumpered dog to 'Sailing' while a perplexed audience looks on. Her boyfriend has been passed out lying across the sofa for well over three hours now.

'RIGHT, I THINK SOMEONE'S DRUG DEALER IS HERE,' I announce irritably to the crowd. 'I'm sorry to be a party pooper – and I don't blame you for wanting to get high at this terrible party – but can you please ask all your drug dealers to wait outside or at least in the hallway.'

The party wraps shortly after midnight.

The next morning over coffee, me and Belle do a two-man Chilcot Inquiry into how it all went so wrong.

I suggest that the preparation I did for the theme might have built up expectations too high.

'You made a Rod for your own back,' she says, nodding sagely.

We keep the Rod Stewart cardboard cut-out in the living room for a while. A reminder to never get ahead of yourself in this life. We deck him out topically – putting a pink bra on him during the Lord Sewel hooker scandal, a leprechaun's hat on St Patrick's Day. When we move flat eight months later and pack up the house, we leave nothing except the Rod Stewart cut-out in the middle of the living room, passing the curse of bad parties on to the future tenants.

Recipe: Got Kicked Out
of the Club Sandwich

(serves two)

Regularly eaten with AJ as we sat on the kitchen counter-top, swinging our legs back and forth, shouting about that dickhead bouncer who said we were too drunk to go back in and that we were 'letting the rest of the group down'.

- 2 eggs
- 4 slices of bread (sourdough preferable, white Hovis acceptable)
- Mayonnaise
- Dijon mustard
- Rocket (optional)
- Olive oil and butter, for frying
- Salt and black pepper, to season

Fry eggs in olive oil and a smidge of butter in a piping-hot pan. Spoon the oil over the eggs once or twice to cook the yolk.

Toast the bread.

For each sandwich, spread one slice with mayonnaise and one slice with mustard.

Fill each sandwich with one fried egg and a handful of rocket. Season with salt and pepper.

Eat in about five big, sloppy bites. Get mustard on your face.

Pour any alcohol left in your flat into two clean receptacles (for us, this was usually the old bottle of Toffee Vodka Farly got given at Christmas 2009 that lived at the back of the freezer).

Play a Marvin Gaye record.

The Bad Date Diaries:
A Mid-morning, Completely
Sober Snog

Spring 2014. I wake up to my alarm on a Saturday at nine a.m., having had five hours' sleep. There is a WhatsApp message from dishy American Martin: 'Doll face – we still on for a cup of joe?' My head feels like it has been turned inside out like a dirty sock, but I tell him I'll be there. We matched on Tinder three days ago and it's been a solid stream of 'No way that's my favourite Springsteen album!', 'I believe in reincarnation too', 'Yes, perhaps we are all wanderers' and so on. In this moment, as I search my room for last night's fake eyelashes and glue them back on, I am convinced he will be my boyfriend by the end of the week and I will move to Seattle with him next month. For this is the only logical solution in the head of a single, hung-over woman who is embarrassed that she fell off a bus the night before – marriage and emigration.

The outfit: a huge Aran jumper so oversized it hangs like a dress, denim hot pants because all my jeans are dirty, a pair of laddered tights and white plimsolls.

'No coat?' my hung-over housemate AJ croaks as I rush past her on the stairs.

'No need,' I say breezily.

'You STINK of Baileys by the way,' she shouts as I close the door.

Martin sits at the bar of Caravan King's Cross. Thankfully, he is identical to his pictures. He is writing in a notebook as I arrive, which I think adds a nice touch of theatre to the whole nomadic lost-soul agenda he pushes with his whimsical Instagram account I've already stalked.

'What you writing?' I ask, over his shoulder. He turns, looks at me and smiles.

'None of your business,' he replies and kisses me on both cheeks. It is already extremely flirty and we haven't even had a coffee, let alone six beers. I think it's because he is American.

Martin tells me the story of his life: illustrator from Seattle nearing forty, earnt a load of money from a big job and decided to use it to travel the world for a year and write a book. He's doing some 'Tinder tourism' to meet new people. He has been in England for a month; he wants a few more weeks in London then he's on his travels again.

(Aside: I noticed at the time that Martin was particularly vague when I asked him what his book was about, other than saying it was non-fiction. I also noticed he wrote a couple of things down when I was talking. He took the notebook with him when he went to the loo and was in there for quite a long time. I decided either A) his bowels had a bad reaction to caffeine and he wanted to pass some time on the loo relaxing with his thoughts; B) he was just a private man and sensed I was a nosey, hung-over person with

no boundaries who might want to read his notebook when he went to the loo; C) he was writing something embarrassing like his cosmic shopping list or how many people he had slept with and didn't want me to read it; or D) he was writing a book about all the women he'd dated in England and I was up next. I have always thought it was option D and to this day am still waiting to see a book called Green and Pleasant Slags: My Time With English Women *on the shelves at Waterstones with an embarrassing paragraph about me in it.)*

After our coffees, we sit outside the cafe on a bench, staring at the water fountains spurting in a rhythmic, pornographic way, and he quotes Hemingway, which I think is a little overkill, but I am enjoying the fanciful tone of the date so I go along with it. He gets out another notebook that he's illustrated with maps of every country he's visited so far, his tracks sketched as twee footprints. I ask if he has a girl in every port. He laughs and says 'something like that' in his annoying, wonderful accent.

He takes me by the hand and leads me down the steps at the front of Central Saint Martins art college to the canal. We walk a little until we stand under the nearest bridge, then he unbuttons his coat, pulls me in and wraps it round me. He kisses my head, my cheeks, my neck and my lips. We kiss for half an hour.

The time is eleven a.m.

Martin and I part ways at eleven thirty and thank each other for the lovely morning. I am back in bed by twelve thirty and sleep all afternoon. I wake up at four, convinced I dreamt the whole thing.

Predictably, Martin falls off-radar after our coffee morning and is vague about when our next date is when he does get in touch. A week later, tanked up on Friday-night Prosecco and encouraged by my friends, I send Martin a WhatsApp message riddled with spelling mistakes asking if I 'may be frank' and suggesting we embark on a 'platonic but sexual relationship' while he is in London. I suggest I become his 'girl in the London port'. I tell him it's 'what Hemingway would do'.

Martin never messages me again.

Everything I Knew About
Love at Twenty-five

Men love a woman who holds it all back. Make them wait five dates to have sex with you, three dates at the very least. That's how you keep them interested.

The boyfriends of your best friends will, annoyingly, stick around. Most of them won't be exactly who you imagined your best friend would end up with.

Suspenders and stockings can be bought cheap and in bulk on eBay.

Online dating is for losers and I include myself in that. Be endlessly suspicious of people who pay to have an embarrassing profile on a dating website.

Forget what I said earlier about using hair-removal cream when you're dating someone. If you go bald, you're letting the sisterhood down. We need to actively take a stand against the patriarchal control of female anatomy.

Never make an album as good as *Blood on the Tracks* 'our album' with a boyfriend because, years after you break up, you still won't be able to listen to it. Don't make that mistake at twenty-one.

If a man loves you because you are thin, he's no man at all.

If you think you want to break up with someone, but

practical matters are getting in the way, this is the test: imagine you could go into a room and press a big red button that would end your relationship with no fuss. No break-up conversations, no tears, no picking up your things from his house. Would you do it? If the answer is yes, you have to break up with them.

If a man has always been single at forty-five – there's a reason. Don't hang around to find out what it is.

The worst feeling in the world is being dumped because they say they don't fancy you any more.

Always bring a man back to your house, then you can trick him into staying for breakfast and trick him into falling in love with you.

Casual sex is rarely good.

Fake orgasms will make you feel guilty and terrible and they're unfair on the guy. Use them sparsely.

Some women get lucky and some women don't. There are good guys and bad guys. It's sheer luck who you end up with and how you get treated.

Your best friends will abandon you for men. It will be a long and slow goodbye, but make your peace with it and make some new friends.

On long, lonely nights when your fears crawl over your brain like cockroaches and you can't get to sleep, dream of the time you were loved – *in another lifetime, one of toil and blood.* Remember how it felt to find shelter in someone's arms. Hope that you'll find it again.

Reasons to Have a Boyfriend and Reasons Not to Have a Boyfriend

Reasons to have a boyfriend
- More likely to get a proper birthday cake
- Access to Sky TV?
- Something to talk about
- Something to talk at
- Sunday afternoons
- More sympathy when you do something really wrong at work
- Someone to grope your bottom in the queue for popcorn
- Holidays for one are very expensive
- And it's impossible to put sunscreen on your own back
- Sometimes you can't manage a whole large pizza to yourself
- Might have a car
- Nice to make a sandwich for someone other than yourself
- Nice to think about someone other than yourself
- Regular sex that isn't weird
- Warmer bed
- Everyone else has one

- If you have one, people will think you're lovable
- If you don't have one, people will think you're shallow and dysfunctional
- The relief of not having to flirt with people
- Fear of dying alone, the void, etc.

Reasons not to have a boyfriend
- Everyone annoys you other than you
- 'Debates'
- They probably won't like Morrissey
- They definitely won't like Joni Mitchell
- They'll point out when you exaggerate stories
- Going to their friends' boring birthday drinks in Finsbury Park
- Being told what you did the night before when you were drunk
- Sharing pudding
- Having to watch any live or televised sports
- Having to spend time with the girlfriends of their friends and talk about *The Voice*
- Constantly walking around in between flats with knickers in your bag
- Being honest about your feelings
- Having to keep your room really clean and tidy
- Not reading as much
- Having to keep your phone fully charged all the time so he knows you're not dead
- You'll probably miss flirting with people
- Hairs all over the bathroom

Tottenham Court Road and Ordering Shit Off Amazon

When I was twenty-one, at the tail end of my last summer spent performing at the Edinburgh Festival before I had to go home and find a job and start an adult life, I went out to celebrate the thirtieth birthday of my friend Hannah. She had been directing me in a comedy sketch show I had been flyering for, and me and two of the other actors took her out to a posh restaurant to mark the occasion. In the run-up to the day, she had made some vague noises about dreading turning thirty, which we all assumed were exaggerated for comedic purposes.

Halfway through dinner, she put down her cutlery and started crying.

'Oh my God, Hannah, are you really *upset*?' I asked, immediately regretting the 'Happy Birthday Granny' card I had given her.

'I'm getting older,' she said. 'I can feel it. I can feel it everywhere in my body; it's already slowing down. And it's only going to get slower.'

'You're still so young!' Margaret said, who was a few years ahead of her, but Hannah continued to sob, unable to catch her breath, tears falling into her plate. 'Do you want to go?' she asked, stroking Hannah's back. Hannah nodded.

As we walked down Princes Street, chatting away about nothing, keen to keep the tone light and Hannah distracted, she stopped in the middle of the road and held her head in her hands. Her tears became wails.

'Is this it?' she asked us, bellowing into the dark night. 'Is this really all life is?'

'Is what all life is?' Margaret asked soothingly, putting her arm round her.

'Fucking . . . Tottenham Court Road and ordering shit off Amazon,' she replied.

For years, those words were stuck on the underside of my brain like a Post-it I couldn't shake off. They hung there like a whispered conversation you overheard between your parents that you didn't understand but you knew to be very important. I always wondered why those two specific things – Tottenham Court Road and Amazon – could cause so much sorrow.

'You'll understand when you're not twenty-one,' Hannah said when I asked.

I finally grasped the machinations and subtext of that phrase the year I turned twenty-five. When you begin to wonder if life is really just waiting for buses on Tottenham Court Road and ordering books you'll never read off Amazon; in short, you are having an existential crisis. You are realizing the mundanity of life. You are finally understanding how little point there is to anything. You are moving out of the realm of fantasy 'when I grow up' and adjusting to the reality that you're there; it's happening. And it wasn't what you thought it might be. You are not who you thought you'd be.

Once you start digging a hole of those questions, it's very difficult to take the day-to-day functionalities of life seriously. Throughout my twenty-fifth year, it was as if I had created a trench of my own thoughts and unanswerable questions, and from the darkness I peered up, watching people care about the things I had cared about: haircuts, the newspaper, parties, dinner, January sales on Tottenham Court Road, deals on Amazon – and I couldn't fathom climbing out and knowing how to immerse myself in any of it again.

I gave up booze for a while to try and even out my mood, but it just left me overthinking even more. I tried Tinder dating, but the mainly platonic encounters left me feeling more disheartened and empty. The once passionate love and focus I had for my work was beginning to wane. My flatmates, AJ and Belle, often came into my room to find me crying whilst still wrapped in a towel from a shower I took three hours previously. I found it impossible to articulate how I was feeling to anyone; I spent huge swathes of time on my own. There was a hum in my body of disinterest, ennui and anxiety, as low and simultaneously disruptive as a washing machine on a spin that won't turn off. All of this reached a crescendo in the early summer when Dilly told me she thought I should leave my job to go be a full-time writer and I had no plan of how to make money and where to go next. And AJ announced that she was moving out to live with her boyfriend, less than a year after Farly had gone. I was depressed, down a job and down a flatmate.

The answer was, of course, what the answer always is for a single twenty-something woman prone to a touch of melodrama: move to a different city. I had always adored New York and often went to visit Alex, who remained a close friend even after her brother Harry had ended our relationship all those years ago. When she got engaged and asked me to be her bridesmaid in the summer of my discontent, it felt fortuitous. She and her fiancé said Farly and I could stay in their Lower East Side apartment for free while they were on honeymoon. We booked our flights, a hotel for the wedding and a one-night break to the Catskill Mountains near the end of our two-week stay. Unbelievably, it would be mine and Farly's first holiday abroad together. And it was a good opportunity for me to recce my potential new home: its day-to-day, its people and how I could see myself fitting into it.

But a week before we were due to fly, Florence was diagnosed with leukaemia. Farly understandably felt she had to stay at home to support her sister and her family. I asked if she needed me there too, but she told me to go to New York on my own and have a much-needed break.

In my first two days in New York, I was caught in a convivial hurricane of bridesmaid duties. All of Alex's British contingent had flown over for the wedding and the run-up was spent making wreaths and arranging chairs and picking things up from the dry-cleaners and catching up with old and familiar acquaintances. I missed Farly terribly, but it was still the busy, new, wonderful embrace of distraction that I had been craving.

On the day of the wedding, I wore a black strappy dress with a thigh-high split (Alex encouraged this – she knew I was in much need of a holiday romance; I also knew I would be seeing Harry for the first time in years) and I read the poem 'The Amorous Shepherd' in the Brooklyn warehouse where they got married. When I said the line *'I don't regret anything I was before because I still am, I only regret not having loved you,'* I couldn't help but cry. For the love Alex and her husband had for each other, and for the depth of loneliness I only then realized I had felt for the past year.

I was one of two single women at the wedding and I counted myself lucky that I had been sat next to the one single male guest: a burly Welshman who built bridges for a living.

'Good poem,' he said to me in his sexy, see-sawing, sing-songy accent. 'The tears were a nice touch.'

'It wasn't planned!' I said.

'That dress certainly was,' he said with a smile.

We drank Negroni after Negroni and ate fried chicken and mac and cheese and flirted in a way that is only acceptable when you're the only two single people at a wedding. We did a rigorous rundown of all our favourite bridges in Britain. I fed him pudding off my fork. He whooped for me when I got up to do my speech and winked when I caught his eye halfway through. He behaved as if he was my boyfriend of many years. Our relationship escalated in familiarity with the gusto of a foot on a pedal pressed right to the floor (in a way that is only acceptable when you're the only two single people at a wedding).

Right before the first dance, my Welshman disappeared to take a call outside. Alex, with her crown of roses and her long, white, kimono-sleeved dress that made her look like a Pre-Raphaelite draped in silk, led her husband to the dance floor. The humming undulation of the most romantic song I had ever heard played – 'Sea Of Love' by Phil Phillips – was a proper, schmaltzy, perfect slow dance.

By the chorus, all the other guests had joined them; tens of couples, including Harry and his new girlfriend, swayed and smiled to the beautifully sentimental song. I sat on the outside, looking in. I tried to imagine what it would feel like to find a sense of security in the person you went to bed with – a notion that was so foreign to me. I looked at the small gaps in between all their bodies and imagined the places that lay between them; the stories they had written together; the memories and the language and the habits and the trust and the future dreams they would have discussed while drinking wine late at night on the sofa. I wondered if I would ever have that with someone or if I was even built to float in a sea of love. Whether I even wanted to. I felt a tap on my shoulder and looked up to see Octavia, a fellow bridesmaid. She smiled and held out her hand; she led me to the dance floor and held me as we danced until the end of the song.

After that, I hit the Negronis even harder. When I went outside for a cigarette and found my Welshman, I was emboldened enough by Campari to push him against the brick wall and kiss him.

'I can't do this,' he said, pulling away.

'Why not?' I asked.

'It doesn't matter,' he muttered. 'But I just can't.'

'No,' I slurred. 'This . . . this is not happening like this. I'm in New York, I'm on holiday, I'm a depressed bridesmaid and I'm in a slaggy dress, the split of which I paid to have taken up even higher at the dry-cleaners. You are my holiday fling, OK? It's been decided.'

'I can't,' he said. 'I'd love to, but I can't.'

'Well then, what was with all the –' I mimed putting pudding in his mouth. 'And the –' I did an exaggerated, theatrical wink.

'I was just . . . flirting,' he offered weakly.

'Yeah, well, it was a total waste of time. You know I was sitting next to a really interesting, really clever actor? I would have loved to have had a conversation with her. She seemed fascinating. I think I said about three words to her all night. I was too busy playing pretend girlfriend with you.'

'Oh well, I'm sorry I was such a waste of time!' he huffed, walking back into the party.

*

The next day, I went to Alex and her new husband's flat in Chinatown, to see them off on their honeymoon and toast their new marriage from the roof. We caught up on the wedding gossip and they explained the Welsh-man's mixed signals (he had a girlfriend – of course he did).

Alex gave me a rundown of the apartment and handed me the keys.

'Are you going to be OK?' she asked.

'I'll be fine,' I replied.

'You've got Octavia's number? She's in the city until the end of the month, so you're not alone.'

'I'll be fine – it's good for me to have some time on my own. Get to know New York better. It will be a great adventure.'

'You call us if you need anything,' she said, hug-ging me.

'I absolutely will not. Go to Mexico and swim naked in the sea and drink tequila and shag yourself into obliv-ion,' I said.

The next morning, I woke up in the flat, fed their two black cats, watered their plants as per their instructions and sat with a notepad to plan how I was going to spend my time here and all the things I would see and do.

But there was one huge problem: a magazine was late paying me for two pieces of work, amounting to just under a thousand pounds, which I had budgeted to be more than enough for my New York spending money. I had £34 in my account and eleven days left in New York.

This was quite a common occurrence as a freelance journalist – I was often chasing accounts departments for payments three months after a piece was published and the invoice filed. But it had never been this urgent. I rang my editor; my editor referred me to the accounts department; that department transferred me from person to person, trying to work out where my overdue payment was. I lay on Alex's bed with my phone on loudspeaker for an hour, the tinny hold music blaring, the long-distance phone call racking up my bill minute by minute. The person I spoke to concluded that I'd be paid 'soon'.

With no money and no friends, it quickly became apparent that New York was a very different place than all the other times I had been there on holiday to visit Alex. It's not a good place to be broke. Unlike London, the museums and galleries all charge a general admission fee, most of which are $25, which would have wiped out my remaining funds. It was also the middle of August, so it was unbearably hot, meaning there was a limited amount of time I could wander around or sit in the park. The city I had always loved, where I had always seemed welcome, felt like it just wanted me out. When I walked down Fifth Avenue, I looked up at the skyscrapers and they felt like large, terrifying, towering monsters trying to chase me to JFK airport.

I began to notice all the small things I hated about New York that had never bothered me before. I realized how inefficient and confusing the subway was. Unlike the London underground with its colourful and at times regal array of line names (Jubilee, Victoria, Piccadilly), the lines have all been given the most indistinguishable and lacklustre names imaginable (A, B, C, 1, 2, 3, etc.). And B can easily sound like D and 1 could probably be 3. It's impossible to keep track of what letter or number you're meant to be catching without writing it down. In a lot of stations the trains only come every ten minutes, so if you're doing three changes and you're unlucky with timings, this could mean an extra half-hour of standing around on sweltering hot platforms. To make this process even more frustrating, the majority of platforms do not have any boards letting you know when the next train is due.

Then there were all those New York 'ball-busters', those loud, pushy people in supermarkets and cafes and queues who snap at you. The ones who are either just incredibly rude or trying to give you 'the full immersive New York experience'. Perhaps, when I'd been feeling secure and happy, I had found it funny. But now, feeling so alone, I hated how much I was being shouted at. 'HEY, LADY – GET OUT OF THE FRIKKIN' WAY!' a passing waiter barked at me in Katz's Deli as I stood at the counter to order a bagel.

I also noticed how much I was shoved in New York. The collective ambition of the place had never felt so overwhelming. Everyone was on their own mission, no one caught each other's eyes. People power-walked, swinging their arms like they were marching, shouting into their hands-free. Even their romance was ambitious; I spent a whole afternoon eavesdropping on two female friends in a cafe jabbering at each other about how they were going to meet men and they made it sound like a military operation – it was all dates, numbers, algebra and rules.

And, Christ, the rules. I'd never noticed how obsessed they all were with rules. I was told off for picking up and smelling an orange in a supermarket before I bought it. I was told off when I visited Apthorp (Nora Ephron's beloved apartment building on which she had written an essay) because I went too near the decorative fountain in the courtyard. I had never considered myself a particularly anarchic creature, but the disciplinarians of New York brought it out in me.

Then there were the humourless hipsters. The people who served you good coffee or worked in cool shops; the people who flatly said, 'That's the funniest thing I've ever heard in my whole life,' with a straight, expressionless face when someone told them a joke, instead of laughing. The ones who looked you up and down for longer than felt comfortable. All the attitude of a twat from Hackney; none of the self-awareness or humour or cynicism. The scenesters in New York who are under thirty are some of the coldest, most uninviting people I have ever met.

A week into my big New York adventure, I realized that places are kingdoms of memories and relationships; that the landscape is only ever a reflection of how you feel inside. I felt more empty, tired and sad there than I had been feeling at home. The fantasy of moving faded day by day. I had the insidious epiphany that 'Tottenham Court Road and Amazon' would follow me wherever I went – I was still the same unfulfilled person on holiday as I had been in my house. When I booked the flights, I thought I was booking a trip out of my head, but I wasn't. The external scenery had changed, but the internal stuff was exactly the same: I was anxious, restless and self-loathing.

One night, as I lay on Alex's sofa making my way through a bottle of leftover wedding Prosecco that she had told me to help myself to, I spent the evening trying 'Tinder tourism' as a way of meeting new people. I right-swiped nearly everyone. I sent out a vague, cheery broadcast message to all my matches, describing myself as a 'visitor from London' looking for some New Yorkers to 'show her a good time'. I opened a second bottle of Prosecco at midnight, just in time to receive a video call from AJ and India.

'Heeeeeeeey!' they shouted in unison from around my kitchen table.

'Hi, guys!' I said. 'Are you pissed?'

'Yeah,' India barked. 'We've just been to the Nisa Local and bought three bottles of wine.'

'Good. I'm pissed too.'

'Who are you with?' AJ asked, peering into the camera. I thought about telling them what a terrible time I was having, but I didn't want to worry them. And, more importantly, my pride wouldn't allow it. I had been giving a very convincing impression on all social media channels that I was having the trip of a fucking lifetime.

'No one,' I replied. 'I'm having some down time tonight.'

We caught up for fifteen minutes and I was happy to see their familiar faces and hear all the minutiae of what they'd been up to.

'Are you OK?' AJ asked when I said goodbye. 'You seem a bit down.'

'I'm fine,' I said. 'I miss you both.'

'We miss you too!' she said. They both blew kisses at me, and then I was alone again.

Halfway through my second bottle of Prosecco, I got a reply from one of my Tinder matches, Jean, an attractive thirty-two-year-old French stockbroker, who asked if I fancied a late drink. I decided *this* man would be my holiday fling; exactly the sort of fun, empowering escapade I needed to turn this trip into an adventure and make me feel like my old self again. But he lived in SoHo, a mile away, which I couldn't walk because outside a thunderstorm had begun, and I had no money left in my account for a taxi.

'I've got money,' he wrote. 'I'll pay for your taxi.' I decided to ignore the *Pretty Woman* subtext of this offer, put on some mascara and a pair of heels and stood in the rain to find a passing cab. As I hailed one, a combination of torrential rain and torrential drunkenness caused my phone to slip out of my hand. The screen smashed into a hundred fragments, the rain drops seeped into the cracks and the screen faded to black.

When I arrived at the address he'd given me he was, thankfully, standing outside. He paid for the cab and he opened the door to let me out.

'Thanks for coming,' he said, pulling my face towards him for a kiss. For a brief moment, the attention of this complete stranger filled me with a light fizz of excitement and the heaviness of my deep-rooted despondency felt like it had exited the building. Then I realized how pathetic and telling this was; and I felt instantly sadder. I needed another drink.

Jean was nice enough. We had nothing in common, but conversation flowed, thanks to the beer he gave me and the packet of Lucky Strike we chain-smoked on his sofa. I got the feeling he did this a lot. After an hour of chatting and snogging, he took me to his bedroom. A stark white box with strange neon lights and a mattress on the floor in lieu of a bed. I tried to ignore the setting as we undressed each other.

'Wait, wait,' he said as I unzipped his jeans. 'I only have group sex.'

'What? What does that mean?' I slurred.

'I can only have sex if someone watches,' he replied as if it were plain logic. 'Or if someone joins us.'

'OK,' I said. 'Well, that's not going to happen now, so –'

'My flatmate is next door,' he said. 'He wants to come in. I'll tell him it's OK?'

'No, it's not OK,' I said, suddenly aware of this not being a big adventure at all. I was in a bedroom with a man who could very well be Patrick Bateman. 'I don't want to do that,' I said, panicked, hearing the fast and heavy beat of my heart in my eardrums and looking for the nearest window.

'Come on, it will be fun,' he said, trying to kiss me. 'You seemed like a party girl.'

'No, I'm not, I don't want to do that.'

'OK, so we don't do that.' He shrugged and rolled over.

I realized just how stupid this was; how irresponsible I had been in the search for a distraction from myself. I was alone in a city I didn't know and I was drunk; no one knew where I was; I had no money and no phone.

'I think I'm going to walk home,' I said, getting out of his bed.

'OK,' he replied. 'It's raining, though. You can stay here if you like.'

I looked at his clock – four a.m. I could sleep until the storm had passed and it was light, then try to navigate my way back to Alex's apartment. I fell asleep as far away from him as I could, my face pressed up against his white wall.

The next morning, I woke at half seven, got dressed and went into the living room to collect my bag. Sitting on the sofa was a very, very angry-looking man in a navy dressing gown. Four electric fans had appeared that hadn't been there the night before and all the windows were open. There were pieces of paper stuck to the wall, all with *FUMER TUE* scrawled on them in red pen, SMOKING KILLS written underneath.

'Good morning!' I said nervously.

'Get. Ze ferk. Out of my apartment,' he said in a French accent heavier than Jean's.

'I'm sorry?'

'I have asthma. You know that? I have severe asthma. So why ze ferk are you in my apartment chain-smoking your disgusting cigarettes at three in ze morning?'

'I'm so sorry, Jean said it was fi–'

'Jean can go ferk 'imself,' he spat.

I went back into Jean's bedroom.

'Hey,' I said, shaking him to wake up. 'Hey – your flatmate is in there and he's going quite nuts.'

Jean opened his eyes and looked at his clock.

'I'm late for work!' he said accusatorially.

'He's going pretty crazy in there,' I said. 'He's angry because we were smoking last night. He's got all these fans on and he's written all these signs. It feels a bit . . . *Rain Man.*'

'He's not angry because we were smoking, he's angry because you wouldn't have sex with him.'

'OK, I'm going,' I said. 'Have a good life.' I walked out of the flat, meekly nodding at the angry French flatmate as I went.

'GET OUT. GET OUT. GET ZE FERK OUT, YOU LITTLE BEETCH!' he shouted after me.

I teetered into the bright SoHo sunshine and felt like

I was going to retch. I went to withdraw ten dollars from the nearest ATM but was informed I had insufficient funds. A wave of sickness rippled through me and I remembered that I hadn't eaten in two days.

As I tried to find my way home, I went into Starbucks, hoping that they left jugs of milk by the sugar sachets. I asked the man behind the counter for a paper cup and filled it with milk, sipping it slowly as I sat at a table.

'Are you OK, honey?' a middle-aged woman asked. 'You look like a . . .' She surveyed my outfit, my eyes ringed with last night's mascara dust, the cup of milk in my hand. 'Like a stray kitten.'

'I'm OK,' I replied. Feeling less OK than ever before.

I walked around in circles for a couple of hours until I finally saw a block of flats that I recognized. I got into Alex's apartment, put my phone in rice and curled up under her duvet with her cats, longing to pull the duvet up over the trip too. But I couldn't afford a sandwich, let alone an early flight home. And I don't think I even wanted to go home – I was trapped between two cities I didn't want to be in. I couldn't ring Farly and ask for help, because she needed my support far more than I needed hers. I couldn't ring my parents, because I couldn't bear to worry them and I was ten years past an appropriate age for being bailed out of anything. Eventually, I rang Octavia, who showed me extraordinary kindness. She took me out for dim sum, held my hand as I talked, gave me a hug and lent me some money.

The next day, I took the three-hour coach trip to a

small town in the Catskills in upstate New York. Farly and I had already paid for the cabin, so I thought I might as well use it, and I was grateful for the opportunity for some space and quiet and some open skies.

I arrived mid-morning, dropped my bags and went for a long hike to clear my head. By the time I'd returned to my cabin in the afternoon, having marvelled at the enormity of the mountains and thought of the possibility of starting again when I returned home, I was already feeling calmer.

In the evening, I walked into the town and ate cheese fries in a local diner. I delighted in the sound of crickets and the warmth and chit-chat of the locals. There was a campfire burning behind my cabin when I got back and I took one of the blankets from my room and sat next to it, looking up at the stars. For what felt like the first time since I had arrived in New York, I breathed.

When I got back to my room, I had a new message on Tinder – a late reply from the 'come one, come all' blanket message I had drunkenly sent two nights before. His name was Adam. He was twenty-six with a perfect, all-American smile complete with Brooklyn beard and man bun.

'Hello, lady,' he messaged. 'So sorry I didn't reply to this sooner – how are you?'

'I wish you had replied sooner,' I said. 'I could have ended up on a date with you and not being strong-armed into a threesome with two Frenchmen.'

'Oh boy,' he wrote. 'New York can be tough. How are you doing?'

'I'm hating it,' I replied. 'I am in the Catskills for a night, and it's a welcome break.'

'How long have you got back in the city before you go home?'

'Three long days. I come back early tomorrow evening.'

'Come hang out with me when you're back,' he said. 'I won't try to have a threesome with you, I promise. I'll just be your friend if you like.'

A friend. Maybe I needed a new friend.

The next day, after another long hike and a swim, I got a late-afternoon coach back to Manhattan, took the subway to Brooklyn and went to Adam's doorstep.

'Hey,' he said, emerging from the front door, his blue eyes sparkling behind horn-rimmed glasses, outstretching his arms for a hug. 'It's so good to meet you. Welcome back to this city you hate.'

'Thanks,' I said, falling into his hug and inhaling the clean, soapy smell of his flannel shirt.

'I'll make you love it.'

Adam showed me round his apartment and we opened a bottle of wine. We talked for hours; told each other all our stories – about our favourite music, our favourite films, about our respective friends and families, about our jobs. He was earnest and bright-eyed and bushy-tailed and curious; he was exactly what I needed.

By mid-evening, we were kissing. By midnight, I was lying in his bed with my face pressed up close against his. It was the soft touch of this man, his generous heart, the tenderness he showed me that was enough to make me open up. So I told him everything; I gave it all away for nothing. I told him about the heartbreak of my early twenties. I told him about the years I had spent starving myself in an attempt to gain some control. I told him about the one time I had been in love; the intimacy that I couldn't bear, the dependence I feared. I told him how my friends, one by one, had fallen in love and left me behind. I told him how my anxiety had crept up on me in catatonic flare-ups since I was a child; how I couldn't stand near windows because I always felt I was moments away from falling to my death. I told him about my best friend's little sister who I had grown up with, who was lying in a hospital bed with cancer. I told him that I felt I was in over my head with adulthood and about my total inability to ring anyone and ask for help. I told him about the ease with which I buried problems in a chaotic rubble of distractions. I only had the right language for my sadness with a stranger; I could only tell these stories in an ephemeral realm of fantasy in which I had no accountability.

'You're so sad,' he said, stroking my cheek. I closed my eyes to stop the tears.

'I'm so lost,' I replied.

'You're not lost now,' he said, pulling me closer to him. And I wanted to believe him, so for that moment, I did.

'I want to say something but it makes no sense,' he said, kissing my head.

'What?'

'I love you,' he sighed. 'And I don't want you to think I'm, like, dangerous or crazy like that insane French guy, and I know I can't *really*, because I've known you for –' he glanced at his watch – 'six hours. But I feel like I could love you. Fuck it, I already love you.'

'I love you too,' I heard myself say. The second the words escaped my mouth, I knew how absurd they were. But I knew I wasn't saying them to him; I was saying them to something else. To the belief in hope and kindness.

Adam took the next day off work, the first sick day in his life, and he took me round the bits of the city I'd never been before. We walked, we talked, we ate, we drank, we kissed. We had a typical holiday romance in two days – we couldn't remember what life was like without each other, but we knew we would never live life with each other. I stayed with him the following night.

The next day, I tore myself away from Adam for three whole hours to meet Octavia, who couldn't believe everything that had happened since I had last seen her. We went to the top of 30 Rock and looked out on the beautiful, relentless, unforgiving city.

'I think I want to go home,' I said, staring out at the lights dancing off the Hudson River.

Adam took me to JFK on my last day. After a long good-bye kiss, he held me by the shoulders and looked at me.

'OK, I have this idea,' he said.

'What?'

'Don't think I'm nuts.'

'OK.'

'Stay,' he said.

'I can't stay.'

'Why not? You're miserable at home. You hate London. You don't have a job. You don't know what you want to do next. Stay here and start again.'

'Where would I live?' I asked.

'With me,' he said.

'How would I pay rent?'

'We'll figure it out,' he said. 'You'll be able to find some work and you can write all the things you've ever wanted to write. I'll give you your own space and your own time. Think about how much freer you'll feel here.'

'What about when your iron-clad immigration system tries to send me home?'

'Then I'll fucking marry you,' he said. 'Is that what you want to hear? Because I'll do it. I'll take you down to City Hall first thing tomorrow morning and I'll marry the hell out of you. And then you can stay for as long as you want.'

'I can't do that,' I said. 'It's completely insane.'

'Why won't you stay?' he said, gently pressing his head against mine. 'You were the one who said you've got nothing waiting for you at home.'

I thought for a while.

'Because I'm the problem,' I replied. 'Not the city. Not any of the circumstances are the problem. I'm the thing that needs changing.' There was quiet between us. And then we kissed for the last time.

'Call me when you land,' he said. 'And don't get drunk on the flight, the plane's not going to crash.'

On the flight home, I daydreamed of Tottenham Court Road and ordering shit off Amazon. I thought of Farly's laugh and the sound of my flatmates getting ready for work in the morning and the smell of my mum's perfume in her hair when I hug her. I thought of the blissful mundanity of life; of what a privilege it was to live it.

It was the day before my twenty-sixth birthday. Belle and AJ were at work when I got home, but there was a wonky home-made cake and a banner wishing me happy birthday. The next evening, we all went out dancing in Camden to celebrate, and I told them about my strange two weeks away. Lauren and I stayed up drinking and playing guitar until the early hours of the next morning, at which point a huge bunch of red roses arrived from Adam.

After I came home, things got easier for a while. The heavy coat of sadness I had been wearing for so long began to lift. I made a proper plan for what I wanted to do next. I fell back in love with my city, wildly. I read Bill Bryson books about England and ate Toffee Crisps. I remembered how lucky I was to live in a place I had grown up in, a place filled with my friends.

Two months into my return, I left my job and went

freelance. A month after that, I was given a column in *The Sunday Times*. Lauren and I made a short film about a directionless twenty-five-year-old who has no idea who she is, and reaches for everything other than into herself to fix the problem. AJ moved out; one of our other brilliant university friends, India, moved in. We left the dilapidated yellow palace of Camden and moved two miles north into a flat with no mice, a working loo and central heating.

Octavia, my saviour, returned to London and became a close friend. Adam and I have always kept in touch and we always will; he sees me when he comes to London and I always have lunch with him when I'm in New York. He reminds me of a tumultuous time in my life, the stories of which I like to remember but never want to recreate. That time when I was twenty-five and so rootless and lost, I nearly moved country for a man I didn't know. He's got his half of the story and I've got mine; we carry them round like those naff teenage necklaces of a heart split in two.

12th December

Dear All,

Happy Christmas from all of us (just me – I live on my own now) here at SE20's overpriced and under-maintained 32 Bracken Street!

What a year it's been. It all kicked off with a flying start when I was given a promotion at the organic juice start-up (Pressed For Lime) I've been working at for the last four years as Social Media Manager. I was upgraded to the rather authoritative and yet nebulous role of Social Media Campaigns Overseer, which basically means I send out four videos on Instagram Stories every day of pieces of fruit with faces drawn on them, wearing miniature knitted hats, on top of all my other responsibilities, for no extra money.

(Dad – if you're reading – no, I'm not going to explain what my job is for the one hundredth time! And, yes, I know my education cost a lot of money. I know I could've 'done anything'! Just pretend I really *am* a lawyer to your friends at the golf club. It's not like they're going to google me to check, and even if they do they won't find my name on anything other than an old Bebo page because no one has even heard of the company I work for! Ha ha!)

As I mentioned at the top of this email, I moved out of my cosy flat-share in Kentish Town with my best friend Katya earlier this year because she and her boyfriend said they were 'ready for some privacy' and they could cover the mortgage without me now (they both have real jobs). So I set up home all by myself in London's trendy Penge.

The area is leafyish – maybe more branchy, actually – and is VERY 'up and coming' (*Metro*, 2016). Which is probably why it's costing me £1,200 to rent a large studio with a mezzanine bedroom above the cooker. Lucky I'm such a foodie – what a treat it is to go to sleep with my whole bedroom smelling of baked salmon!

After a long and happy seven years together, Jordan and I broke up amicably this year. We were both a bit jealous of our friends having tons of casual sex with strangers from Tinder and our shared death anxiety and choking FOMO meant we were increasingly aware that, when the end comes, we didn't want to have had a total of three sexual partners between us. We read a few books on polyamory and gave that a good go, but what with our respective work schedules, we couldn't synchronize our diaries to make time for each other as well as all the others, so we thought it would be less time-consuming if we just parted ways. He took the cat.

So now I am being shown the delights of online dating! The men won't commit, all the sex is pornographic and my phone never has any storage because of all the photos of fully shaven penises I'm sent on WhatsApp. I'm Penge's very own Carrie Bradshaw!

(Please read my sexploits on www.theadventures ofandrea.org. 'Amusing, desperate' – *Huffington Post*.)

Health-wise, my hypochondria continues to thrive in direct correlation with my anxiety. In the past year alone, I have self-diagnosed five types of cancer, three sexually transmitted diseases and four mental health conditions.

I have also stopped walking in grassy or woodland areas since reading about Lyme disease (I still think I have it – do you?).

My Uber rating has fallen to 3.5, which is disappointing, but I am hoping to face this challenge head-on in the New Year with renewed optimism and alacrity.

Over on social media, it's been one hell of a ride. I managed to reach 2,000 followers on Twitter in November – hitting my projected target (you might remember this was my main goal in last year's round-robin letter). And, even more excitingly, I've had four Instagram photos receive less than seven likes and I've managed not to immediately book an emergency discussion with my online therapist as a result. So, progress all round!

My goals for this year include getting off anti-depressants, getting out of overdraft and finding the perfect shade of cream blusher to suit my skin tone. Wish me luck on the next chapter of this ever-changing, unpredictable journey we call life.

That's all for this year – wishing you a very merry Christmas and a New Year full of happiness!

Andrea xxx

Weekly Shopping List

- Loo roll
- New knickers
- Paper
- Desire to read all sections of the paper
- Coffee capsules
- Marmite
- Apples
- Sanitary products that aren't scented with a Britney Spears perfume
- Time-management skills
- Puppy (dachshund, miniature)
- Tap dispensing strong but milky Yorkshire tea
- A better toaster with a more reliable timer
- Flatmates who will watch *Countryfile* with me
- My own driver, just for me
- Bin liners
- Puppy (Norfolk Terrier, soft-coated)
- Jarvis Cocker
- An endless supply of Cheddar
- The time to watch every *Seinfeld* episode three times
- My own cinema
- Better grammar

- Thicker skin
- Better ability to say 'no' to things
- Twenty pairs of tights with no ladders
- Milk

Florence

When I first met Florence, she was six years old and I was barely a teenager. Farly opened the front door to see her little sister standing on the step swaying side to side, her hair cut into a tufty mop on her little head.

'FLORENCE!' she yelped. 'WHAT HAVE YOU DONE TO YOUR HAIR?!'

Florence smiled cheekily.

'DAD, I CANNOT BELIEVE YOU'VE LET HER DO THIS!' Farly shouted in her teenage bellow to her dad, Richard, standing by the car. 'SHE LOOKS LIKE A LITTLE BOY!' Florence carried on grinning.

'She begged to have it that way, angel,' Richard said, shrugging. 'What could I do?'

I adored her instantly.

Florence and I grew closer when she approached adolescence. Like me, she always felt like she was ready to be a grown-up. She wanted her own identity and independence. She was weary of her peers. She escaped into books and films and music. She was an obsessive; always tracking down every word ever written by her new favourite writers, watching every film ever made by her favourite directors back-to-back. Like me, she found being a teenager at an all-girls school tough and I always wanted to reassure her that the best was yet to come; that being an adult, no matter how difficult or boring at times, was the best thing in the world.

'You know when people say schooldays are the best days of your life?' I said to her one weekend afternoon as we lay in the sunshine of their family's garden.

'Yeah?' she said.

'They're talking shit.'

'Really?' she asked, stroking my arm – always a condition of her being able to hang out with Farly and me when we were in our late teens.

'Yes. It's the biggest load of rubbish I ever heard. Schooldays are the *worst* days of your life, Floss. All the good stuff only begins when you leave.'

'Thanks, Aldermaston,' she said (it was their family nickname for me – anyone who walked through the doors of their home got a nickname).

But Florence had nothing to worry about, because she grew into a completely sensational teenager. Far better than I had ever been: like most teenagers, I was mainly concerned with myself, but Florence's worldview was wide-reaching and empathetic, especially for someone so young and who had lived a fairly sheltered life. Floss was creative and angry and curious and passionate. She wrote a blog on film, dissecting American indie cinema and bemoaning modern Hollywood. She wrote daily diaries. She wrote half a novel. She wrote and directed plays that she put on at school. She gave a talk on LGBT issues in her buttoned-up school assembly.

She went on marches. She once came round to our house in Camden with a camera and two friends and asked if she could use it as a location to shoot a short film to raise awareness about domestic violence.

She also became delightfully, wonderfully disruptive at the dinner table. A meal with Farly's family was nearly always punctuated by Florence shouting 'MISOGYN-IST!' at someone during a heated discussion. During one particularly memorable dinner, she went hell for leather on Scott when he dared to question the artistry of Wes Anderson's films and said he found his work to be a purely aesthetic experience. Floss went into a long, passionate piece of oratory, informing him why he was wrong, before leaving the table in a rage and returning with a huge hardback book about cinema and slamming it on the table with a thud.

Florence was diagnosed with leukaemia in the summer she left school. She'd finally got to the finish line of adolescence and stood on the cusp of life, only to be told she had cancer. But, from everything the doctors said, though the treatment and recovery from the treatment would be very serious, the outlook was positive. And so was she – magnificently so. She went straight to Kingston Hospital for chemotherapy and made best friends with the nurses and cleaners; she would raise her bed as high as she could so she could chat to them and give them advice. She was told she wouldn't be able to have children, a fact that many around her found devastating, but she responded with characteristic grace and good humour, stating that the world was overpopulated anyway.

She started a funny, honest blog documenting her journey with cancer that garnered thousands of readers. She took selfies of her newly shaved head and made funny videos of herself dancing around her bed. She was inundated with emails and letters from supporters. I couldn't have been prouder of her and regularly sent her texts telling her she had no right to be such a good writer at the age of nineteen.

One particular post read:

The worst thing I heard that night [on the date of her diagnosis, 8 August] wasn't actually the diagnosis but the following words: 'We want you to stay in overnight.' I didn't expect that at all. And then the doctor said, 'And in the morning the haematologist will perform a bone marrow extraction on you.' That's when I knew something was not right. They don't just DO those kind of things.

The haematologist came in to see me to say hello and introduce himself before he went home for the night. I just wanted an answer, really, so I asked him plainly, 'What do you think this is?' (gesturing to my lumpy and swollen neck). He breathed a sigh before plainly replying, '50/50 it's cancer.'

When you hear the word cancer you hear death. You think of all the prospects of your future shrivelling into non-existence. And you cry. And cry I did. This lovely

man, evidently not so great with others' emotions, pat-
ted my back and attempted to comfort me with words
of 'I didn't come in here to make you cry.' Well what do
you expect someone to do when you tell them they've
probably got cancer?! Leap in the air and yell, 'Yippee!
My life just got so much better!' No, of course they're
going to be upset. And I was. And I was angry. And I
was worried about my parents who were crying just as
much as I was.

And I remember saying, 'I'm not ready to die yet. I
haven't even lived yet.' And then later on, 'And I haven't
had sex yet! It's not fair.'

But I got over that stage. And now it's more like,
'When I'm done with this cancer, I'm going to kick the
world in the arse and be the best thing anyone's ever
seen.' I mean who can reject me, I'll have beaten cancer. Everything else is easy.

I texted her to tell her how much I loved it and assured
her that she'd definitely have sex once all of this was over.

'We'll go on the pull,' she replied. 'I'm going to find
you one cracking fella, I promise.'

She celebrated her nineteenth birthday in hospital;
the nurses made her a banner that they hung outside her
room. She found out she got into York University to
read film studies and they said she could delay her place
for a year until she'd made a full recovery. She came
home after her last cycle of chemo and made chocolate
Guinness cake for the nurses who'd cared for her.

199

Farly shrunk her world during this time; she was either at the primary school where she was now a teacher, at the hospital or with her family. Scott was with her for everything and I loved him for being such a steadfast, sturdy pillar of support for her and her family. We texted and called each other regularly and he'd let me know how she was doing – it brought us closer, and I felt lucky that my best friend had someone so strong and loving at her side.

Floss carried on blogging when she came home from Kingston. Her brother, Freddie, was a bone marrow match, which was fantastic news as it enabled him to be a donor for her, though she had to recover from chemotherapy before having the operation at a hospital in central London. But, quite suddenly, her health started deteriorating and she was rushed into the hospital prematurely. A series of issues followed in succession, one never being solved before the next problem came. Her kidneys weren't working, she couldn't speak, her organs started failing and she was put in intensive care and on a ventilator to breathe. Farly was given some time off school to be at the hospital with her family every day.

I had just left my job of over three years to be a full-time writer, which meant I was working from home and could get a bus to meet her. We met for lunch most days for a month, always going to the cafe above Heal's on Tottenham Court Road and ordering the same thing each time, two Caesar salads and a plate of chips to share. She'd tell me how Floss was doing that day, but the news never seemed to get better. Everything was up in the air and no one had any clear idea of what was going to happen next – the bone marrow transplant seemed like it was getting further and further away. I tried to calm her with the same repeated platitudes: she's in the best place she can be, she's in safe hands, the doctors know what they're doing. I knew she was being inundated with stats and science every day from experts, so I felt it was my job as an ignorant friend to be a positive cradle for her hope. But the truth was, I had no idea what was happening.

Every day she asked me my news, desperate for some normality to distract and rejuvenate her before heading into the hospital room for the afternoon. I told her about the articles I was writing that week. I showed her boys on Tinder. She bought me a glass of Prosecco the day I found out I'd been given my first column, telling me she was just happy to celebrate something.

At one point, it seemed like Floss was showing small signs of progress and Farly said I should come to the hospital to visit her. I said I would love to, although I was nervous I wouldn't be able to keep it together. As I sanitized my hands before I went in, I realized I'd never visited anyone in hospital before.

'Someone's come to see you,' Farly said as I entered the room. Floss couldn't speak, but she smiled at me, and I was filled with relief and a rush of love for this girl who was the closest thing I'd ever known to a little sister. I stood at the end of her bed and babbled at her, hoping it would provide some sort of distraction; I told her about the new series of *Girls* that I knew she was going to love, about a new band I'd been listening to that I thought she would like. Farly asked me to tell her about all the stuff I was writing, and she smiled again as I told her about the short film Lauren and I were working on, the script of which she'd have to edit for me sometime soon. After fifteen minutes, I said goodbye to this spectacular, beautiful, electric thunderstorm of a girl, knowing it could be the last time I ever saw her.

'I feel like I'm watching her slip away,' Farly said to me one day soon after my visit during one of our lunches. 'I can feel it, I know it's happening.'

'You don't know that,' I said. 'People go to the darkest edge and come back to full health. You hear the stories all the time.' But, having seen Floss so ill and being told that was her best day, I knew why Farly was having those thoughts and it was important that I let her express them.

The following week, early one afternoon, I was writing at my kitchen table when Farly called.

'She's gone,' she said, gasping for breath. 'She died.'

I've never seen as many people gathered at a funeral as there were the day we said goodbye to Florence. All of our friends came to the service, along with masses of teachers and girls from her school, family, friends she met on her travels; people who had been touched by her warmth and wit and intelligence and kindness over the years, of which there were hundreds. There were so many attendees, many of them had to stand outside the crematorium and watch the service from a screen. I smiled up at the sky when I realized this, hoping it would have made her happy, and hoping she knew just how loved she was. Freddie gave the eulogy; the rabbi – who'd known her since she was a kid – spoke admiringly of her charisma and courage. Her best friend did a reading of a breathtaking piece Florence had written for her year-book page. 'It may seem that life is difficult at times but it's really as simple as breathing in and out,' she read. 'Rip open hearts with your fury and tear down egos with your modesty. Be the person you wish you could be, not the person you feel you are doomed to be. Let yourself run away with your feelings. You were made so that someone could love you. Let them love you.'

In between the funeral and the shiva – a period of mourning in the Jewish faith that happens at home – all the girls came back to our place. We went to Ivan's and picked up some wine. I made a huge pan of scrambled eggs while India produced endless rounds of toast. We talked about Florence – everything that was funny and brilliant and outrageous about her – we cried and we laughed and we raised our glasses to her memory.

The family house was just as packed for the shiva as it had been for the funeral. We all stood in the kitchen and the rabbi said prayers and spoke again of Florence. Farly began to read a poem and I watched her speak the lines into the microphone, looking so much smaller than I'd ever seen her. She stopped at a particular line and began to cry, so she passed the poem to the rabbi, who continued to read it aloud. I looked across the crowded kitchen at this small, birdlike creature, snapping into pieces, all her bones and words crumbling, and I wanted to barge through the room to hold her. It was the worst moment of my life.

People stayed on late into the evening. Her school friends all sat in Florence's bedroom among her books and clothes. I had been tasked with the condolences book. India, AJ and Lacey were chugging Bristol Cream Sherry that Aunty Laura had plied them with from plastic glasses. All of Farly's colleagues from the school where she taught had come to pay their respects, including the head teacher. Halfway through the evening, as is Jewish tradition, the grieving family sat on chairs in a line and the mourners wished them a long life.

I got to Farly and crouched down to her level to hug her.

'I love you very much,' I said. 'And I wish you a very long and happy life.'

'Thank you,' she said, squeezing me back. 'Have you seen all the teachers from my school?'

'Yes. They're lovely. I've just been talking to your deputy head.'

'Do you like her?'

'I do. We had a great chat, what a nice woman.'

'I'm pleased you like her,' she said, smiling. 'What did you guys talk about?'

'I asked her to look after you when you go back to work,' I said. 'I asked her to make sure someone's always looking after you.'

'I'll be OK, Doll,' she said, her huge brown eyes brimming with tears until one escaped through her lashes and ran down her cheek. 'I just have to find a way to live without her.'

I spent the following days at the family home with Farly. There wasn't much talking, but I made tea and we helped her stepmum, Annie, with any bits that needed doing around the house. After Florence died, a *Telegraph* journalist found her blog and got in touch with the family to ask if they could run extracts of it in the paper, as well as an accompanying piece about her. They agreed, as they knew it's what she would have wanted, and the article meant even more people got in touch with Annie and Richard to express their sorrow at the loss of someone so full of life.

'Send letters,' Annie said one morning as she sat reading through a huge pile of cards and letters from people offering their condolences. 'I used to always worry when I heard something bad had happened to someone that writing would be an intrusion. It's never an intrusion, it always helps. If there's one thing we can learn from this, it's to always just send the letter.'

That afternoon, we all took the dog for a walk. Farly and I walked side by side. We wore matching bobble hats that we'd bought a few days earlier when we'd gone to Kew retail park to pick up insoles for the shoes she wore to the funeral. What with the intense week of inseparable company, these matching hats and the adults behind us, it felt like we were teenagers again. Except this time we weren't talking about boys on MSN. Somewhere in our fifteen years of walking side by side, from school to university lectures, to the streets around our first place in London, we had stopped playing at being grown-ups and accidentally become grown-ups.

'She told me once that she never wanted to be forgotten. I feel bad about resuming life as normal,' she said.

'She said that before she knew she was dying,' I reasoned. 'I know she would have hated the thought of you mourning her for ever.'

'I suppose.'

'You can find a way of keeping her close to you and living with her without stopping your life.'

'Everything will be so strange without her.'

'It will be a new normality,' I said. 'But she made fucking sure she won't be forgotten, don't worry.'

'Well, that's true,' she said.

'You have to live. You don't have a choice. You move forward or you go under.'

We continued walking along the river. It was so cold and sunny, as still and clear as a day in an unshaken snow globe. We walked past a row of cottages in Chiswick with bright-coloured doors. Whitewashed pubs faced the cool, watery breeze. Other than the bridges with tube trains careering over, we could have been in a seaside village.

'Ant and Dec live down here,' she said, gesturing at the cottages. 'In one of these ones.'

'No they don't.'

'They do, I promise.'

'They don't, you're just saying that because the front doors are so small.'

'I PROMISE you they live here.'

'Together?'

'No, not together, they live next door to each other.'

We carried on walking.

'I don't ever want to live far away from you,' I said.

'Me neither.'

'I don't really care where I live when I'm older, I just want to live near you.'

'Me too.'

'Even now it feels like we're too far away from each other. I want us to make sure our houses are really close. I want it to be a priority from now on.'

'So do I,' she said.

We continued down the riverside, the December sun still flooding the sky.

'I always think of you when the weather is like this. This is your favourite kind of day,' I said.

'It is. Cold and bright.'

'Yes. Whereas my favourite is dark and wet because I'm a self-indulgent neurotic and you're always bouncy and buoyant.'

'Ha.'

'You are. We got it wrong when we were kids. We

always thought you were the sensitive one, but it turns out I'm the one that's always a mess. You're so much more resilient than you think you are.'

'I don't know about that,' she said.

'You are. You're made of the strongest stuff. I wouldn't cope if this were me.'

'You don't know that. You never know how you're going to react to something until it happens to you.' We continued to pace alongside each other, watching the sunlight shimmy off the water. 'It's been like this every day since she died.'

'She's here,' I said. 'She's with us. She'll be here every time you call out an injustice or laugh at your favourite film. She will be there.'

We walked along Kew Bridge, Annie and her sister still in view behind us, the bruiser of a dog trotting beside them, tail merrily swooshing from side to side.

'Do you want to be cremated?' she asked.

'I do,' I said. 'And I want to be scattered in Devon. On Mothecombe Beach.'

'Me too,' she said. 'But I want to be scattered where Floss will be, in Cornwall. Although I feel bad I won't be with you.'

'Oh, it's fine, we'll be together wherever we go next. We'll just have to meet each other there.'

'Definitely.'

'Do you think it's a bit loner-y for me to be on a beach on my own? What about Hampstead Heath? It's my favourite place in London and my mum and dad used to take me there when I was a kid.'

'No, definitely not, you'll be stamped on.'

'Yeah, you're right. And too posh and predictable.'

'That's why I think it's nice to be scattered in the sea,' she said pensively. 'Although I am scared of sharks.'

'But you'll be dead already.'

'Oh yeah.'

'That's the whole point, the shark could do its worst and you'd be fine. You're past the point of no return.'

'OK, at sea then.'

We walked home in the beautiful light and I felt grateful for Florence's life and everything she had taught me. I was grateful for the sun on Kew Bridge as I placed each foot in front of the other. I was grateful for understanding in that moment that life can really be as simple as just breathing in and out. And I was thankful to know what it was to love the person walking next to me as much as I did. So deeply, so furiously. So impossibly.

Recipe: Scrambled Eggs

(serves two)

All you need is butter, eggs and bread. No scrambled eggs need milk or cream. Keep it simple and they're easy to both cook and eat when you're sad.

- 2 knobs of salted butter
- 4 fresh eggs (plus one yolk if you're feeling indulgent), lightly beaten with a fork
- Salt and black pepper, to season

Melt one knob of butter slowly, on a low heat, in a wide saucepan.

Pour eggs into the saucepan.

Move them around with a wooden spoon, slowly and quite constantly.

Take the pan off the heat when slightly too wet.

Season and stir in the other knob of butter.

Texts That My Flatmate India Has Let Me Send Off Her Phone Pretending to Be Her

(I don't know why she agrees to it either)

A text to Sam, her ex-colleague

India 20.47
Top of the morning to you, Sam! How's life? Bit of a random one but I was wondering what borough of London you currently reside in?

Sam 20.48
Richmond. Why do you ask? Are you moving South?

India 20.50
Alas, no. Staying in Highgate. We are having some problems at the moment with our bin collection. They are only taking general refuse every other week, and we are filling them up quite rapidly. How would you feel about me bringing two of our bins down to Richmond every other week? I'll pick them up and bring them back the next day, so don't worry about that.

Sam 20.51

Um . . . what?

You want to bring some bins 15 miles every
other week?

Why don't you just dump it somewhere?

India 20.51

Because I like to know it's in safe hands.

Sam 20.52

Bins?

India 20.52

Yes.

It won't be a big problem for you, you'll barely
notice.

Sam 20.53

Stop it.

India 20.53

OK, no worries, I'll text my friend in Peckham.

Sam 20.54

Can you only complete this job in places that are
over 10 miles away?

Seems quite drastic.

Why don't you text a friend in Camden?

Seems more suitable.

India 20.56

It's about being in a different borough, Sam. North

London is no good for me. I need a completely different borough in a completely different part of town.

The following day

India 21.00
Hey. How you bin doing?

> **Sam 21.01**
> Oh my God.
> Is this about bins again? Bin there, done that.

India 21.01
Stop talking rubbish!

> **Sam 21.02**
> Hahahahaha. Good one.

India 21.02
No but seriously are we good to start this arrangement next week?

> **Sam 21.03**
> Oh my God. Is this for real?

India 21.03
My bins go on Tuesday, so I can pop them down on the overground train on Mon? xx

> **Sam 21.05**
> I thought you'd been drinking, India. I live in
> Barnes.

India 21.05
Bins?

Sam 21.06
It's over an hour away.

India 21.06
You're right, it's too long on the tube.

Sam 21.07
It's not even on the tube.

India 21.07
I'll bring them in a large cab.

Sam 21.08
Stop this. I don't want your bins.

India 21.09
OK. Bit lost with what to do now, but I guess you don't want the hassle.

Sam 21.09
Why don't you just dump them somewhere? Unless you put personal documents in, no one is going to know.

India 21.10
I suppose.
I just wish I could bring them to Barnes as it's more practical.

> **Sam 21.10**
> It's not, it's ludicrous.

India 21.11
I get it if you want your privacy, etc.
And don't want me coming back and forth.

> **Sam 21.11**
> I don't want to be a bin crèche, no. It's weird.
> But if you ever fancy a drink in Barnes you're
> more than welcome.
> Just don't bring any bins.

A text to Shaun, an acquaintance from university

India 19.21
Hi. I get the impression that you have the nose
for an entrepreneurial venture. Am I right?

> **Shaun 19.22**
> Who is this?

India 19.22
India Masters, BA Hons.

> **Shaun 19.53**
> How can I help?

India 19.54
I've identified a gap in the market – and it's a
fairly big gap – to sell mini fridges in a variety of

colours. I've got a business plan, all I need is a silent partner. Could that man be you?

A text to Zac, a university friend

India 18.53
Can I ask you a favour??

Zac 18.54
Sure, babe.

India 18.54
Can I borrow a pair of your trousers for a work meeting this week?

Zac 18.54
Haha. Yeah.
What sort of trousers? And why?

India 18.55
Just noticed you wear nice ones.
And can't be bothered to buy new ones.
And it's a really important meeting with a client.

Zac 18.55
Mine will be too long.

India 18.55
I don't think they will be?

Zac 18.55
You are v weird.
Indy, how tall are you?

India 18.56
I'm five foot two.

Zac 18.57
I'm five foot eleven.

India 18.57
I can roll them up.
Don't worry about any of that, just meet me with the trousers.

A text to Paul, a man India once snogged

India 19.02
Hi. How are you?

Paul 19.16
Good thanks! How are you?

India 19.18
Great to hear from you. I have a request – I'm in the middle of starting a dance troupe, mainly traditional Irish dancing but don't let that put you off, there will most certainly be a modern twist. Anyway, it can make you a lot of money come wedding season and I wondered if you

fancied a piece of the pie? It wouldn't take you long to learn the routines and frankly we need someone tall at the back. Let me know what you think.

Paul 19.56
Hi, wow thanks so much for thinking of me.
As fun as that does sound unfortunately my calendar for this year is looking pretty busy and I don't think I'd be able to commit to this.
Really sorry about that.
Be sure to take pictures.
Take care and hopefully see you soon x

India 19.58
But do you want a piece of the pie though?

23rd March

Hello any woman Emily has known for the last twenty-eight years!

I hope you're well and excited about next weekend's festivities. We thought it would be useful for all of you ladies to know what the shape of the day looks like.

Saturday will begin promptly at 8.00 a.m. Please join us in the Tower of London for a Tudor cooking course. We will be making stuffed, roasted venison with stewed pears. This will be breakfast at 9.00 a.m. along with a generous pint of mead.

At 10 we will make our way up north to Kentish Town Sports Centre, where we will be playing a game of dildo football. It's very simple – we split into two teams and play a friendly game but all while wearing big black strap-ons. (PLEASE if you haven't already, send us a sentence of your favourite memory of you and Emily – we will write these in Tippex on her strap-on so she can keep it for ever.)

At 12 p.m. **sharp** we will change into our first fancy-dress outfits (disco meets Kenan & Kel), leave the sports centre and make our way to Emily's favourite pub she went to twice ten years ago, the Sparrow and Ape in Camden.

12.30 p.m. Lunch (included in the money you've already transferred) will be a delicious mezze sharing platter entitling you to one falafel, three olives and half a flatbread each and a glass of Prosecco. If you don't drink Prosecco or any type of fizzy wine, you're advised to organize your own alcohol for the entire day.

2.00 p.m. After lunch, we thought it would be fun to play a game of 'how close are we actually?' We will form a circle and Emily will go round and have to answer questions about us. If she gets more than one wrong, you will be evicted from the hen do and be asked to make your way home (e.g. for the first round, she'll be asked what our jobs are; in the second round she'll be asked what our middle names are, etc.). Not only do we think this will raise the stakes of the day, we need to get the group down from thirty-five to thirty for the dinner venue later as thirty is its capacity. This seems like the only fair option.

3.00 p.m. We are super excited to have had chocolate moulds made of a variety of male anuses by artisan chocolate company Sucre et Crème (massive thanks to bridesmaid Linda for organizing this). It will be Emily's job to guess which anus belongs to her fiancé.

4.00 p.m. We think this would be a good time to change into our second fancy-dress outfit – 'My Favourite Emily'. I've had a lot of concerned emails over the last few weeks from people about what they should come as and, honestly, we can't stress enough: **this is meant to be fun**. So don't worry too much about it! Lacrosse Emily, gap-year Emily and unemployed fat Emily all work great! Someone mentioned The Priory Emily and this is the only idea we're not sure about – bear in mind, we've got mums and grannies there for this portion of the day.

5.00 p.m. Before everyone gets too tipsy to remember anything, we want to present Emily with her Tampon Tree. I hope you all got the email about saving a used tampon and bringing it in an envelope. We'll have a fig tree to present to Emily decorated with all our tampons to symbolize how we will always be connected by womanhood and friendship. We think it will be a really special moment for her.

6.00 p.m. We say goodbye to the grannies and the mums and order them an Uber.

6.30 p.m. We head to Ribs N Bibs in Stockwell.

7.15 p.m. Arrive at restaurant and immediately change into our going-out clothes. (Heels, please!! Want to make it as glam as possible for Emily.)

7.30 p.m. Starters.

8.30 p.m. Surprise performance by a nude cast of the Blue Man Group. Emily was very keen to impress that she didn't want an embarrassing stripper, so we thought this was a good compromise. (NB Bridesmaids remember to bring change of clothes for Emily because she will be covered in paint by the end of this.)

9.00 p.m. Main courses.

10.00 p.m. Pudding and a DIY millinery crash course. We have world-famous hatter Madame Meringue arriving who has agreed to teach us all how to make disposable fascinators from our leftover pudding. You can watch her amazing banoffee pie beret tutorials **here** for a sense of what we're in for.

11.00 p.m. Walk to FLUID club in Vauxhall where we have reserved a chair (no tables left).

4.00 a.m. Club closes.

And that's that!

All that's left to say is, Emily wanted us to let you all know that unfortunately an invitation to the hen do **DOES NOT GUARANTEE** an invitation to the wedding. It's going to be a small(ish) affair and they can't accommodate everyone, but she still hopes you'll be there to celebrate her last days as an unmarried gal.

Anyone found talking to Emily about the wedding or angling for an invitation will be immediately removed from the hen do – this is meant to be a fun day for her, not another day of logistical wedmin.

Thank you everyone for transferring £378.23 – this covers the entire cost of the day other than transport, main courses at the restaurant, drinks at the restaurant and drinks at the club.

We're yet to receive money from the following girls:

EMILY BAKER

JENNIFER THOMAS

SARAH CARMICHAEL

CHARLOTTE FOSTER

If those girls don't transfer the money by 11.00 p.m. tonight, they unfortunately won't be able to attend and everyone will have to cover the cost of their places.

Let's get ready to roost!!

The Bridesmaids xxx

My Therapist Says

'Why are you here?'

Why was I there? I never thought I would be there. In a small room just behind Oxford Circus, with cream carpets and a burgundy sofa. Where it always smelt of molecule perfume and nothing else, no matter how hard I sniffed when I came in – no leftover lunch, no cooling coffee – no evidence of a life outside this room other than this woman's perfume. The smell that would for ever make my heart sink and think of one p.m. on a Friday afternoon whenever I got a whiff of it on a woman at a party. I was there for a price by the hour. In a vacuum of life where nothing existed but conversation between two people – a commentator's box, the TV studio of post-match analysis. The less popular discussion show that runs alongside the big thing. This was *Strictly: It Takes Two*. This was *Dancing on Ice: Defrosted*. This was the room I would always think of when I was on the verge of making a bad decision; in the loo of a pub, with a man in the back of a taxi. This room that promised that my life would change in it.

I always promised myself I would never be in a room like this. But I didn't know where to be but there. I had run clean out of other options. I was twenty-seven and I felt like I was toppling from a gale of anxiety. It was nine months since I went freelance and I had spent nearly every day alone with my thoughts. I had pushed away the concerns of my friends and family; I was always on the verge of tears, but I was unable to talk to anyone. I woke up every morning with no idea of where I was or what was happening; I came round to my life every morning like the previous night's sleep was a punch in the head that left me bloody.

I was there because I had to be there. I was there because I had put off being there; because I always said I didn't have any money or time; because it was indulgent and silly. I told a friend that I felt on the verge of an implosion and she gave me a woman's number to call. I had run out of excuses.

'I think I'm going to fall and die,' I replied. She – Eleanor – peered over her glasses and then back to her page, furiously writing notes. She had a dark, semi-parted seventies-style flicky fringe, brown, feline eyes and a strong nose. She must have been in her early forties. She looked like a young Lauren Hutton. I noted that her arms were muscular and tanned and elegant. I thought that she probably thought I was a silly crybaby. A big, fat loser. An over-privileged girl, needlessly spaffing all her hard-earned cash so she could blabber on about herself for an hour a week. She probably saw women like me coming a mile off.

'I can't open or close any windows in my flat, I have to ask someone else to do it,' I continued, clipped and quiet to hold in tears that felt like they were pressing up behind the back wall of my eyeballs like water to a flood barrier.

'Sometimes I can't go into a room at all if a window is open because I'm so scared of falling out of it. And I have to stand with my back pressed against the wall when a train pulls into a tube station from the tunnel. I see myself falling in front of it and dying. I see it happening every time I blink. Then I'll spend all night replaying it over and over again in my head and I can't sleep.'

'Right,' she replied in an Australian accent. 'And how long have you felt like this?'

'It's all got really bad in the last six months,' I said. 'But on and off for the best part of ten years. The drinking gets bad when I'm very anxious. Same with the death obsession. The flavour of the month fixation is falling.'

I guided her through The Greatest Hits of My Recurring Emotional Turmoil. I talked about my weight that had been as ever-changing as cloud formations – the fact that I could look at every photo taken of me since 2009 and tell her exactly to the pound how much I weighed in each one. I told her about my obsession with alcohol that hadn't waned since I was a teenager, my unquenchable thirst when most people my age now knew when to stop, how I'd always been known for knocking it back at record speed, the vast black holes in my memory from these nights over the years; my increasing shame and distress over these lost hours and that unrecognizable madwoman running around town who I was meant to be responsible for, but who I had no recollection of being or knowing.

I told her about my inability to commit to a

relationship; my obsession with male attention and my simultaneous fear of getting too close to someone. How difficult I had found watching all my friends, one by one, ease into long-term partnerships like they were lowering themselves into a cool swimming pool on a scorching day. How every boyfriend I'd had has asked why I can't do the same; how I'd always feared that I was romantically wired wrong.

We talked about how I had spread myself like the last teaspoon of Marmite across the width of as many lives as possible. I told her that I gave almost all of my energy away to other people when no one had asked it of me. I described the control I thought this gave me over what other people thought of me, and yet it left me feeling more and more like a fraud. I told her how I fantasized about what people said about me behind my back; how I would probably agree with almost any insult thrown at me anyway. I told her the lengths I had gone to for approval: spending all my money on rounds of drinks for people I'd never met and not being able to pay my rent the next week; starting Saturday nights at four p.m. and ending them at four a.m. to attend six different birthday parties of people I barely knew. How tired and heavy and spineless and self-loathing this had made me feel. The pathetic irony that I had the greatest circle of friends around me and yet I felt I couldn't tell them any of this. How deep-rooted my fear of dependency was. That I could cry in the bed of a stranger I met in New York, but I couldn't ask my best friends for help.

'But none of this is having a visible effect on my life,' I said. 'I feel silly for coming here because it all could be so much worse. I have great friends, a great family. My work is going well. No one would know that anything is wrong with me from the outside. I just feel shit. All the time.'

'If you feel shit all the time,' she said, 'it's having a very, very big effect on your life.'

'I guess.'

'You feel like you're going to fall because you're broken into a hundred different floating pieces,' she told me. 'You're all over the place. You've got no rooting. You don't know how to be with yourself.' The back wall of my eyeballs finally gave way and tears poured out from the deepest well in the pit of my stomach.

'I feel like nothing is holding me together any more,' I told her, my breathlessness punctuating my sentence like hiccups, the stream of my tears on my cheeks as hot and free-flowing as blood.

'Of course you do,' she said with a new softness. 'You've got no sense of self.'

So that's why I was there. The penny dropped. I thought I had a fear of falling, but really I just didn't know who I was. And the stuff I used to fill up that empty space no longer worked; it just made me feel even more removed from myself. This overwhelming anxiety had been in the post for a while and it had finally arrived, fluttered through the letter box and landed at my feet. I was surprised by this diagnosis; there I was thinking my sense of self was rock solid. I am Generation Sense of

Self, this is what we do. We have been filling in 'About Me' sections since 2006. I thought I was the most sensiest of selfiest of anyone I knew.

'You will never know what I truly think of you,' she said, just as I was about to leave, letting me know she had already sensed how I work. 'You might be able to guess from my demeanour if I like you, but you'll never know exactly what I think of you on a personal level. You need to let go of that thought if we're going to make any progress.'

At first I was filled with an uncomfortable paranoia; then an almost immediate sense of total relief. She was telling me to stop making crap jokes. She was telling me to stop saying sorry for ploughing through her Kleenex supply on the table next to me. She was telling me that this was a room where I didn't have to labour over every word and gesture and anecdote to accommodate her in the hope that she would like me. This woman with no sense of self, no self-regard, no self-esteem – a shapeshifting, people-pleasing presence; a tangled knot of anxiety – was being given permission to just *be*. She was telling me I was safe to let go in this room just behind Oxford Circus, with the cream carpet and the burgundy sofa.

I left her office and walked the five and a half miles home. I was both liberated with the relief that I had finally found my way to that room and unbearably heavy with the weight of what was to come. I told myself that everything could be ironed out in three months.

'She thinks I've got no sense of self,' I told India as she made our dinner that night.

'That's bullshit,' she replied indignantly. 'You've got a stronger sense of self than anyone I know.'

'Yeah, but not that kind of sense of self,' I said. 'Not, like, how I will vote in the EU referendum or what my favourite way of serving potato is. She means I break myself off into different bits to give to different people, rather than being whole. I'm so restless and unsettled. I don't know how to be without all the things I use to prop me up.'

'I didn't know you felt like this.'

'I feel like I'm falling apart,' I told her.

'I don't want you to be sad,' India said, holding me, barefoot in our kitchen, as the spaghetti boiled on the stove with a gentle bubbling sound. 'I don't want you to do this if it's going to make you sad.'

The following Friday, I told Eleanor that India said she didn't want me to go through this process because she was worried it would make me sad. I told her that I half agreed.

'OK, well, news flash,' she barked in her reassuringly plain-speaking, sarcastic tone that I would come to crave as the year went on. 'You're already sad. You're really fucking sad.'

'I know, I know,' I replied, reaching for the Kleenex again. 'Sorry for using all these. I bet you really get through a lot, in your line of work.' She assured me that was what they were there for.

*

And so the process began. Every week I went in and we did detective work on myself to answer the question of how I came to be who I was in twenty-seven years. We did a forensic search of my past, sometimes discussing a thing that happened the night before, sometimes a thing that happened at school in a PE lesson twenty years ago. Therapy is a great big archaeological dig on your psyche until you hit something. It's a personal weekly episode of *Time Team*, a joint effort of expert and presenter – the therapist, Mick Aston, the patient, Tony Robinson.

We talked and we talked until she posed a cause-and-effect theory that fitted; then, crucially, we worked out how to change it. Sometimes she set me tasks – things to try, stuff to work on, questions to answer, thoughts to mull over, conversations I had to have. For two months I cried every Friday afternoon. Every Friday night I slept for ten hours.

The big myth of therapy is that it's all about pointing the blame at other people; but as the weeks passed, I found the opposite to be true. I heard about some people's therapists who took on a sort of defensive, deluded mum role in their patients' lives, always reassuring them that it was not their fault, but the fault of the boyfriend or the boss or the best friend. Eleanor rarely let me pass the accountability on to someone else and always forced me to question what I had done to end up in a particularly bad situation, which is why I always dreaded our sessions. 'Unless someone dies,' she told me one Friday, 'if something bad happens in a relationship, you have played a part in it.'

A couple of months in and me and Eleanor properly laughed together for the first time. I came in – a mess – after a bad work week. I was low on money and self-esteem and I was worried about paying my rent and I was worried my career was going nowhere. My paranoia was spinning out of control; I had imagined that anyone I had ever worked for thought I was incompetent, untalented and useless. I didn't leave the flat for three days. I described a vivid fantasy to her in which a boardroom of people who I didn't know talked about what a terrible, incapable writer I was. She stared at me while I talked, then her face contorted in disbelief.

'I mean –' she breathed out and raised her eyebrows – 'I think it's *insane* that you think that.' I noticed that she got more broadly, brashly Australian the tougher she was being. I looked up from my tissue; not the reaction I was hoping for.

'*Whole boardrooms of people you've never met?*' she said, shaking her head in disbelief. 'That's INCREDIBLY narcissistic.'

'Well,' I said, managing to snort with laughter. 'Yeah. When you put it like that. It's ridiculous.'

'No one is talking about you.'

'Yeah,' I said, patting at my tears with the tissue, suddenly feeling like a character Woody Allen would play. 'You're right.'

'Seriously!' she said, still flabbergasted, flicking her fringe away from her high cheekbones. 'You're not all that interesting, Dolly.'

When I got into my third month, I had my first

tear-free session. The box of Kleenex went untouched. A therapy milestone.

While my closest friends were encouraging of the process, soon it became apparent that self-examination made me boring to the wrong people. I started to drink less and less – always questioning whether I was doing it to have fun or doing it to distract myself from a problem. I tried to put a stop to people-pleasing, aware that giving my time and energy away so freely was what was chipping away at the void that I didn't want to turn into a quarry. I was more honest; I told people when I was upset or offended or angry and valued the sense of calm that came with integrity, paid with the small price of an uncomfortable conversation. I became more self-aware, so inevitably I made a tit of myself for the amusement of other people far less.

I felt like I was growing week by week; I felt my insides photosynthesize with every day I put new habits into practice. I developed an indoor plant obsession; a sort of verdant pathetic fallacy. I read up on what I should put in every corner of light and shade and I filled my flat with an abundance of green; pothos plants crawled down bookshelves, a Boston fern sat on top of my fridge, a Swiss cheese plant fanned against my bright, white bedroom wall. I hung a perfect philodendron above my bed and at night the odd cold droplet of water fell off the heart-shaped point of its leaves and on to my head. India and Belle questioned how healthy this was for me, comparing it to Chinese water torture. But I'd read that it was guttation – a process where a plant sheds unnecessary water at night; it works hard to get rid of everything putting pressure on its roots. And I told them that meant something to me. Me and the philodendron were doing a thing together.

'Any more plants in here,' Farly said one day, looking around my bedroom, 'and it's going to turn into *Little Shop of Horrors.*'

When I didn't drink as much, I experienced the brand-new sensation of waking up with a linear recollection of the night. The things people said; the way they looked; the signals between each other that they thought were discreet. I noticed that whenever I turned up to a social event, people wanted the bad stuff. If it was at the pub table, they wanted another bottle of wine, they wanted to call a drug dealer, they wanted to sit outside and chain-smoke, they wanted to drunkenly trade nasty gossip about someone we knew. Without realizing, I had become a black-market tradesman on a night out. I was everyone's green light for bad behaviour – and I hadn't realized until I stopped.

Eleanor's most brutal and brilliant takedown was delivered when we were talking about this one Friday afternoon.

'People want me to gossip, I've realized,' I told her. 'It's the thing they expect of me when I arrive somewhere, particularly if they're getting wrecked.'

'And did you gossip?'

'A bit, yeah,' I said. 'I didn't realize how much I used to do it.'

'Why did you do it?'

'I don't know. To feel close to people? To make conversation? Maybe to feel powerful,' I said. 'That's the only reason people gossip. I obviously did it to feel powerful.'

'Yes, you did,' she said with the slight smile she reserved for when she was pleased I had got there before she did. 'It's putting other people down so you could feel big.'

'Yes, I suppose it is.'

'Do you know who else does that?' There was a pause. 'Donald Trump.' I burst out laughing.

'Eleanor. I have come to really appreciate your brand of tough love,' I told her. 'But even for you, that's a bit of a stretch.'

'Fine, a Nigel Farage then,' she said, shrugging slightly as if I was being pedantic.

'My therapist compared me to Donald Trump today,' I texted Farly as I walked out on to Regent Street. 'I think I'm making real progress.'

Then around five months into therapy, I suddenly felt like we'd hit a brick wall. My development plateaued. I found myself being defensive with her. She told me I was being defensive with her. In one session, I proposed that perhaps there was no answer to be found in dissecting the events and decisions of my life; in going over and over the thing that happened with that boyfriend once or the thing that my parents did or didn't say when I was growing up. That perhaps it was a futile exercise; that perhaps I was just born this way. Did she think there was a chance I was just born this way? She looked at me blankly.

'No, I don't,' she replied.

'Well, *obviously* you don't,' I said in a surly fashion. 'Because otherwise there would be literally no need for your job.'

If I fucked up that week, I sometimes worked out the story I was going to give her so she'd go easy on me. Then I remembered how much I was paying to see her; all the masses of extra work I'd had to take on to afford it; what a privilege it was to be able to afford it at all. And what a complete waste of money it was if I didn't tell her the truth. I spoke to some friends in analysis who said they got nervous before their sessions because they tried to come up with something juicy enough to tell the therapist. I felt the total opposite. I always contemplated what I could keep from her or what positive spin I could wrap a story in so it didn't seem as bad as it really was.

But, of course, she always saw right through it. Because I'd let her in on how I worked. And I always resented how well she knew me and I always burst into tears when she challenged me. Not because I disliked her for questioning something I'd done but because I disliked myself for doing it in the first place.

At six months, I got to the point where I nearly said: 'Well what makes YOU so fucking wise about all this stuff? Come on. Tell me how perfect YOU are,' in a session. And I realized I needed a break from it, but I didn't tell her. She told me she 'sensed some anger'; I told her

I was fine. I started cancelling sessions. I missed a month and a half.

When I returned to her, I found she was far more understanding than I remembered and I wondered if I had invented her dogged and unforgiving line of inquiry. Perhaps she had become the blank canvas at which I threw all the anger and judgement I felt towards myself. In the middle of our hour, she asked me why I'd stopped coming regularly without discussing it with her. I thought about making an excuse; I thought about the money and time I was spending on this; how it was too late to back out now.

'I don't know,' I said.

'Is it because it's all getting too intimate?' she asked me. 'Is this a dependence issue? You don't want to depend on this?'

'Yeah,' I said, sighing. 'I think that's it, I think I wanted to control it.'

'Yeah, I think that might be it,' she said, thinking out loud. 'What's going on in your outside life is reflected in here.'

'That makes sense.'

'What are you trying to control?'

'Everything,' I said, realizing it as I said it out loud. 'I'm trying to have a hand in everyone's opinion of me. How everyone behaves towards me. I'm trying to stop bad things happening. Death, disaster, disappointment. I'm trying to control it all.'

Her epiphany was my epiphany; I decided to give way

to the process. I handed myself over to Eleanor, with trust, and began a new cycle of our time together.

'You need to keep coming here and we need to keep talking,' she told me. 'We need to talk and talk and talk until we join everything together.'

I think part of the problem was that I had reached a point where I couldn't bear that Eleanor got to know so much about me – the darkest recesses of who I am, my most sacred, embarrassing, humiliating, awful, precious experiences. And I didn't get anything about her in return. Sometimes I imagined Eleanor at home; I thought about what her life might be like when she wasn't being a therapist. I wondered what she said about me to her friends, whether she ever read my articles or looked at my social media feeds or googled me like I googled her the first time I received an invoice with her full name on it.

A few weeks later, she asked me how I was finding therapy and I revealed that I resented not knowing anything about her. I told her that I understood this was the appropriate exchange, but sometimes I felt like that exchange was unfair. Why did I have to be naked every week and she always got to be fully clothed?

'What do you mean, you don't know anything about me?' she asked, genuinely puzzled.

'I don't know anything about you as a person.'

'Yes you do,' she said.

'No I don't, I couldn't tell my friends one thing about you.'

'You come in here every week and we talk about

love, sex, family, friendship, happiness, sadness. You know exactly what I think about all these things.'

'But I don't know if you're married, I don't know if you have children, I don't know where you live. I don't know where you go out. I don't know if you go to the gym,' I said, thinking specifically about her toned arms that I always found myself looking at in particularly difficult moments, wondering what weights she used.

'And do you think knowing any of that stuff would help you understand who I am?' she asked. 'You know a lot about me.'

Over time, I learnt Eleanor language. After a particularly weepy session, she always said: 'Take *good* care' – emphasis on the 'good'. That meant: 'Don't get completely leathered this weekend.' It was also bad when she said 'Oh boy' when I told her something. But the worst by far was: 'I've been worried about you this week.' When Eleanor said she'd been worried about me that week, it meant I had given her a *real* shit show the previous Friday.

I never stopped dreading Fridays, but I dreaded them less and less. Eleanor and I laughed together more. I told her that sometimes after our sessions I went straight into Pret and ate a brownie in about five seconds flat or went into a shop and bought a piece of ten-quid crap that I absolutely didn't need. She said it was because I was worried about what she thought of me – and I agreed. It's not a natural thing to sit in a small room with someone removed from the rest of your life and tell them all your raw, uncensored stories – the ones you've never said aloud before, the ones you've never told anyone, maybe not even yourself. But the healthier I got, the less judgement I projected on her. Her true form started to take shape in front of me: a woman who was on my side.

When a friend told me that it is the relationship between patient and therapist that brings healing, rather than the talking, I understood. My incremental sense of calm and peace felt like something we were building together – like a physio who strengthened a muscle. I carried a small part of her with me and I'm sure I always will. The work helped me develop a new understanding of myself that I'll never be able to dismiss and bury. That's what she called it: 'the work'. And that's what it always felt like. My time with Eleanor was challenging and confronting and hard. She didn't let me get away with anything. She made me think about the part I played in everything. I sometimes tried to remember a time when my behaviour had no consequence; after particularly difficult Friday afternoons, I wondered what life would be like if I hadn't decided to go on this hike into myself. Would it have been easier to have just carried on being a drunk dick in a taxi hurtling down the M1 at four a.m.? A person whose behaviour was never examined, but shoved to one side, only to repeat again the following weekend?

Eleanor loved to tell me that life is shit. She told me every week. She told me it was going to disappoint me.

She reminded me that there was nothing I could do to control it. I relaxed into that inevitability.

When we came up to our one-year anniversary, our conversations began to flow with familiarity and ease; she recommended books she thought I would find helpful. She mostly said 'Goodbye' instead of 'Take *good* care'. She stopped saying 'Oh no' in a concerned way when I told her a story and I started hearing a genuinely ecstatic 'Well, this all sounds GREAT!' fairly regularly. One Friday I actually ran out of stuff to tell her.

I didn't know exactly how long I wanted to be there or how free I wanted to feel. But I knew that the longer I spent there, the more things came together. I talked myself into some harmony, just as she had predicted. I joined the dots; I noticed the patterns. The talking started connecting with the action. The gap between how I felt inside and how I behaved got smaller. I learnt to sit with problems, to go deeply, uncomfortably internal instead of on a trek to the Outer Hebrides of Experience when things went wrong. The drinking happened less and less frequently and, when it did, the intention was celebration rather than escape, so the outcome was never disastrous.

I felt steadier; I felt stronger. The doors inside me unlocked one by one, I emptied the rooms of all my shit and talked her through every piece of old toot I found in there; then I threw everything out. Every room I unlocked, I knew I was getting closer. To a sense of self, a sense of calm. And a sense of home.

12th June

Dear Dolly Something Alderton,

Congratulations! You have won a place to the wedding of Jack Harvey-Jones and Emily White. Well done for getting this far – you got down to the last two for the final invite to the actual wedding as well as the reception along with Emily's cousin Rose. We chose you in the end because you're loud and drink quite a lot, which we thought could liven up the table of Jack's introverted friends from LSE. Rose will now only be coming to the reception but that's fine as we weren't invited to her wedding when she and her husband 'eloped' and Rose has got a prominent birthmark on her face so she'd ruin the daytime pictures anyway.

So! Drum roll please! Mr and Mrs Keith White request the pleasure of your company at the marriage of their daughter Emily to Mr Jack Harvey-Jones in the Vale of Nowhere.

(I know it sounds a bit mental saying 'Mr and Mrs Keith White' but Jack's posh parents have insisted that's what you write and they are paying for the welcome booze so we can't be bothered to fight them on it.)

You are cordially invited to watch Emily's father give her away and be enthusiastically received by another man like he's selling a second-hand car. When Emily's rad-fem friends question her on this, she will lie and say the church said we had to and it wasn't our choice, and we'd appreciate it if you could give this same party line.

Now – *please* – we beg of you, no presents, just your presence! OK, well if you ABSOLUTELY INSIST then you can choose a little token gift from our registry at Liberty, where you will have the privilege of ordering something banal – like the fifty-pound salad mixer – or decadent – like the giant porcelain rabbit figurine wearing a top hat. Really, your choice.

Also donate to a charity if you want, not bothered which one, we just thought it would be good to suggest it. (Please someone buy the chesterfield for our living room!!)

We are aware, Dolly Something Alderton, you are single with an income of £30,000 at best while we have a joint annual earning of £230,000. We also understand that we live in a £700,000 flat in Battersea, the deposit on which was paid in its entirety by our parents, while you struggle to scrape together £668 every month to pay your rent, so by this logic we thought it would make sense for *you* to be the one to give *us* expensive presents to adorn our already fully furnished home.

No, but seriously, we just want you there, so don't worry at all about the present or the charity thing or whatever. If you turn up empty-handed we'll just make barbed comments about it at dinner parties to our mutual friends when you're not there for the following year. And, actually, that suits us fine, because we need to carry on talking about the wedding until we get pregnant, so hopefully your selfish decision to not celebrate our love with a Le Creuset set will give us enough material to bring it up in every conversation until we can move on to trimesters and water births, so thanks.

On to the booze! Every guest will receive a glass of champagne/unidentified fizzy white wine in a champagne flute on arrival. Then there's a cash bar, I'm afraid. We tried to make the £75,000 wedding budget stretch to booze for 120 people, but sadly it didn't quite cut it. Bloody weddings!

Attached are the details of an extremely overpriced bed and breakfast that comes highly recommended from all of us; it's where we've had many a lovely Sunday lunch. No pressure to stay there though, you can stay wherever you like in the rural and remote village where we're getting married.

Enjoy it and book fast!

So, see you there. Oh, and by the way, I know that every person you know has been given a plus one because they're all in relationships. And no, we don't know half of their partners, we just thought it would be nice for them to have someone there, you know, because people in relationships like being together. Sadly, you are not granted this kind of support (☹) and you have to come on your own. Sorry about that, it's just a numbers thing. Please ring Jack's pervy brother because I *think* he's the only other single guest so might be fun to get on a train and share a room with him! Although he might be bringing that French girl he met on that conference, so maybe let us double-check first.

Dress code: morning dress, whatever that means.

Getting there: the church and venue are utterly picturesque, so we'd ideally like no cars on the day as we don't want to ruin the photos or the calm atmosphere. We recommend getting a train from London – the nearest station to the Vale of Nowhere is twenty-two miles away. There is a local taxi company to get you to the church but please ring in advance as they are only in possession of three vehicles.

Other formalities: we want the vibe of the wedding to be very relaxed, so we encourage some super-fun confetti throwing outside the church. PLEASE DO NOT BRING YOUR OWN CONFETTI. There will be a Tupperware container of confetti HANDED OUT BY ALISON, MOTHER OF THE BRIDE, who has been air-drying delphinium petals one by one for four years for this occasion. Delphiniums look great on camera, are cheaper than rose petals but are also environmentally friendly – paper confetti will cause distress to the local wildlife and the reception venue have said if there are ANY PIECES OF PAPER CONFETTI found in the grounds, the reception will be immediately cancelled, the catering staff will be ordered to leave and the evening won't go ahead. So wait your turn and you'll all get a SMALL HANDFUL of confetti (please, only small, we want everyone to have a go) for you to throw over the happy bride and groom as they enter the world as man and wife.

Please write your favourite song on the RSVP and our DJ will try his very best to play it, but only if it's 'I Would Walk 500 Miles' by the Proclaimers or 'Umbrella' by Rihanna.

We have a hashtag for Instagram pictures on the day which is 'jemily2016'. We wanted to have just 'jemily', but sadly that's the name of a brand of personal lubricant, as we discovered when we searched the hashtag, so 'jemily2016' will have to do.

Kids welcome!

Absolutely *no lounge suits* – no tie, no entry. It's our special day, not a cricket dinner.

If you can't make it, don't worry, as we're going to do another casual reception party in the city next month, for our less close but highly Instagrammable London friends. Then the following month we're going to do another ceremony and party in Austria, where a lot of Jack's family come from. Then we are going to do a blessing in Ibiza, along with a group holiday which you'll all be invited to. Basically, our wedding is going to be like a band on tour for the next year, so just find one of the dates that suits and ~~book a ticket~~ come along.

All our love and can't wait to see you guys there!

Jack and Emily xxx

PS Sorry you had to pay to receive this invitation, we were in a bit of a mad rush when we posted them and got the wrong stamps for their weight. This means you all paid £0.79 which will be reimbursed on entrance to the venue. Jack's brother, Mark, is in charge of the kitty and will be standing by the topiary arch. NO RECEIPT – NO REFUND.

PPS Sorry about the heart-shaped sequins that have fallen out of the envelope and gone all over your carpet you only just hoovered today.

Heartbreak Hotel

I woke up to three missed calls from Farly before seven a.m. and a message asking to call her. Before I had a chance to dial her number, she was ringing again. I knew it wasn't good. I thought about the last eighteen months since Florence had died and the way Farly had pulled away from all her closest friends and buried her grief in the distance. How I had tried to bring her back to me; to know what to say to soothe her. Those moments when we would laugh about something and I'd see a flash of her old self, then the laughing would turn to guttural sobs and she would apologize for not understanding how her entire mind or body was working any more. Selfishly, I had just one thought: *I don't know how I'll get her through this again.* I took a deep breath and picked up the phone.

'Dolly?'

'What's happened?'

'No one's died,' she said, noting the panic in my voice.

'OK.'

'It's Scott. I think we're breaking up.'

It was eight weeks before their wedding.

Farly was alone in their flat when I arrived an hour later; Scott had gone to work and she had been given a few days' compassionate leave by her boss. She talked me through the conversation they had had the night before, moment by moment. She told me that she hadn't seen this coming – that right now the wedding was the least of her worries and she would do anything to save her relationship. Her dad and her stepmum were at their house in Cornwall for the weekend and we decided to drive down there so she and Scott could have some time apart to think.

We worked out a plan of what she wanted to say to him on the phone. She asked if I could sit in the same room as her when he called – she was a nervous wreck and wanted to have me in her eyeline to steady herself. I sat on their sofa as she paced about their flat on the phone and I looked around at the home they shared; the life they'd built together. There was a fresh-faced photo of them in their respective early and mid-twenties, grasping each other lovingly; a photo of them on their last holiday with Florence. The burnt-orange rug I had helped them pick out; the sofa the three of us lay on drinking red wine until dawn while watching election results on the telly. The Morrissey print we bought for their engagement hanging on the wall.

I had a strange and difficult thought. For so many years, this was all I had wanted. I used to hope that, at some point, one of them would move on from the other, we'd always talk fondly about Scott the First Love and I'd get my best friend back. But now that moment was here and I felt nothing but wrenching sadness and longing for her. They had been through so much together and I wanted desperately for them to make it work.

We had all thought of Farly and Scott's upcoming wedding as a sort of Polyfilla over the hole that was left in their family. Whenever her family or any of our friends talked about what the day would be like we all agreed it would be full of both great soaring happiness and inescapable sadness – but it would definitely mark a new chapter in their lives. A beginning rather than an ending.

After Florence's death, I had taken on the role of her maid of honour as if it held the gravitas of a knighthood. AJ, Lacey and I organized a hen do with the same ambition and scale as the Olympic Opening Ceremony. After months and months of begging and negotiating, an East London hotel gave us their top-floor function room overlooking the city at a highly discounted rate to host a big dinner. I booked the London Gay Men's Chorus to come sing a surprise set of wedding-related songs to Farly while wearing T-shirts on which her face was printed. I devised a cocktail called The Farly with a mixologist. I ordered a life-size cardboard cut-out man from eBay and stuck a photo of Scott's face on it, for people to have their photo taken with him. I recorded dozens of video messages from people wishing her good luck with her marriage to screen on the night like a *This Is Your Life* VT. These included 1990s *EastEnders* actor Dean Gaffney, two cast members of *Made in Chelsea*, the boy she lost her virginity to and the manager of her local dry-cleaners.

I drifted back into the conversation she was having with Scott.

'Perhaps the wedding got too big,' she said. 'You know? Perhaps we let the wedding get out of control. Maybe we need to just forget about all that and focus on us.'

At that exact moment I received an email from the office of Farly's local MP.

Dear Dolly,

Thank you for your email. Andy would be delighted to help – it sounds like you are going above and beyond to make sure your friend has a very special hen do! Would you be able to pop by Andy's constituency office next Monday at 11.30 a.m. to film?

If that isn't convenient, I will have a look in his diary to find another day.

Best wishes,

Kristin

I deleted it quietly.

We drove up to my flat, I flung a few things in a bag and texted India and Belle to tell them that Farly was ill with tonsillitis and Scott was away with work so I was staying with her for a few days. I felt bad for lying, but as everything was still so up in the air and no final decision had been made, it was better to keep things vague so she could avoid any questions. I put up an out-of-office and we got in her car to go to Cornwall.

It was a car journey we had done together many times: M25, M4, M5. For holidays at the house in Cornwall, for the summer road trips we took aged sixteen and seventeen, and the journeys we did back and forth from London to university when we were at Exeter. Farly had a rigorous ranking system for all the motorway service stations according to their snack outlets and she liked testing me on her order of preference (Chieveley, Heston, Leigh Delamere).

A long car journey, strangely, felt like just what we needed in that moment. Her car was the home of our teenage relationship. In the years I was so desperate to be a grown-up, Farly's driving licence was our passport to freedom. It was our first shared flat; it was our shelter from the rest of the world. There was a viewpoint on a hill in Stanmore that looked out over the sparkling city as if it were Oz. We would drive there after school and share a packet of Silk Cut and a tub of Ben & Jerry's while listening to Magic FM.

'What do you see when you look at that?' she asked me once, a few weeks before we left school.

'I see all the boys I'm going to fall in love with and the books I'm going to write and the flats I'm going to live in and the days and the nights that lie ahead. What do you see?'

'Something completely terrifying,' she replied.

The drive – five hours – felt even longer than usual.

Perhaps because it wasn't accompanied with chit-chat or radio or our scratched Joni Mitchell CDs, but a silence that wasn't a silence; I could hear the noise in Farly's head. We rested her mobile phone on the dashboard and both waited for Scott to call and say he'd made a terrible mistake. Every time her phone lit up her eyes would briefly flicker down from the road to the screen.

'Check it for me,' she would say quickly. It was always another message from one of our friends wishing her and her tonsillitis better and asking if she wanted them to come round with soup and magazines.

'For fuck's sake,' she said, managing a weak laugh. 'Me and him have spent the last six years texting constantly about the most mundane stuff and now all I am desperate for is to hear from him and all I get is a load of texts of support about a fake illness.'

'At least you know you're loved,' I offered. There was more restless silence.

'What am I going to tell everyone?' she asked. 'All those wedding guests.'

'You don't have to think about that yet,' I said. 'And if that situation does arise – you won't have to tell anyone anything. We can do it all for you.'

'I don't know how I could survive this without you,' she said. 'As long as I have you, everything will be OK.'

'I'm right here,' I told her. 'I'm not going anywhere. I'm right here for ever, mate. And we'll get through to the other side together, no matter what that place looks like.'

Tears ran down her cheeks as she looked straight ahead into the darkness of the M5.

'I'm sorry if I ever made you feel like you were second best, Dolly.'

When we arrived just after midnight, Richard and Annie were waiting up for us. I made tea – in the week after Floss died, I learnt by heart how everyone took theirs, it was the only useful thing I could do – and we sat on the sofa talking through everything that had been said and all the possible outcomes.

Farly and I lay in the same bed with the lights turned out.

'Do you know what the real tragedy in all this is?'

'Go on,' she said.

'Me and Lauren have finally nailed all the chords and harmonies of "One Day Like This" for the ceremony.'

'Oh, I know, don't. I loved that recording you sent me.'

'*And* the string quartet have just confirmed they could do the intro.'

'I know, I know.'

'It may be a blessing in disguise,' I said. 'I actually think that song makes everyone think of *X Factor* montages now.'

'Are you going to lose money for the hen do?'

'Don't worry about any of that,' I said. 'We'll sort it out.' There was silence in the darkness and I waited for her next sentence.

'Go on,' she said. 'I'm ninety per cent sure it's not happening now so you might as well tell me.'

'But is it going to make you sad?'

'No, it will cheer me up.'

I told her about the weekend we had planned for her. With every absurd detail, she groaned like a child missing out on sweets. We watched the videos of the Great and the Good of Britain's D-List give their well wishes on my phone.

'Thank you for planning it,' she said. 'It would have been wonderful. I would have loved it.'

'We'll do it for you all again.'

'I won't get married again.'

'You don't know that. And even if you don't, I'll just lazily transfer all those plans to a birthday. I'll do you a great fortieth.' I heard her breathing deepen and slow; years of bed-sharing and bickering over her falling asleep before the end of a film meant I knew she was drifting off. 'Wake me up in the night if you need me,' I said.

'Thanks, Dolls. I wish we could just be in a relationship sometimes,' she said sleepily. 'Everything would be easier.'

'Yeah, but you're not my type I'm afraid, Farly.'

She laughed and then a few minutes later she cried. I stroked her back and said nothing.

The next few days were spent going for long walks, talking through the same details of their last conversation over and over again, trying to trace back where things might have gone wrong. I made tea that Farly didn't drink, Richard cooked meals she barely ate and we watched TV while she stared into the middle distance. After a few days, I had to go back to London for work. A couple of days later, Farly came back to the city too, where she and Scott agreed to meet in their local park, walk and talk everything through.

On the morning of their meeting, I couldn't concentrate on anything and I watched my phone like a television, waiting for a message from her. Finally, after three hours, I decided to call her. She picked up before the first ring had finished.

'It's over,' she said hurriedly. 'Tell everyone the wedding is off. I'll call you later.'

The phone went dead.

I rang our close friends one by one and explained what had happened; each of them was as shocked as the last. I wrote a carefully worded message explaining that the wedding was off and sent it to Farly's side of the guest list. And then it was done. Extinguished in a copy-and-pasted message in an email and a few calls. The day, that future, their story was finished. I dismantled every elaborate component of her hen do, due to happen in less than a month, and cancelled everything. Everyone I called – who already knew the wedding had been put back a year due to a family tragedy – had nothing to say but how sorry they were.

Farly left the flat the day of their conversation and

went to stay with Annie and Richard in their family home a few miles away. I went to the house, my positivity bank account totally out of funds and well into my overdraft of cheering platitudes.

'I feel like I'm in jail for something I didn't do,' she told me. 'I feel like my life is somewhere over there and I'm locked somewhere over here, being told I can't reach it. I want my old life back.'

'You'll get there. It won't be like this for ever, I promise.'

'I'm cursed.'

'No,' I said. 'You're not cursed. You've had a terrible, awful, unbearable bout of bad luck. You've had more darkness in eighteen months than a lot of people get in a lifetime. But you've got so much light ahead of you – you've got to hold on to that.'

'That's what everyone said after Florence died. I don't think I can take much more.'

With everyone's encouragement, Farly went back to work immediately and our friends kicked a military operation of keeping her distracted into action. Even though it was the most time we'd spent together since we were teenagers, I also sent her a postcard every other day so she'd always have something nice to come home to from work. The bridesmaids took her away for a weekend of wine and cooking in the countryside for what would have been her hen do. I booked us a holiday in Sardinia for the week of her wedding. We all took turns to spend the evenings with her after work in the month after they broke up; there wasn't a night that passed without at least one of us there. Sometimes we talked about what was happening and sometimes we just sat eating Lebanese takeaway and watching trashy TV. Whoever visited would send a message out to the rest of us on the way home, update us on how she was and check who was seeing her next. We were a circle of keepers; nurses on shift. Our first-aid kit was Maltesers and episodes of *Gogglebox*.

It was at this time that I was reminded of the chain of support that keeps a sufferer afloat – the person at the core of a crisis needs the support of their family and best friends, while those people need support from their friends, partners and family. Then even those people twice removed might need to talk to someone about it too. It takes a village to mend a broken heart.

I drove back to the flat with Farly and waited in the car while she picked up more of her belongings and had one final discussion with Scott. Their flat went on the market. Farly unpacked everything into her childhood bedroom – this was somewhere more than temporary but less than for ever, now.

The first moment any of us glimpsed an ember of Farly's old self was on an utterly disastrous Sunday that saw me roping my friends into doing a photo shoot for a fake dinner party. It was to accompany a piece I had written for a broadsheet culture section about the death of the traditional dinner party and the editor wanted a photo of me 'entertaining guests' in my flat. I had warned him that I didn't have any male friends available that day and he had reluctantly agreed that an all-female gathering would be fine. However, when the photographer arrived, it seemed he was under new instruction to definitely make sure there were men in the photo.

Farly, who had been mainlining white wine since she'd arrived at noon, went knocking door-to-door along my street trying to find a willing male neighbour, but to no avail. Meanwhile, Belle and AJ drove to our local pub, went in, tapped a glass for everyone's attention and made a rather limp announcement that they were looking for a handful of men to be photographed in return for some slow-roast lamb and their picture in the paper.

'If this sounds like something you would be interested in,' Belle bellowed, 'then we will be waiting in the red Seat Ibiza outside.'

Five minutes later, a group of sweaty and inebriated men in their thirties and forties trundled out of the pub and into the car.

When we were all squeezed round the table, clinking glasses and trying to look like old friends, it became clear that one of the gentlemen was far drunker than the others, eating the roast lamb with his hands, like a Roman emperor. The photographer was standing on a chair so he could get all of us into the shot in my rather cramped living room, a light broke and one of the men started bellowing for more wine. It was a sort of slapstick caper of people running around and things breaking with a low-level manic energy.

'This is a disaster,' I said under my breath to the girls.

'Oh, I don't think it's a disaster AT ALL,' Farly barked drunkenly. 'I got jilted by my boyfriend of seven years a month ago, so this is a walk in the park!' The photographer looked at me for reassurance and even the drunken emperor stopped his masticating. 'Cheers,' she said merrily, raising her glass to all of us.

We quickly learnt how to deal with this sort of suicide bomb of a joke that became a familiar, well-worn piece of furniture in our conversations with Farly. You couldn't join in the banter as you didn't know where the black comedy was capped and tipped over into cruelty; but you couldn't ignore it either. You just had to laugh loudly.

We left for Sardinia a few days before what would have been Farly's wedding. We landed late and drove up to the north-west of the island in our uninsured hire car, carefully winding up coastal roads with the same Joni Mitchell album on the stereo that we'd played on our first road trip over ten years before. A time when a relationship seemed liked the most laughably unreachable thing, let alone a cancelled wedding.

We stayed in a pretty basic hotel that had a pool, a bar and a room with a view over the sea – it was all we wanted. Farly – the girl who loved school and went on to become a teacher – is and always has been a routine-based creature and we quickly created one of our own. We woke up early every morning, went straight to the beach where we'd do some exercise in the bright, white light of the early-morning sun, then swim in the sea before breakfast. Well, I'd swim. Farly would sit on the sand and watch. A characteristic where Farly and I clash most is the subject of outdoor swimming; I strip off at the sight of nearly any body of open water for a dip whereas Farly's a strictly chlorinated-pool-only person.

'Come on!' I shouted at the shore one morning, when the sea was as still and warm as bathwater. 'You've got to come in! It's so lovely.'

'But what if there are fish?' she shouted at me with a grimace.

'There aren't any fish!' I bellowed. 'All right, there may be some fish.'

'You know I'm scared of fish,' she barked back.

'How can you be scared of them – you eat them.'

'I don't like the thought of them swimming around underneath me.'

'You sound so bloody suburban, Farly,' I shouted at her. 'You don't want to miss out on life because you only shop in shopping centres because you're scared of rain ruining your blow-dry and only swim in pools because you're scared of fish.'

'We *are* suburban, Dolly. That's literally what we are.'

'Come on! It's natural! It's God's own swimming pool! It's healing! God is in the ocean!'

'If there's one thing I know for sure,' she stood up and wiped the sand off her legs, 'it's that there is no God, Doll!' She shouted it joyfully, while paddling into the sea.

We'd spend all morning reading our books and listening to music, then we'd have our first drink of the day at noon. We napped all afternoon in the sun, then we'd shower and take our tans out for dinner in the town. We'd come back to the hotel afterwards, drink Amaretto Sours on the terrace in the thick blanket of evening heat and play cards and write tipsy postcards to our friends.

On the day of the wedding, Farly was awake before I got up. She stared at the ceiling.

'Are you OK?' I asked as soon as my eyes opened.

'Yeah,' she said, turning away and pulling up the cover. 'I just want today to be over.'

'Today will be one of the hardest days,' I said. 'And then it will be finished. At midnight, it's done. And you'll never have to go through it again.'

'Yeah,' she said quietly. I sat on the end of her bed.

'What do you want to do today?' I asked. 'I've booked a restaurant for tonight that has those sort of glowing five-star Trip Advisor reviews that include disgusting close-up photos of the food like it's a crime scene.'

'Sounds good,' she said with a sigh. 'I think I just want to lie on a sun lounger like a basic bitch.'

We spent most of the day in silence, reading our books and taking an earplug each to listen to podcasts together. Occasionally she would look around and say something like 'I'd be having breakfast with my bridesmaids now' or 'I'd probably be putting my wedding dress on.' Mid-afternoon, she picked up her phone and checked the time.

'Ten to four in England. In exactly ten minutes, I would have been getting married.'

'Yeah, but at least you're here sunbathing in beautiful Italy rather than floating down a lake with your dad in rainy Oxfordshire.'

'I was never *actually* going to arrive on a gondola,' she said exasperatedly. 'I just told you about it as a potential possibility because the venue said that's what some of the other brides had done.'

'You did consider it, though.'

'No I didn't.'

'Yes you did because when you told me about it I could hear in your voice that you were waiting for me to say I thought it was a good idea.'

'No I wasn't!'

'It would have been so awkward, everyone staring at you while you floated down a lake in a massive dress then someone heaving you out of it, the sailor clattering about with the oars.'

'It didn't have a sailor,' she sighed. 'And it didn't have oars.'

I went to the bar and ordered a bottle of Prosecco.

'Right,' I said, pouring the ice-cold fizz into poolside plastic flutes. 'You would've been making vows now. I think we should make vows.'

'To who?'

'To ourselves,' I said. 'And to each other.'

'OK,' she said, putting her sunglasses on top of her head. 'You go first.'

'I vow to not judge however you handle this when we get home,' I said. 'If you want to have a really heavy amphetamine and casual sex phase, that's fine. If you lock yourself in your house for a year, that's fine too. You've got my support whatever you do, because I can't imagine what it must be like to lose the people you've lost.'

'Thank you,' she said, taking a sip of her Prosecco and pausing to think. 'I vow to always let you grow. I'll never tell you that I know who you really are just because we've known each other since we were kids. I know you're going through a period of big change and I'll only ever encourage that.'

'That's a good one,' I said, clinking her glass. 'OK, I vow to always tell you when you have something in your teeth.'

'Oh, always.'

'Particularly as we get older and our gums start receding. That's when the leafy greens can really get lodged.'

'Don't make me more depressed than I am,' she said.

'Do a vow to yourself.'

'I vow to never lose sight of my friends if I fall in love again,' she said. 'I'll never forget how important you all are and how much we need each other.'

On what would have been the night of Farly's wedding reception for over two hundred people, we got a taxi up to a hilltop restaurant with a view over the sea.

'You would have been making your speech now,' she said. 'Did you ever write it?'

'No,' I said. 'Whenever I've been a bit pissed and emotional I've written some ideas for it in my iPhone notes. But I hadn't written it up yet.'

'I wonder if I would have been happy for the whole day or whether I would have found any of it stressful.'

I thought about an article I had read about premature death after Florence died; the one in which an agony aunt advised a grieving father not to think of the life his teenage son would have led had he not been killed in a car crash. This fantasy, she said, was an exercise of torture rather than of comfort.

'You know, that life isn't happening elsewhere,' I said. 'It doesn't exist in another realm. Your relationship with that man was seven years long. That was it, that's what it was.'

'I know.'

'Your life is here, now. You're not about to live a tracing-paper copy of it.'

'Yeah, I suppose it's better not to dwell on what could have been.'

'Don't think of it as *Sliding Doors*.'

'I love that film.'

'And thank God it's not because no one could ever pull off that blonde haircut Gwyneth Paltrow had in it.'

'I'd look like Myra Hindley,' Farly said flatly, signalling for another carafe of wine. 'Did you have doubts about me and him?'

'Do you want to know honestly?'

'Yes, I really do,' she said. 'It doesn't matter now anyway, and I'd like to know.'

'Yes,' I said. 'I grew to truly love him and I believed by the end that there was a future where you could be very happy. But, yes, I always had doubts.'

She looked out on the setting sun, sitting on the horizon of the deep-blue Mediterranean like a perfect peach balancing on a ledge.

'Thank you for never telling me.'

The sea swallowed the sun and the sky slowly turned to dusky blue and then night as if operated by a dimmer. It never was as bad as that day again.

After a week together, we drove down to another coastal town where Sabrina and Belle met us. The holiday continued in a similar vein: we drank Aperol, we played cards, we lay on the beach. Belle and I left the apartment at six a.m. one morning, stripped at the beach and swam naked in the light of the sunrise. Farly had good days and quiet days for our final week, which was to be expected. We all talked a lot about what had happened – the underlying reason for the holiday itself. But she also started talking about the future rather than the past; where she was going to live, what her new routine would look like. Over the course of the fortnight it felt like she shed one of her skins of melancholy. One night she even got so drunk – more drunk than since we'd been teenagers – she started hitting on the manager of a local restaurant who looked like a sixty-something

Italian John Candy; surely the most recognizable rite of passage and one that indicates you're into a new phase of getting over a break-up.

Things felt very different when we returned to London. Her twenty-ninth birthday marked three months since that morning I woke up to three missed calls. It felt like a milestone and we celebrated it properly; we went to one of our favourite pubs for dinner then we went out dancing. She wore the dress I'd found her for the hen do that never happened. It was black and cut low at either side and flashed a tattoo she got when she was nineteen, a disastrous, impulsive mistake at a parlour in Watford. Two small stars – one coloured in pink and one coloured in an ill-thought-through yellow ('A Jew with a yellow star tattooed on her! I ask you!' her mother despaired).

On the afternoon of her birthday, she went to another tattoo parlour to amend her error from a decade ago. She had the stars filled in with dark ink; she painted it black. She put an 'F' next to one of them for Florence and a 'D' for me. A reminder that no matter what we lose, no matter how uncertain and unpredictable life gets, some people really do walk next to you for ever.

I Got Gurued

Early in the summer of Farly's heartbreak, I was asked to write a first piece for a magazine about the dangers of people-pleasing. The editor I was working for suggested that I speak to a man who had written a new book on the subject. His name was David, he was nearing fifty; he was an actor turned writer. I googled him before we spoke on the phone and noticed he was also very handsome: olive skin, salt-and-pepper hair, gentle brown eyes. His publisher sent me a PDF of the book and it was a frustratingly brilliant read. His work focused on the human need for validation and how it cuts happiness short. Reading it felt like something – or someone – had grabbed my shoulders with a pair of strong, trusted hands and given me one big, sharp, much-needed shake.

We emailed back and forth for a while then organized a time to speak. His voice was deep and soft; far more pronounced and theatrical than I had imagined. His general vibe seemed to be that of an out-and-out hippie, but he spoke like an RSC ensemble member. I asked him questions about the book and the things that had really stuck with me; he told me that when we are children, we are constantly told to contain our behaviour. He described how being told not to be bossy or not to show off or not to be a clever-clogs puts up barriers around certain recesses of who we are; and we're scared to ever revisit them again as adults. Instead, we hide those parts of ourselves, the bits that are dark or loud or eccentric or twisted, for fear of not being liked. It was those parts of ourselves, he argued, that were the most beautiful.

Because the piece was written from a personal angle, we had to talk about my own experiences. I told him I had started seeing a therapist this year.

'The danger of a person like you doing therapy is that you seem clever,' he said. 'You will get the theory of it all very easily. You'll be able to be academic about yourself in conversation. But, you know, all the talky-talky stuff will only take you so far. You need to really feel it in your core, that change. It can't just be stuff you discuss with a therapist. You need to feel it in your body –' his voice slowed – 'you need to feel it in the backs of your knees, in your womb, in your toes, in your fingertips.'

'Hmm,' I said in agreement.

We talked for about forty-five minutes, drifting from passages in the book to the research and work he'd done for years and to my own experiences. He spoke to me directly, with no formalities or politeness. I felt like he had somehow got straight to my inner equator, just through a phone call.

'Pinch that little cheek of yours,' he said as if he'd known me for years. 'You don't need someone else to tell you what to do or who to be. You're your own mother now. You have to listen to what you want.'

'Hmm,' I managed again.

'And for every day for the rest of your life, I want you to take that job seriously.'

'But what about being appropriate? How does that work when you're being yourself all the time?'

'Have you ever fallen in love with a man because he's appropriate?'

'Well, no.'

'Oooh, that Greg,' he said in a lustful voice. 'He turns me on, he's so fucking *appropriate.*'

'No, no,' I said, laughing.

'I'm not interested in appropriate. Darkness and edges and corners is where buried treasure lies. Fuck appropriate.'

I felt like he was flirting with me, but I couldn't tell if he was talking to me so intimately simply for the sake of good quotes for the piece. By the end of our conversation we had drifted into a general chat that didn't feel at all like an interview. I could tell he also wanted me to disclose if I was in a relationship, but I kept that information vague. He told me he thought I could use a one-on-one session with him.

'If you feel like you can show all of yourself to someone without fear of being judged,' he said, 'your intimacy will go through the roof.'

'Yeah, that's always been a huge problem for me,' I said. 'Intimacy.'

'I know, I can feel that in you.' There was a sudden silence between us. Maybe he was talking guru bullshit; maybe everything I had always pushed down was far more visible than I thought.

'Hmm,' I managed once more.

'I hope you have someone in your life who really holds you, Dolly.'

'I have a therapist,' I replied.

'That's not what I meant,' he said.

I came out of my flat and blinked into the light like I had just woken up.

'I've just had the most extraordinary conversation,' I said to India and Belle, who were sunbathing in our garden.

'With who?' India asked, taking her earphones out.

'That guy for the article – that guru guy.'

'What did he say?'

'I don't know, it was like he was speaking to something inside me that hadn't been spoken to before; it was like something was yawning and waking up for the first time.'

'That's what they do though, isn't it, they make you think that's the power they have,' India said lugubriously, turning on to her front. 'I'd never trust anyone who called themselves a guru.'

'To be fair, he doesn't call himself a guru,' I said.

'Everyone else does.'

'OK, well that's better,' she replied.

'It's a bit like being a "maven",' I continued. 'Or a "mogul". You have to wait for someone else to say it, I think. You can't say it about yourself.' I took my top off and joined them on the towels they had thrown on the grass.

'Did you get what you needed from him?' Belle asked.

'Yeah,' I said. 'He was a great interviewee.' I closed my eyes and let the strong English sunshine give me a rare hug. 'Jesus, I am not going to be able to stop thinking about him.'

'In, like, a sex way?' India asked.

'No, I don't think so. In a I-want-to-eat-your-soul way. I just want to find out everything about him, I want to listen to everything he has to say.'

'Ask for his number,' she said.

'I already have his number. I just interviewed him on the phone.'

'Oh yeah,' she said. 'Well then, just text him.'

'I can't "just text" someone I interviewed for a piece.'

'Why not?' Belle asked.

'Because it would be inappropriate,' I said, catching the words in my mouth. 'But whoever fell in love with appropriate?'

I listened to the recording again when I was in bed that night, his words bouncing through me like a ping-pong ball. The next morning I wrote up the piece, sent it to the editor and forgot about him.

*

A couple of months later, I was coming home late from a party when I got a WhatsApp message from David. He told me he was on holiday in France and had just been for a long walk under the stars and suddenly remembered our interview and that he hadn't seen it anywhere.

'This is obviously my narcissism speaking – when is the piece out?'

'Not narcissistic at all,' I replied. 'It's been held over for an issue, sorry. I'll text you the day it's out next month. I can send you a copy if you're not in the country.'

'I'll be back by then. How are you?' he asked. 'You seemed on the edge of something the last time we spoke.'

'Still on the edge of something,' I typed. 'Still trying to shift into a different paradigm. Easy-peasy. How are you?'

'Same.'

He told me that he was a few weeks out of a very long-term relationship. He said it was the right thing – an amicable and mutual separation. He told me that sometimes a break-up can be nothing but a relief for both parties; like an air-conditioning unit has finally been turned off, the low, relentless hum of which you hadn't realized was there until everything is silent.

We texted for hours that night, learning the fundamentals of each other we hadn't gleaned in our first conversation. We both grew up in North London, we both went to conservative boarding schools, which is why he had a voice I suspected he hated as much as I hated mine. He had four kids – two boys, two girls – and he was obviously very taken with all of them. I could spot a man using his kids as a chat-up line from a mile away – this was not one. He knew every tiny detail of each child's character and passions and dreams and daily life and he talked about all of them with genuine fascination and devotion.

We talked about music, song lyrics. I told him that my favourite singer was John Martyn; that his music had been the only love affair I'd had with a man that had lasted longer than a handful of years. He told me a story of how he bought one of John Martyn's guitars off his ex-wife and said I could have it if I liked, as he could tell how besotted I was with his music. We talked about a book we'd both read that turned me vegetarian; we both got angry about the same stats and passages. We talked about our childhood holidays spent in France. We talked about our parents. We talked about the rain. I told him how much I loved it; more than blue skies and sunshine. I told him how the rain had always cradled and calmed me – how as a kid I would ask my mum if I could sit in the boot of her car parked outside when it rained. I told him that when I read in Rod Stewart's autobiography that he would stand in the middle of the street with his arms outstretched when it rained once a year in LA, all because he missed it so much, I realized I could never leave England. We said goodnight at three a.m.

The next morning I woke up and felt I was recovering from a vivid dream. But sure enough, there was a new message from David on my phone waiting for me under my pillow like a bright, shining pound coin from the tooth fairy.

'You woke me up at about five this morning,' it read.

'What do you mean?' I replied. He sent me a recording of the sound of rainfall, hard and then soft, on the window of his bedroom.

'Am I the rain?' I asked, suspending my well-worn cynicism in a way that would become a fixture of our interactions.

'Yeah, you are,' he replied. 'I felt you come closer.'

I had to tell my friends about David because I never got off my phone to him. We messaged each other from the moment we woke up to the moment we went to bed. I reserved about five hours of the day for working, eating and washing, but even in those enforced windows of time, I was thinking about him. I had lunch with Sabrina and she told me she could tell my eye was on my phone screen for the entire time.

'Right, enough with the phone,' she said.

'I'm not on my phone!' I said defensively.

'You're not physically on your phone, but I can tell all you're thinking about is speaking to him.'

'No I'm not.'

'You are, it's like I've taken my thirteen-year-old daughter out for lunch who wants to be back on MSN Messenger talking to her foreign exchange student boyfriend.'

'I'm sorry,' I said. 'I'm not thinking about him, I promise.' My phone lit up.

'What's that he's sent there?' Sabrina asked, peering down at the screen. I showed her the photo of an elaborate illustration of a lion.

'He thinks my inner spirit is a lion.'

Sabrina gave me a few bewildered blinks.

'Yeah, I don't think we'll have much in common, me and your new boyfriend,' she said flatly.

'No, you will, you will. He's not a serious, humourless guru, he's really funny.'

'OK, just cool down all the texting,' she said. 'Please. For your sake. You're going to ruin your relationship before it's even started. It's like he's a human Tamagotchi.'

'But he's in France for three weeks,' I said. 'I'm not going to not speak to him until he's back and we can meet.'

'Oh my God, I bet he's told you to fly to France, hasn't he?' she asked, shaking her head. 'Why is it always *so extreme* with you and men?'

'Come on, I'm not actually going to go,' I said. I didn't tell her that I had looked at flights, out of curiosity.

My friends, quite rightly, thought I was insane to have become so quickly obsessed with someone I didn't know. But they were also used to it – me finding a new love interest had always been like a greedy child opening a toy on Christmas Day. I ripped the packaging open, got frustrated trying to make it work, played with it obsessively until it broke, then chucked the broken pieces of plastic in the back of a cupboard on Boxing Day.

I emailed Farly the recording of me and David's original interview.

'Listen to this,' I wrote. 'And then you'll understand why I'm acting so nuts about this man.' An hour later I received an email back from her.

'OK, I understand why you're acting so nuts about this man,' it read.

A week after we started texting, we spoke on the phone. With the dynamic of interviewer and interviewee changed, everything felt different to the last time we spoke months before. It was late and quiet and I could hear his breathing and the crickets in the French countryside. I closed my eyes and could almost feel him next to me; the magic of this strange intimacy we'd created in the last week.

'It's kind of great we're getting to know each other like this before we meet,' he said. 'Shelley Winters said: "Whenever you want to marry someone, go have lunch with his ex-wife."'

'Are you suggesting I have lunch with your ex-wife before I have lunch with you?'

'No, I just think people give such an edited sales pitch of themselves on a first date, you don't really get to see any of who that person really is.'

'Yes, I suppose it will be too late for a sales pitch by the time we meet.'

Another week passed, thousands of messages, dozens of calls. He became increasingly fascinating to me and I wanted to know his thoughts on everything. There was no detail that was spared; I was seduced by the hair-splitting of our dialogue. On the subject of anything I was interested in, he had something new to say. Having the light of this man's interest shine on me made me feel energized and new. There weren't enough hours in the day to talk to David. I needed more, more, more.

Soon, texts and calls weren't enough. We sent each other all our work. He sent me unpublished chapters of his new book; I sent him drafts of articles and screenplays. We told each other the things we wouldn't know from talking and googling for pictures – that my nails were always bitten down from my anxious disposition, that his fingertips were hard from playing guitar. I watched short films he had appeared in with singular concentration; I thought he was a genius and told him so, writing down lines that stuck with me and shots that I loved and calling him afterwards to talk about them.

'Go look at the moon,' he said late one night as we were talking on the phone. I slipped my feet into my trainers and pulled a coat over my T-shirt and knickers. I walked to the end of my road and into Hampstead Heath. He told me about a wild-haired woman he'd once dated who lived in Highgate who gave him a thirty-second start on running into the Heath at night and then chased after him. They'd had sex in the woods, up against an oak tree. I sat on a bench on a viewpoint overlooking the city skyline, stretched my bare legs out under the light of the moon and told him about another bench I'd seen here that had made me cry when I read the tribute carved into it. It was on the meadow next to the Ladies' Pond, where I swam all summer, in remembrance of Wynn Cornwell – a woman who swam there right up into her nineties.

'It says: "In memory of Wynn Cornwell, who swam here for over fifty years, and Vic Cornwell, who waited for her." He must have stood by the gate while she swam every day. Isn't that beautiful?'

'You know . . .' he began to speak.

'What?'

'Nothing,' he said.

'No, go on, tell me.'

'You're just such a fascinating girl. You're this wide-open book in so many ways. Why do you do all this petulant "I'm an island" stuff?' he asked.

'I don't realize I do it, it's not a conscious affectation.'

'You might not feel like you can have that, but you can. It can all be yours if you want it.'

'I can be moved by something and not know if I want it for myself,' I said. 'And I'm just a sap anyway. It's like every year a cleaner comes in to hoover the channel between my heart and my tear ducts. One day it will be just one huge clear passage of disgusting, gushing feelings and by the time I'm your age I will probably cry at the sight of a leaf in the breeze.'

'If you're lucky.'

'Sometimes the gap between the little faith you have compared to the unwavering faith of others is a very moving thing.'

'I don't know. Maybe you just have an unfillable void,' he said with a gentle sigh. 'Maybe no man will ever be able to fill it.' I looked above me at the same side of the moon we both gazed at and wished on a star that I would go to bed that night and forget what he had said.

I was aware that I was investing huge amounts of time and energy in a perfect stranger, but I had every reason to trust him. I counted down the days until there was just air between us and in the meantime enjoyed this place of our own making; he was like a portal at the side entrance of boring, daily life that allowed me to slip into a magical technicolour world. If I had a problem, I asked him for advice. If I found myself searching for the end of a sentence when I was writing, I would ask his opinion.

'Thank you for being more open with me,' he messaged me one afternoon. 'It's sexy.'

Obviously, I would continue to do just about anything if a man I liked told me he thought it was sexy.

We regularly talked about how strange the intensity of our communication had been; for him it was completely new and entirely peculiar. I had never formed such an intense bond with someone I'd never met, but I was more used to the idea of chatting with strangers, what with my formative training on MSN and the subsequent adult years of online dating.

'Isn't it weird?' he messaged me. 'You and I have never met and yet – the places we've been! The realms of intimacy and tenderness and Sundays and laughter and music.'

'I know!'

'And we've woven it all out of invisible energy. Only using pixels.'

'We're magicians.'

'Look what we are doing with these pixels,' he wrote. 'Bouncing each other off satellites.'

I barely slept the night before David landed back in England. He was going to drop his kids off at their mother's house, drive to London and sleep at a mate's house, then the next day we had our perfect date planned. The weather was set to be good; I was going to meet him on Hampstead Heath in the early afternoon with a bottle of wine and two plastic cups. India and Belle helped me pick an outfit – a blue tea dress and white plimsolls. I cleaned my flat. I got some good bread in for the inevitable morning after.

'She means business,' India observed as she watched me carefully remove the books from my shelf, clean the ledges and rearrange the books in an order of titles that I imagined he'd find most impressive (Dworkin, Larkin, *Eat, Pray, Love*).

But the night before our hot afternoon date, I had to go on a date. It was a blind set-up by a matchmaking agency who wanted me to write about them in my dating column. It was organized weeks before David and I had started our virtual relationship and at the time had made total sense – they needed the exposure, I needed a date and copy. I didn't want to blow the poor guy off, so we arranged a very early evening drink somewhere central. I knew I could be home by nine.

'Call me later, heartbreaker,' were David's parting words to me.

I didn't turn out to be a heartbreaker at all – quite the opposite. Just as I've found with most set-ups, neither of us wanted to be there. He was still in love with his ex-girlfriend with whom he'd regrettably messed things up, while I was besotted with a man I'd never met. We told each other our respective stories. I told him to go to his ex's house with flowers and tell her he'd never stopped loving her; he told me to go home and get an early night because tomorrow I was going to meet the man I was quite clearly going to marry. We left after one cocktail, got on the same tube home and parted with a hug.

'GOOD LUCK!' he shouted at me as the tube doors closed between us.

'You too!' I mouthed through the glass.

When I got home, I rang David and told him about the date. He had driven down to London earlier than planned and was sleeping on his mate's sofa in a flat that was about two miles west of my flat.

'Come round and stay here,' I said.

'What about tomorrow's perfect date?' he asked.

'I know, I know, it just seems so silly, you being a ten-minute drive from me.'

We agreed to stick to the original plan, then five minutes later I looked at my phone and saw a message from him.

'I'm coming round.'

I tiptoed out of the flat and down the iron outdoor stairs and there he stood on my silent street, with only the moonlight making out his tall, broad silhouette and the curls of his dark hair. I paused on the steps for just a moment to take him in, feeling like I had jumped off a cliff and was about to hit the still water's surface. I ran up to him, flung my arms round his neck and we kissed.

'Let me look at this girl,' he said, holding my face with his eyes intently darting around my features, as if memorizing me for an exam.

'It's nice to meet you,' I said.

'Well, it's nice to meet you too.' We carried on kissing, in the middle of my road in the middle of the night, as I stood on my bare toes on the tarmac, the twit-twoo of a suburban owl in a nearby tree. He pulled me into him and I pressed my face against his navy shirt, as rumpled as his curls.

'You're not six foot,' he whispered into my forehead.

'Yes I am,' I replied, standing up straighter.

'No you're not and I knew you weren't, you fucking liar.'

I took his hand and we crept up the stairs to my flat.

The next few hours passed exactly how I had imagined they would. We drank, we talked, we listened to music, we lay next to each other and kissed. I breathed in his naked, tattooed skin – walnut-brown and dusty from the French sun – and the smell of tobacco and the earth. I studied his mannerisms that a phone and a photo couldn't catch; the fold of his eyelids, the way an 's' slid through his teeth. He listened to me closely, he talked to me directly; I was open and trusting and marvelled at my ability to feel such intimacy with someone I barely knew.

'Do you know what's funny?' he said, kissing my head.

'What?'

'You're just like I thought you'd be. Like the kid in the playground who covers her eyes with her hands and thinks no one can see her.'

'What do you mean?'

'You can't hide from me,' he said. I knew already that this was someone I would never be able to lie to. I knew I was fucked.

'Are you annoyed we didn't do the perfect date first?' I asked as I transitioned into the dreamy, mumbling fallow field between consciousness and sleep.

'No,' he said, stroking my hair. 'Not at all. What are you doing tomorrow?'

'Meeting with an editor at one,' I said.

'I could come meet you afterwards?' he suggested.

I closed my eyes and fell into an instant, peaceful sleep.

A few hours later, I was woken by a sound. David was standing at the end of my bed, getting dressed.

'Are you OK?' I asked sleepily.

'I'm fine,' he bristled.

'Where are you going?'

'For a drive.'

I looked at my clock – five a.m.

'What – now?'

'Yes, I fancy a drive.'

'OK,' I said. 'Do you want me to give you my keys so you can get back in?'

'No,' he said. He leant down to the bed and kissed along my arm; from my elbow to my shoulder. 'Go back to sleep.'

He closed the door. I heard him leave the flat, get in his car and drive off.

I stared at the white ceiling of my bedroom, trying to piece together what had happened. I was filled with a sour feeling of violent rejection. I felt it from my stomach to my throat: self-disgust, self-loathing, self-pity, squared. It's how I felt all those years ago when I got that call from Harry.

At seven a.m., I crawled into India's bed and told her everything that had happened.

'It sounds like he had a freak-out,' India said.

'What about?'

'Maybe it was suddenly too real. Too intimate.'

'I mean, the man is an intimacy coach,' I said. 'That's quite literally his job.'

'Well, it might be a case of "Those who can, do . . ."'

'I still can't believe this has happened,' I said.

'Whatever his reason is, he has a fuck-load of explaining to do today.'

'But maybe he'll never speak to me again.'

'Surely not,' she said. 'He's a father of four, surely he has more compassion than that.'

'If I didn't have the texts on my phone saying he was

coming over, I would honestly think I just dreamt last night,' I said. 'I've been lying awake, torturing myself with these fragments of him; his eyes and his freckles and the tattoo on his chest –'

'Oh, of course he has a tattoo on his chest,' India said, rolling her eyes. 'What is it?'

'I can't. The irony is too awful.'

'Go on,' she said.

'Some symbol thing that means respect to womankind.'

'Jesus wept.'

'He should get it amended with a footnote,' I said. 'An asterisk next to it. "Apart from Dolly Alderton."'

'Are you OK?' India asked, stroking my arm. 'This must be a big shock.'

'I'm just confused,' I said. 'Is that it?'

A couple of hours later, I received a riddle-like message from David.

'Hey,' it read. 'Sorry if that was weird, a bit of an odd exit. It was so beautiful to see you, touch you – it sent me very inner, felt this chasm between the amazing intimacy we've created in the last days and also the opposite, not "knowing" each other.' I watched him type and refused to reply until I got something that made a morsel of sense. 'It sent me into some big questions. Fuck. I hope you're not in pain, maybe you're just "Whatever". But maybe you're weirded out.' I stared at my phone, still unsure of what to respond. 'I hope you didn't wake up sad,' he wrote.

'I did wake up sad,' I replied. 'It's not often I let people close to me.'

'I know. I'm really sorry. It wasn't an abandonment of you.'

I thought about the last call I ever had with Harry. How I begged him to love me; how I persuaded him through tears that I was good enough for him. How I listened to any wavering in his voice that would lead me to believe I could cling on to him desperately, my fingers turning purple from the grip. That wasn't my story any more. That wasn't who I wanted to be.

'I don't really understand what the above means but I'm fine to leave it here if it's something you don't feel comfortable continuing,' I wrote.

'I need to press pause and get my head straight when it comes to you,' he replied. 'I'm not saying it should be the end.'

'I am,' I wrote. 'I have to press stop now.'

'Shit, I've hurt you. I can feel it.'

'It's OK,' I replied. 'We're both in weird times in our lives. You've just come out of a relationship, I'm going through all this analysis. But I have to self-protect.'

'OK,' he responded.

I deleted our conversations and call history, then I deleted David's number.

As the days passed, I felt a combination of loneliness, embarrassment, grief and anger. I felt like an idiot; like a sort of frumpy female character on *The Archers* who gets wooed by a dastardly, beautiful stranger before he leaves, taking all her money. Friends exchanged similarly embarrassing stories to make me feel better, tales of being tricked into false intimacy with strangers. One of the editors of my dating column sent me an article called 'Virtual Love' published in a 1997 issue of the *New Yorker* about the curious new phenomenon of falling in love online; a first-person piece from a female journalist who began a phone and email relationship with a stranger. 'I may not have known my suitor,' she wrote. 'But, for the first time in my life, I knew the deal: I was a desired person, the object of a blind man's gaze . . . if we met on the street, we wouldn't recognize each other, our particular version of intimacy now obscured by the branches and bodies and falling debris that make up the physical world.'

Two days after David left me in the middle of the night, the magazine came out with the piece that had originally led me to him. I had completely forgotten about it; but seeing it on the shelves of newsagents felt like everything had come full circle. I didn't text him to let him know it was out, as I had initially promised in the message that started this disaster. I never spoke to David again.

My friends reeled in the aftermath of the encounter, the whole thing becoming even more absurd the further away in time it drifted. Sometimes, weeks and weeks after it all happened, we'd sit in the pub and India would suddenly put down her glass of wine and bark: 'Can you BELIEVE that David guy?' Belle contemplated reporting him for abusing his position of trust.

'But who could you even report him to?' I asked.

'There must be some guru council, some sort of Equity thing where they qualify,' India said.

'Maybe we just call Haringey Council,' Belle suggested. 'Tell them there is a guru at large who is a danger to impressionable young women.'

Some friends thought he was just a misogynist who saw the challenge of a woman with trust issues, got what he wanted and left; a wolf in Glastonbury stall-owner's clothing. Others, more generously, thought that he was less comfortable with the reality of virtual seduction than a millennial. I was quite used to chatting to people I hadn't met and creating a rapport with them. Meeting them in the flesh for the first time was always jarring, but getting to know someone was just the art of closing that gap; that 'chasm' he referred to. That's the entire premise of online dating.

Helen devised another theory: that he was going through a midlife crisis off the back of his break-up and I was nothing more than an impulse buy for his ego. I was a leather jacket or a fast car that he liked the idea of, but knew after purchasing that it would never work for him or fit into his life.

But mourning the loss of David would be like a child mourning the loss of an invisible friend. None of it was real. It was hypothetical; it was fiction. We played intensity chicken with each other, sluts for overblown, artificial sentiment and a desperate need to feel something deep in the dark, damp basement of ourselves. It was words and spaces. It was pixels. A game of *The Sims*; a game of dress-up love. It was bouncing off satellites in a tightly choreographed dance.

Only now, after hours of dissection, do I realize who David was. He was neither a trickster, nor a walking midlife crisis, nor a caddish Don Juan disguised in Birkenstocks and linen. He was the little boy in the playground who covered his eyes and thought no one could see him. But finally I could see him – because we were two of a kind; kids as bad as each other. He was lost and looking for a lifeboat. He was sad and he needed a distraction. We were two lonely people who needed a fantasy to escape ourselves. Perhaps, having twenty years on me, he should have known better – but he didn't. I hope to never be complicit in a game like that again. And I hope he finds what he's looking for.

18th October

Good morning to Karen's fertile and barren friends!!

I thought I'd send over the plan for the completely unnecessary, mawkish and expensive non-tradition borrowed from America that is our friend Karen's baby shower! Karen thinks it's always good to demand money and time from people to celebrate her own personal life choices and we felt you hadn't given her quite enough in recent history what with the £1,500 hen do in Ibiza, wedding in Majorca with a strict dress code and gift registry at Selfridges. (NB Ladies – if you get a new job or buy a flat on your own, you get a card and that's it. We want to make sure there is no precedent set. We're not made of money!!)

The good news is, after Karen gives birth she won't see any of her childless friends unless all they want to do is talk about her baby and nothing else, so you can treat this as her farewell party as well as her baby shower and save those pennies for a couple of years! That is of course until she comes back to you when she's stopped breastfeeding and is bored out of her mind, demands you all go out to drink, dance and take loads of drugs, then sends you an offish text the following week saying she can't really have a night out like that again because 'I'M A MOTHER NOW'.

When you arrive at my flat (Karen's BFF) in Belsize Park, I would like you to really take in its size, layout and period features, because that will make up a large portion of the afternoon's conversation. I'll talk at length and with boastful authority about getting my kitchen redone, making every renter in the room feel like a piece of shit, and I'd appreciate it if none of you pointed out that my dad paid for the flat in full. That's right – not even a mortgage! Please take your shoes off at the door.

We will begin the embarrassing, time-consuming and infantile games promptly at 14.00. The first is a round of pin the vomit on the baby. The second is guess the poo (we'll melt different brands of chocolate into nappies and mummy-to-be will have to guess which bar is in which nappy!). We'll then go on to baby charades, in which we will all have to act out a different stage of parenting, e.g. falling out with your overbearing mother because you won't have your child christened and fighting with your partner about whether it's too mollycoddling to claim there is a hamster afterlife.

We'll round off three hours later with a game of pass the breast pump. I've had some worried emails about this so let me clear something up now: YOU DO NOT HAVE TO BE ACTIVELY LACTATING TO ENJOY THIS GAME. Karen has made it very clear to me that non-mothers are only marginally less welcome than those guests who are also pregnant or have had children. We'll pass the breast pump round and whoever has it when the music stops attaches it to their tit for a bit of a laugh. It's supposed to be fun!

There will be one bottle of warm welcome Prosecco to be shared between twenty-five guests; other than that it's a dry event. Instead, you can binge on the predictable afternoon tea, of which everything will be in miniature.

The gifts will be opened at 17.00 (registry attached).

To the hippies, freelancers, unemployed and those who work in media, the arts or creative industries for less than £25,000 P/A: no one wants your home-made shit. If you really care about Karen and her unborn child then you will go to the White Company registry like everyone else. There are cashmere hats on there for as little as £80, so there's no excuse for your attempts at knitting. No one will find it cute.

We will watch Karen open every single present like a five-year-old at a birthday tea party and she'll explain what every present does. This will be not only tedious but completely horrifying for those of us who haven't given birth and don't yet know the specifics of nipple creams, post-birth nappies for mum, placenta broth and fishing for poo in a water-birth pool. There will be a trained PTSD therapist on site for the childless women as well as a manicurist for everyone else.

The big event of the day will happen at 19.00 – the gender reveal cake. Karen and her husband, Josh, do not know the gender of their baby and instead have asked the doctor to direct the information straight to an artisanal bakery in Hackney. All the team at Bake 'n' Bites have been working exceptionally hard to produce a four-tier creation covered in salted-caramel icing, Karen's favourite. When she slices into the cake, the colour of the sponge will reveal the sex: pink for a girl, blue for a boy or green for a bit of both. It will be a very special (not to mention delicious!) moment for all of us.

We're hoping for an expensive and boring day full of love and laughs, preparing our best friend for motherhood, hopefully while making all her friends without children feel alienated and all her friends with children feel inadequate.

See you then!!

Love,

Natalia XXXXXXXXXXXXXX

Enough

In the weeks after I met David, feeling exposed and embarrassed, I made a loud, defensive declaration of celibacy. Of course, it wasn't celibacy at all because, firstly, it lasted just shy of three months. Secondly, it was mainly a tool to get male attention; a sort of born-again-virgin fantasy challenge. Which is the complete opposite of the intended outcome of celibacy. No nun has ever taken a vow of celibacy so she seems irresistibly hard to get.

And then came the disastrous Christmas Special. The 'Christmas Special' was a phrase coined by my friends to describe a particular type of drunken carefree fling that only happens in the run-up to Christmas; when everyone is high on merriment and goodwill and advocaat and all bets are off. In the run-up to Christmas, I decided I'd earnt an instant fix of validation; a Pot Noodle of self-esteem.

After a work party, I texted a bloke I'd been chatting to on a dating app for a couple of weeks, a Geordie who worked in the music industry with a cheeky smile and good chat-up lines.

'Do you fancy doing our date now?' I messaged him with an aggressive nonchalance. It was half past one in the morning.

'Sure,' he replied.

He arrived at my flat with a bottle of organic red wine at two a.m. and we made small talk on the sofa like we were just two sophisticated metropolitans enjoying an early-evening dinner date rather than the tragic reality of desperation. After precisely one hour of talking, we started kissing. Then we went to my bedroom and had perfunctory, nondescript sex. It was the physical equivalent of a rushed sandwich in a motorway service station – something you thought you were looking forward to then the minute you get to it you wonder why.

I hadn't had sex with a stranger since the night I met Adam in New York. I had accidentally grown out of one-night stands, like a little girl who realizes one day that she no longer wants to play with her Barbies. As soon as it was over, I knew I never wanted to do it again. The sex itself was fine; but his presence was unbearable. The false intimacy of casual sex that I once relished as a student felt like a laughable farce. This was not his fault at all, but I wanted him out of my flat, out of my room, out of my bed with its letters from my friends on the table next to it and its nice memory foam mattress topper I had saved up for. Seeing the outline of this stranger's sleeping face in the darkness made me feel queasy. The night passed like a slug.

I woke up with a terrible hangover and the Geordie was still in my bed. He wanted to spend the morning lying around together, drinking tea and playing Fleetwood Mac albums – I had on my hands a 'boyfriend experience' guy. The 'boyfriend experience', I had noted over the years, was a thing certain men offered after a one-night stand where they behaved in an inappropri-ately romantic way the morning after to either make you fall in love with them or quell their personal feelings of guilt for having had sex with a person whose surname they didn't know. They spent the morning after spoon-ing you and making you breakfast and watching *Friends* episodes before eventually leaving at dusk. They never called again. It was a seemingly free service with a hid-den high emotional charge. I never took the 'boyfriend experience' if it was being offered.

'Have a nice life,' I said as I stood at the door, having finally got him out of my home with the excuse of some fake lunch plans.

'Don't say that,' he said, giving me a hug.

'Sorry,' I replied, not knowing what else to say. 'Merry Christmas.'

I lay on the sofa in Leo's jumper that I had never thrown away and watched daytime television. India's lovely boy-friend came into the living room, bearded and smiling and wearing the cosy Fair Isle scarf India had lovingly picked out for him for Christmas. He was a picture of familiarity and love; and it had never felt so far away from me.

'Morning, Doll,' he said.

'Nice scarf.'

'Yeah, it is, isn't it?' he said, looking down at it with a smile. 'India tells me you commissioned a Christmas Special last night.'

'Yeah,' I said, my face half buried in the cushion of the sofa, my eyes still staring at the *Loose Women* panel.

'Good?'

'No. Awful. Depressing,' I said. 'It was the *EastEnders* Christmas Special.'

'Oh dear,' he said. 'So there won't be a recommission?'

'No. It was a one-off.'

The following month, my dating column finally came to an end – giving me no excuse to be always looking for the next bloke under the guise of it being my profession. The end of the column could easily have marked the beginning of a new phase in my life; one that wasn't governed by late-night calls from old boyfriends and right-swiping and left-swiping and cornering men at dinner parties and coordinating cigarette breaks in the pub when there was an attractive man outside.

The truth is, the column had been an enabler, but I was an addict. I always had been, long before I was even sexually active. There's this thing that Jilly Cooper says in her episode of *Desert Island Discs* – that when she was at an all-girls school, she was so obsessed with boys that she would even fantasize about the eighty-year-old male gardener who would sometimes work in the grounds. I was that girl growing up and, in a way, I never stopped being that girl. Boys fascinated me and frightened me in equal measure; I didn't understand them and neither did I want to. Their function was for gratification, whereas female friends provided everything else that mattered. It was a way of keeping boys at arm's length.

*

When Farly and I came back from Sardinia and she began her new life as a single woman for the first time since her early twenties, I gave her quite the imperious TED talk on the complexities of modern dating.

'The first thing you've got to realize,' I said, 'is no one meets in real life any more. Things have changed since you were last on the market, Farly, and, unfortunately, you've got no choice but to change with them.'

'OK,' she said, nodding and taking mental notes.

'The good news is, no one actually likes online dating. We all do it, but everyone hates it, so we're all in the same boat.'

'Right.'

'But you mustn't get upset if you find you're in a pub or wherever and not being chatted up. It's completely normal. In fact, sometimes a man will like the look of you at a party and not speak to you, but then Facebook message you afterwards saying he wishes he had spoken to you.'

'Weird.'

'Very, but you get used to it. It's just a new way of making that initial connection with someone.'

'What about tit-wanks?' she asked.

'Well, what about them?'

'Do people still do tit-wanks?'

'No,' I said authoritatively. 'No one has given or received one since 2009. It won't ever be expected of you.'

'OK, that's one good thing at least,' she said.

*

Farly met a bloke in a bar a week later. They exchanged numbers. They immediately started seeing each other.

'Farly's met someone,' I told India over a Saturday-morning breakfast.

'Good for her,' she replied. 'One slice of toast or two?'

'Two. You'll never believe where. Guess.'

'I don't know,' she said, eating a spoonful of lemon curd.

'In a bar.'

'What do you mean "in a bar"?'

'In, like, real life. He came over to her and started talking and now they're dating. Can you believe it? I'm happy for her but I'm also so angry. I mean, when did you last meet someone in a bar?'

'How RIDICULOUS!' India said, with genuine outrage.

'I know,' I said. 'I know.'

Belle schlepped into the kitchen in her dressing gown.

'Morning, kittens,' she said sleepily.

'Did you hear about this?' India asked indignantly. 'About Farly's new bloke?'

'No?' she replied.

'They met in *a bar*.'

'What bar?'

'I don't know,' I said. 'Richmond, I think. Can you believe it? I don't think someone has given me their number on a night out in about five years and it happens to her in five minutes.'

'Maybe it's a south of the river thing,' Belle mused.

'I think it's a Farly thing,' I said.

The differences between Farly and me are never more apparent than when it comes to love. Farly is a cosy, cohabiting, committed, long-term, textbook monogamist. The part of a relationship I find most thrilling – the unknown, the high-risk, the exciting first few months where you can barely eat because of butterflies in your stomach – is the bit she hates the most. The bit I live in fear of – barbecues at a boyfriend's family home, two baked potatoes on the sofa on a Saturday night in front of the telly, long car journeys on motorways together – is absolute heaven for her. She would happily trade in the first three months of romance for a lifetime of domesticity, intimacy, practical plans and baked potatoes. I would give anything for a lifetime of those first three months on repeat and a guarantee that I would never have to go to an Ikea, a National Express coach station or a relative's home outside of the M25 with a sexual partner.

'Projecting': this is one of those therapy words you learn along the way. It means you accuse someone else of doing or being exactly what you fear you are as a way of deflecting responsibility; it's 'watch-the-birdie' blaming. I did it a lot when it came to Farly's relationship choices. I had always thought of my perpetual resistance to commitment as an act of liberation; I hadn't ever realized it was the thing that made me feel trapped. Farly may have always needed to be in a relationship, but at least she knew what she wanted and was clear about it. I needed something, but I had absolutely no idea what, and I hated myself for wanting it.

Farly and I went for a long walk and I told her my plans to take a proper break from sex – along with all its prologues and epilogues of flirting, texting, dating and kissing – to try and find some autonomy. I told her that, despite being single for most of my life, I'd realized I hadn't *really* been single for a moment since I was a teenager. She agreed, and told me she thought it was a good idea.

'Do you think I'll ever feel settled with someone?' I asked her as we hopped over logs in Hampstead Heath's woods.

'Of course I do. You just haven't met the right man.'

'Yes, but that's the thing. I don't think it's about the right man at all, I think it's about me. I think the men are sort of immaterial until I sort all this out.' I gestured at myself with exhaustion, like I was a teenager's messy bedroom.

'Well, I think it's good you're taking the time to do it. I think it will be short-term work for a long-term reward.'

'Why do you find it so easy?' I asked her. 'I was always so jealous of how easy you found it with Scott. You were just there, *in*, boom. Committed.'

'I don't know, really.'

'When you were engaged, did you ever think about how you'd never sleep with anyone else? Did that never bother you?'

'Do you know,' she said, 'now that you've said that, I don't think I ever thought about it once.'

'That can't be true,' I said, jumping like a child as I walked so my fingertips touched a tree's branch.

'Honestly – I know it sounds weird – but I don't think that thought ever crossed my mind,' she said. 'All I wanted was a future with him.'

'I want to know what that feels like, to be truly committed to someone, rather than having one foot out the door.'

'You're too hard on yourself,' she said. 'You can do long-term love. You've done it better than anyone I know.'

'How? My longest relationship was two years and that was over when I was twenty-four.'

'I'm talking about you and me,' she said.

I couldn't stop thinking about Farly's words in the following few days; I thought about how we'd known each other for twenty years and how, in all that time, I'd never got bored of her. I thought of how I'd only fallen more and more in love with her the older we grew and the more experiences we shared. I thought about how excited I always am to tell her about a good piece of news or get her view when a crisis happens; how she's still my favourite person to go dancing with. How her value increased, the more history we shared together, like a beautiful, precious work of art hanging in my living room. The familiarity and security and sense of calm that her love bathed me in. All this time, I had been led to believe that my value in a relationship was my sexuality, which was why I always behaved like a sort of cartoon nymphomaniac. I hadn't ever thought that a man could love me in the same way my friends love me; that I could love a man with the same commitment and care with which I love them. Maybe all this time I had been in a great marriage without even realizing. Maybe Farly was what a good relationship felt like.

I threw myself into abstinence like I was doing a PhD on it. The more books and stories and blogs I read on sex and love addiction, the more I realized where I had gone so wrong. Dating had become a source of instant gratification, an extension of narcissism, and nothing to do with connection with another person. Time and time again, I had created intensity with a man and confused it with intimacy. A stranger proposing to me at JFK. A middle-aged guru asking to fly me out to France to spend a week with him. It was overblown, needless intensity, not a close connection with another person. Intensity and intimacy. How could I have got them so mixed up?

A month passed – I felt nothing but total, unbridled relief. I deleted the dating apps on my phone. I deleted the numbers I booty-called. I stopped replying to ex-boyfriends who would send me messages at three a.m. asking seemingly casual questions like 'How's it hangin' m'lady?' or 'What's the dealio smith?' I stopped stalking potential conquests online; I deleted my Facebook account mainly for this reason. I stopped living with secrets. I stopped with the midnight hours. I invested all my time in my work and my friendships.

Two months passed. I discovered what it was to go to

a wedding and actually be there to witness your friends getting married, rather than treating it like an eight-hour meat market. I found out what it was like to enjoy the beautiful, bell-like sound of a choir singing in church, and not manically scan the pews, checking the fingers of all the men to work out which were unmarried. I learnt how to enjoy the conversation of a man next to me at dinner regardless of his marital status; to resist fighting for the attention of the only single man at the table by saying something inappropriate in a vaguely threatening tone of Sid James bawdiness. I saw Leo for the first time in five years at a party and met his new wife – I gave them both a hug, then I left them alone. Harry got engaged – I felt no anger at all. Adam moved in with a girl – I sent him a text to congratulate him. Their stories had nothing to do with me any more, I didn't need their attention. I felt like I was finally jogging along on my own path, gathering my own pace and momentum.

I sat on tubes and got lost in my book, rather than try-ing to catch any man's eye. I left parties when I wanted to leave them, instead of desperately doing circuits of the room until the bitter end in the hope that I'd find some-one I fancied. I didn't go to events just because I knew certain people would be there; I didn't engineer chance encounters with people I fancied. I went out dancing with Lauren one night and when she was chatted up, instead of trying to find a bloke of my own, I stayed in the centre of the dance floor for an hour and danced by myself, sweat-ing and swaying and spinning and spinning.

'Are you waiting for someone?' a bloke asked, pulling me towards him.

'No, she's right here,' I said, and removed his hands from me.

'I never thought I would use this word in relation to you, and I don't want you to take offence at this,' Farly said, three drinks down in the pub a few weeks later. 'But I've found your company so calming these last few months.'

'When was the last time you saw me calm?' I asked.

'Well, I just haven't,' she replied, before draining the dregs of her vodka tonic and crunching on an ice cube. 'Ever. In nearly twenty years.'

In the late spring, I took two flights to the Orkney Islands to write a piece for a travel magazine about holidaying on your own. I stayed above a pub that looked over the port of Stromness and at night, after I'd had a beer and a steaming bowl of mussels downstairs, I'd go for a long walk along the seafront and look up at the vast open skies – vaster than any sky I'd ever seen.

One night, having spent a few days in peaceful solitude with my thoughts, I walked under the stars and along the cobbled streets and an idea crept all over me like arresting, vibrant blooms of wisteria. I don't need a dazzlingly charismatic musician to write a line about me in a song. I don't need a guru to tell me things about myself I think I don't know. I don't need to cut all my hair off because a boy told me it would suit me. I don't need to change my shape to make myself worthy of someone's love. I don't need any words or looks or comments from a man to believe I'm visible; to believe I'm here. I don't need to run away from discomfort and into a male eyeline. That's not where I come alive.

Because I am enough. My heart is enough. The stories and the sentences twisting around my mind are enough. I am fizzing and frothing and buzzing and exploding. I'm bubbling over and burning up. My early-morning walks and my late-night baths are enough. My loud laugh at the pub is enough. My piercing whistle, my singing in the shower, my double-jointed toes are enough. I am a just-pulled pint with a good, frothy head on it. I am my own universe; a galaxy; a solar system. I am the warm-up act, the main event and the backing singers.

And if this is it, if this is all there is – just me and the trees and the sky and the seas – I know now that that's enough.

I am enough. I am enough. The words ricocheted through me, shaking every cell as they travelled. I felt them; I understood them; they fused into my bones. The thought galloped and jumped through my system like a race horse. I called it out to the dark sky. I watched my proclamation bounce from star to star, swinging like Tarzan from carbon to carbon. I am whole and complete. I will never run out.

And I am more than enough.

(I think they call it 'a breakthrough'.)

Twenty-eight Lessons Learnt in Twenty-eight Years

1. It is 1 in 100 people who can take hard drugs and binge-drink regularly over a long period of time and not feel deep, dark longing or emptiness. It is 1 in 200 who will not be negatively affected by it. After many years of trying to work this out, I have decided Keith Richards is the exception, not the rule. He should be admired, but copied with caution.

2. It is 1 in 300 people who can have sex with three different strangers a week and it not be because they're desperately avoiding something. It might be their thoughts, their happiness or their body; it might be loneliness, love, aging or death. After many years of trying to work this out, I have decided Rod Stewart is the exception, not the rule. He should be admired, but copied with caution.

3. The lyrics of the Smiths' 'Heaven Knows I'm Miserable Now' is the most neatly worded explanation of the reality of life and summarizes the initial optimism then

crashing bathos that is the first five years of
one's twenties with elegant concision.

4. Life is a difficult, hard, sad, unreasonable,
   irrational thing. So little of it makes sense. So
   much of it is unfair. And a lot of it simply
   boils down to the unsatisfying formula of
   good and bad luck.

5. Life is a wonderful, mesmerizing, magical,
   fun, silly thing. And humans are astounding.
   We all know we're going to die, and yet we
   still live. We shout and curse and care when
   the full bin bag breaks, yet with every minute
   that passes we edge closer to the end. We
   marvel at a nectarine sunset over the M25 or
   the smell of a baby's head or the efficiency of
   flat-pack furniture, even though we know that
   everyone we love will cease to exist one day. I
   don't know how we do it.

6. You are the sum total of everything that has
   happened to you up until that last slurp of
   that cup of tea you just put down. How your
   parents hugged you, that thing your first
   boyfriend once said about your thighs – these
   are all bricks that have been laid from the
   soles of your feet up. Your eccentricities,
   foibles and fuck-ups are a butterfly effect of
   things you saw on telly, things teachers said to
   you and the way people have looked at you

since the first moment you opened your eyes. Being a detective for your past – tracing back through all of it to get to the source with the help of a professional – can be incredibly useful and freeing.

7. But therapy can only get you so far. It's like the theory test when you're learning to drive. You can work out as much as you like on paper, but at some point you're going to have to get in the car and really fucking feel how it all works.

8. Not everyone needs to navigate their insides with therapy. Absolutely everyone is dysfunctional on some level, but a lot of people can function dysfunctionally.

9. No one is ever, ever obliged to be in a relationship they don't want to be in.

10. A holiday is completely and utterly ruined if you don't buy two cans of Boots insect repellent at the airport on your way there. You will never buy it when you get to the other end and every night you'll sit around having dinner outside with your holidaying partners all saying 'I'm being bitten to pieces' passive-aggressively to each other because you're all annoyed someone else didn't remember to bring it. Just buy it at the airport on your way out there and then it's done.

11. Don't eat sugar every day. Sugar turns everything on the outside and inside of your body to shit. Three litres of water makes everything work properly. A glass of red wine is medicinal.

12. No one has ever asked you to make a floor-to-ceiling-sized friendship collage for their birthday. Or ring them three times a day. No one will cry if you don't invite them to dinner because you don't have enough chairs. If you feel exhausted by people, it's because you're willingly playing the martyr to make them like you. It's your problem, not theirs.

13. It is futile and knackering to try and make all your tiny choices representative of your moral compass then beat yourself up when this plan inevitably fails. Feminists can get waxed. Priests can swear. Vegetarians can wear leather shoes. Do as much good as you can. The weighty representation of the world cannot rest on every decision you make.

14. Everyone should own a Paul Simon album, a William Boyd book and a Wes Anderson film. If those are the only three things you have on your shelf, you will get through the longest, coldest, loneliest night.

15. If you're in a rented flat, paint your walls white, not cream. Cheap cream is grubby,

EVERYTHING I KNOW ABOUT LOVE

suburban and chintzy. Cheap brilliant white is
cool, clean and calming.

16. If you press shift and F3, it makes something
either all capitals or all lower case.

17. Let people laugh at you. Let yourself be a tit.
Pronounce things wrong. Spill yoghurt down
your shirt. It is the greatest relief to finally let
it happen.

18. You probably don't have a wheat intolerance,
you're just not eating wheat in a normal-sized
portion: 90–100g of pasta or two slices of
bread. Everyone feels weird after eating a
whole pack of Hovis; you'd feel weird after
eating an entire watermelon in one go too.

19. There is no quicker way to bond a group of
women than to bring up the subject of rogue,
coarse chin hairs.

20. Sex really, really does get better with age. If it
keeps improving like it has done so far, I'll be
in a state of constant coitus aged ninety. There
will be no point in doing anything else. Apart
from maybe pausing in the afternoon to eat a
Bakewell slice.

21. It's completely OK to focus on yourself.
You're allowed to travel and live on your own
and spend all your money on yourself and flirt
with whoever you like and be as consumed
with your work as you want. You don't have to
get married and you don't have to have

children. It doesn't make you shallow if you
don't want to open up and share your life with
a partner. But it's also completely not OK to
be in a relationship if you know that you want
to be on your own.

22. Gender, age and size regardless: everyone
looks good in a white shirt or a thick polo
neck or brown leather boots or a denim jacket
or a navy pea coat.

23. No matter how awful your neighbours are, try
to stay on their good side. Or make an ally
with at least one occupier of the flat next door
who you can respectfully nod to by the bins.
There will be gas leaks and break-ins and
packages that need to be delivered when
you're out and it will all be so much easier if
you've always got someone whose door you
can knock on. Grin and bear them. And give
them an emergency spare set of your keys.

24. Try to pretend Wi-Fi on the tube doesn't
exist. It's completely shit anyway. Always have
a book in your bag.

25. If you're feeling wildly overwhelmed with
everything, try this: clean your room, answer
all your unanswered emails, listen to a
podcast, have a bath, go to bed before eleven.

26. Swim naked in the sea at every possible
opportunity. Go out of your way to do it. If
you are driving somewhere faintly near the

coast and you smell the salty lick of the sea in the air, park the car, take off your clothes and don't stop running until you're tits-deep in icy ocean.

27. You're going to have to make a lifestyle choice between gel nail manicures and playing guitar. No woman can have both.

27a. Other than Dolly Parton.

28. Things will change more radically than you could ever imagine. Things will end up 300 miles north of your wildest predictions. Healthy people drop dead in supermarket queues. The future love of your life could be the man sitting next to you on the bus. Your secondary school maths teacher and rugby coach might now go by the name of Susan. Everything will change. And it could happen any morning.

Homecoming

There's a whole lot of stuff I don't know about love. First and foremost, I don't know what a relationship feels like for longer than a couple of years. Sometimes I hear married people refer to a 'phase' of their relationship as being a period that lasted longer than my longest ever relationship. Apparently, this is common. I've heard people describe the first ten years of their relationship as 'the honeymoon phase'. My honeymoon phases have been known to last little more than ten minutes. I have friends who describe their relationship as if it is the third person in their partnership; a living thing that twists and morphs and moves and grows the longer they're together. An organism that changes just as much as two humans who spend a life together change. I don't know what it is to nurture that third being. I don't really know what really long-term love feels or looks like from the inside.

I also don't know what it is to live with someone you're in love with. I don't know what it is like to go hunting for a home together; to plot against an estate agent in a conspiratorial whisper from the loo. I don't know what it's like to sleepily choreograph my way round someone every morning in the bathroom as we take turns to brush our teeth and use the shower in a familiar routine. I don't know what it's like to know you never get to leave and go home again; that your home is lying right next to you every morning and night.

In fact, I don't know what it is to be a proper team with a partner; I've never really leant on a romantic relationship for support or relaxed into its pace. But I've been in love and I've lost love, known what it's like to leave and be left. I hope all the rest will follow one day.

Nearly everything I know about love, I've learnt in my long-term friendships with women. Particularly the ones I have lived with at one point or another. I know what it is to know every tiny detail about a person and revel in that knowledge as if it were an academic subject. When it comes to the girls I've built homes with, I'm like the woman who can predict what her husband will order at every restaurant. I know that India doesn't drink tea, AJ's favourite sandwich is cheese and celery, pastry gives Belle heartburn and Farly likes her toast cold so the butter spreads but doesn't melt. AJ needs eight hours sleep to function, Farly seven, Belle around six and India can power through the day on a Thatcherite four or five. Farly's wake-up alarm is 'So Far Away' by Carole King and she loves watching narrative-driven programmes about obesity called things like *Half-Ton Mom* or *My Son, The Killer Whale*. AJ watches old *Home and Away* episodes on YouTube (astonishing) and buys books of sudoku to do in bed. Belle does exercise videos in her bedroom before work and listens to trance music while in the bath. India does jigsaw puzzles in her bedroom and watches *Fawlty Towers* every single weekend. ('I just don't know how she gets the mileage out of it,' Belle once privately commented to me. 'There are only twelve episodes.')

I know what it is to enthusiastically strap on an oxygen tank and dive deep into a person's eccentricities and fallibilities and enjoy every fascinating moment of discovery. Like the fact that Farly has always slept in a *skirt* for as long as I've known her. Why does she do that? What's the point of it? Or that Belle rips her flesh-coloured tights off on a Friday night when she gets home from the office – is it a mark of her quiet rage against the corporate system or just a ritual she's grown fond of? AJ wraps a scarf round her head when she's tired – it's certainly not cultural appropriation so what is it? Was she overly swaddled as an infant and it brings her a peaceful sense of infantilization? India has a comfort blanket, a frayed old navy jumper she calls Nigh Nigh that she likes to sleep with. Why does she call it 'he'? And how old was she when she decided it was a boy? In fact, I would love nothing more than to conduct a sort of literary salon in which all my beloved friends bring their comfort blankets from childhood to the table and we discuss the gender identities of all of them. I would, believe it or not, find that completely compelling.

I know what it is to collaboratively set up and run a home. I know what a shared economy of trust is; to know there will always be someone who will lend you

£50 until pay day and that as soon as you've paid it back they might need to borrow the same off you ('We're like primary school kids constantly swapping sandwiches,' Belle once said of our salaries. 'One week you need my tuna and sweetcorn, the next I want your egg and cress'). I know the thrill of post in December and cards shooting through the letter box with three names written on the front that really make you feel like a family. I know the strange sense of security to be felt in seeing three surnames on one account when you log into online banking.

I know how it feels for identity to be bigger than just you; to be part of an 'us'. I know what it's like to overhear Farly saying, 'We don't really eat red meat,' to someone across the table or to hear Lauren say, 'That's our favourite Van Morrison album,' to a boy she's chatting up at a party. I know how surprisingly good that feels.

I know what it's like to weather a bad experience and then turn it into shared mythology. Like the couple who theatrically tell the story of their luggage getting lost on their last holiday, taking a line each, we do the same with our own micro-disasters. Like the time India, Belle and I moved house and everything that could possibly go wrong went wrong. The reality was lost keys and borrowing money from friends and sleeping on sofas and putting stuff into storage. The story is a great one.

I know what it is to love someone and accept that you can't change certain things about them; Lauren is a grammatical pedant, Belle is messy, Sabrina's texts are incessant, AJ will never reply to me, Farly will always be moody when tired or hungry. And I know how liberating it feels to be loved and accepted with all my flaws in return (I'm always late, my phone's never charged, I'm oversensitive, I obsess over things, I let the bin overflow).

I know what it is to hear someone you love tell a story you've heard approximately five thousand times to an enraptured audience. I know what it's like for that person (Lauren) to embellish it more flamboyantly each time like an anecdotal Fabergé egg ('it happened at eleven' becomes 'so this was around four a.m.'; 'I was sitting on a plastic chair' becomes 'and I'm on this sort of chaise longue hand-crafted from glass'). I know what it's like to love someone so much that this doesn't really annoy you at all; to let them sing this well-rehearsed tune and maybe even come in with the supportive high-hat to boost the story's pace when they need it.

I know what a crisis point in a relationship feels like. When you think: we either confront this thing and try to fix it or we go our separate ways. I know what it is to agree to meet in a bar on the South Bank, begin bristly then end three hours later, weeping in each other's arms and promising to never make the same mistakes again (people only ever meet on the South Bank to reconcile or break up – I've done some of my finest dumping and being dumped in the National Theatre bar).

I know what it is to feel like you've always got a lighthouse – lighthous*es* – to guide you back to dry land; to feel the warmth of its beam as it squeezes your hand standing next to you at a funeral of someone you loved. Or to follow its flash across a crowded room at a terrible party where your ex-boyfriend and his new wife turned up unexpectedly; the flash that says *Let's get chips and the night bus home.*

I know that love can be loud and jubilant. It can be dancing in the swampy mud and the pouring rain at a festival and shouting 'YOU ARE FUCKING AMAZING' over the band. It's introducing them to your colleagues at a work event and basking in pride as they make people laugh and make you look lovable just by dint of being loved by them. It's laughing until you wheeze. It's waking up in a country neither of you have been in before. It's skinny-dipping at dawn. It's walking along the street together on a Saturday night and feeling an entire city is just yours. It's a big, beautiful, ebullient force of nature.

And I also know that love is a pretty quiet thing. It's lying on the sofa together drinking coffee, talking about where you're going to go that morning to drink more coffee. It's folding down pages of books you think they'd find interesting. It's hanging up their laundry when they leave the house having moronically forgotten to take it out of the washing machine. It's saying, 'You're safer here than in a car, you're more likely to die in one of your Fitness First Body Pump classes than in the next hour,' as they hyperventilate on an easyJet flight to Dublin. It's the texts: 'Hope today goes well', 'How did today go?', 'Thinking of you today' and 'Picked up loo roll'. I know that love happens under the splendour of moon and stars and fireworks and sunsets but it also happens when you're lying on blow-up air beds in a childhood bedroom, sitting in A&E or in the queue for a passport or in a traffic jam. Love is a quiet, reassuring, relaxing, pottering, pedantic, harmonious hum of a thing; something you can easily forget is there, even though its palms are outstretched beneath you in case you fall.

I had lived with my friends for five years before it came to an end. First Farly had left me for her boyfriend, then AJ left, and then India rang me one day to tell me she was ready to do the same, before bursting into tears.

'Why are you crying?' I asked her. 'Is this because of how I was with Farly when she met Scott? Were you scared I was going to go mad? Do you guys all think I'm nuts? That was, like, four years ago, I'm better equipped at handling this now.'

'No, no,' she sniffed. 'I'm just going to miss you.'

'I know,' I said. 'I'm going to miss you too. But you're thirty this year. And it's great that your relationship is ready to move forward. It's completely right and normal for things to change.' I was surprised at my own rationality on the whole thing and quietly awarded myself a CBE for services to friendship.

'What are you going to do?' she asked. 'You've always talked about how much you'd like to try living on your own.'

'I don't know. I don't know if I'm ready for it,' I said.

'Maybe I should live with Belle until she decides to move in with her boyfriend. It gives me at least six months to work out what to do next.'

'Dolly – you're not *The Hunger Games*,' she said. 'It shouldn't be an endurance test amongst our friends to see who can stick you out the longest.'

I realized that I had been presented with an opportunity. I could wait until every single one of my friends had found a man and moved out. I could rent with strangers from Gumtree who kept shaving cream in the fridge in the hope that I'd soon find a man and move out. Or I could start a new story on my own.

Finding a one-bedroom flat to rent within my budget wasn't easy; I was taken to a number of places that had beds next to the ovens and showerheads balanced over a loo in a 'wet room'. There was the 'spacious one-bed' that was twenty square metres big, there was the one with police tape round the front door. India came along with me to viewings, negotiating and interrogating the bluster of estate agents and asking me if I *really* believed I could manage without a wardrobe and instead keep all my clothes in a suitcase under the bed.

But, eventually, I found a place I could just about afford right in the middle of Camden. It was a ground-floor flat with a bedroom, bathroom and living room, enough space for a wardrobe and a shower that hung over an actual bath. At the back, there was a sunken, damp kitchen with absolutely no drawers that was so small I could barely turn in it, with a porthole window and a canal view that made it feel like I was in a boat. It was not perfect, but it would be mine.

All of us who had lived together did a 'farewell flat-sharing' pub crawl on our twenty-something stomping ground. We came dressed as an element of flat-sharing in our twenties, which was just as deranged as it sounds. AJ came as Gordon, our first landlord, complete with midlife-crisis leather biker jacket, white trainers, a short brown wig and permanent smarmy grin. As the resident obsessive cleaner, Farly came as a giant Henry vacuum in a spherical costume with a pipe attached that dragged along the ground the more she drank. Belle came as our loud nightmare neighbour, with smudged lipstick and a Cher wig. India came as a giant bin – as emptying or relining or taking one out seemed to be the most constant motif of our time together – with bin liners tied round her shoes, a lid for a hat and empty face-wipe and Monster Munch packets stuck to her body. I came as a giant packet of cigarettes and immediately regretted it as people kept coming up to me asking for free fags, assuming I was some sort of promo girl for Marlboro Lights hammering the streets of Kentish Town.

We went from pub to pub before ending back outside our first yellow-brick house. We even dropped in on Ivan at the corner shop, only to find out from his colleague that he'd mysteriously 'gone abroad for some unfinished business' and left 'without a trace'.

'The artists have gone,' Belle slurred wistfully as we

walked along the crescent, day turning into dusk. 'Now the bankers will move in.'

A week later, I packed my pot plants and paperbacks into cardboard boxes and taped them up for my new home. On the last night we lived together, India, Belle and I drank discounted Prosecco – the tipple of a bloody decade – and drunkenly danced to Paul Simon around our empty living room. As we waited for our respective moving vans the next morning, we huddled in the corner of our wine-stained carpet, our knees knocking together as we sat side by side, saying very little.

Farly, the most efficient and organized person I will ever know, came over to help me get started with unpacking the day I moved into my new place ('Are you sure you want to do this?' I texted her. 'Please – this is like cocaine to me,' she replied). We ordered Vietnamese food and sat on my living-room floor slurping pho and dipping summer rolls into sriracha sauce while we talked through where we should put the sofa and chairs and lamps and shelves, and where I would sit and write every day. We unpacked into the night before crashing out on my mattress pushed up against the bedroom wall, surrounded by cardboard boxes of shoes, bags of clothes and stacks of books.

When I woke up, Farly had left for work already and there was a note on the pillow, scrawled in her rotund childlike handwriting that hadn't changed since she wrote notes on my lever-arch files in Tipp-Ex during science GCSE classes. 'I love your new home and I love you,' it read.

The morning sun leaked into my bedroom and poured on to my mattress in a bright white puddle. I stretched out diagonally in my bed, across the cool sheet. I was completely alone, but I had never felt safer. It wasn't the bricks around me that I'd somehow managed to rent or the roof over my head that I was most grateful for. It was the home I now carried on my back like a snail. The sense that I was finally in responsible and loving hands.

Love was there in my empty bed. It was piled up in the records Lauren bought me when we were teenagers. It was in the smudged recipe cards from my mum in between the pages of cookbooks in my kitchen cabin. Love was in the bottle of gin tied with a ribbon that India had packed me off with; in the smeary photo-strips with curled corners that would end up stuck to my fridge. It was in the note that lay on the pillow next to me, the one I would fold up and keep in the shoebox of all the other notes she had written before.

I woke up safe in my one-woman boat. I was gliding into a new horizon; floating in a sea of love.

There it was. Who knew? It had been there all along.

Everything I Know About
Love at Twenty-eight

Any decent man would take a woman at peace with herself over a woman who performs tricks to impress him. You should never have to work to hold a man's attention. If a man needs to be 'kept interested' in you, he's got problems that are not your business to manage.

You probably won't be best friends with your best friend's boyfriend. Relinquish that dream, say so long to that fantasy. As long as he makes your friend happy and you can stand his company for the length of a long lunch, all is well.

Men love a naked woman. All other bells and whistles are an expensive waste of time.

Online dating is for the brave. It's increasingly hard to meet people in real life and those who take matters into their own hands – who pay a monthly fee for the chance to edge closer to love, who fill out an embarrassing profile saying they're looking for a special someone to hold hands with in the supermarket – are towering romantic heroes.

Get a Brazilian wax if you want a Brazilian wax. If you don't, don't. If you like feeling bare and you've got the money to spend, get waxed all year round. Don't ever get one for a man. And don't ever not get one for 'the sisterhood' – the sisterhood doesn't give a shit. Volunteer at a bloody women's shelter if you want to be useful, don't spend hours debating the politics of your pubic hair. And don't ever get one because you think not having one is unclean or unsightly – if that were true, every unwaxed male alive would be unclean. (Salary permitting, never go near hair-removal cream again.)

You may not be able to listen to the songs of past relationships in the first few years after the end, but soon the albums will find their way back to you. All those memories of Saturdays by the sea and Sunday-night spaghetti on the sofa will slowly unfurl from around the chords and lift, floating up out of the songs until they disappear. There will always be a faint recognition somewhere deep in the tissue of your guts that tells you that for a week this song, that man, was at the centre of your universe, but at some point it won't make your heart burn.

If you're still getting drunk and flirting with other people in front of your boyfriend, there's something wrong with your relationship. Or more likely, with you. Address why you need this level of attention sooner rather than later. Because no man on earth has a large enough supply of instant gratification to fill that emptiness you feel.

More often than not, the love someone gives you will be a reflection of the love you give yourself. If you can't treat yourself with kindness, care and patience, chances are someone else won't either.

However thin or fat you are is no indicator of the love you deserve or will receive.

Break-ups get harder with every year you get older. When you're young, you lose a boyfriend. As you get older, you lose a life together.

No practical matter is important enough to keep you in the wrong relationship. Holidays can be cancelled, weddings can be called off, houses can be sold. Don't hide your cowardice in practical matters.

If you lose respect for someone, you won't be able to fall back in love with them.

Integration into each other's lives should be completely equal; you should both make an effort to be involved with your respective friends, families, interests and careers. If it's unbalanced, resentment is on its way to you.

You should have sex on the first date if it feels right. You should never take any advice from a sassy, self-help school of thought that makes the man the donkey and you the carrot. You're not an object to be won, you're a human made of flesh and blood and guts and gut feelings. Sex isn't a game of power play – it's a consensual, respectful, joyful, creative, collaborative experience.

There is no feeling as awful as breaking up with someone. Being dumped is a violently intense pain that can, at some point, be converted into a new energy. The guilt and sadness of breaking up with someone goes nowhere but inside you and, if you let it, will do circuits of your mind for eternity. I'm with Auden on this one:

'If equal affection cannot be / Let the more loving one be me.'

There are so many reasons a person might be single at thirty or forty or a hundred and forty and it doesn't make them ineligible. Everyone has history. Take the time to hear theirs.

Sex with a total stranger is always weird, but staying in someone's flat – in their bed sheets, in their bedroom, or having them stay in yours – is even weirder.

It is no person's job to be the sole provider of your happiness. Sorry.

The perfect man is kind, funny and generous. He bends down to say hello to dogs and puts up shelves. Looking like a tall Jewish pirate with Clive Owen's eyes and David Gandy's biceps should be an added bonus and not a starting point.

Anyone can be fucking fancied. It is a far greater thing to be loved.

Don't fake orgasms. It does nobody any good at all. He is more than equipped to handle the truth.

If you're doing it for the right reasons and both parties are fully aware of the nature of the encounter, casual sex can be really good. If you're using it like an over-the-counter prescription to feel better about yourself, it will be a horribly unsatisfying experience.

The most exciting bit of a relationship is the first three months, when you don't yet know if that person is yours. A great bit that comes right after that is when you know that person is yours. The bit that comes a few years after that is something I've never experienced. Apparently it's not always exciting, but I've heard it's the best.

Unless someone dies, if a relationship goes wrong, you somehow had a part to play in it. How simultaneously freeing and overwhelming it is to know this. Men aren't bad, women aren't good. People are people and we all make, allow and enable mistakes.

Intimacy is the goal; laziness is not.

Let your friends abandon you for a relationship once. The good ones will always come back.

To lower your heart rate and drift off on nights when sleep feels impossible, dream of all the adventures that lie ahead of you and the distances you've travelled so far. Wrap your arms tightly round your body and, as you hold yourself, hold this one thought in your head: *I've got you.*

Acknowledgements

Thank you to my agent Clare Conville who shaped this book when it was just Post-its and pieces of stories and bits of ideas. I am so grateful to be represented by a friend whose kindness is as abundant as their skill.

Thank you to Juliet Annan who completely understood the book, and me, from our first meeting, whose instincts and insight have astounded me from start to finish. I couldn't have asked for more good humour, experience and guidance; I couldn't have dreamed up a better editor.

Thank you to Anna Steadman for her brilliant work on the book and her ongoing encouragement of my writing over the years.

Thank you to Poppy North, Rose Poole and Elke Desanghere at Penguin for their boundless energy, enthusiasm and collaboration. You are solid-gold members of the sisterhood.

Thank you to Marian Keyes and Elizabeth Day for reading the book early on and being so generous and big-hearted with their support for it.

Thank you to Sarah Dillistone, Will Macdonald and David Granger for taking a chance on a 22-year-old with a Billy Idol haircut and giving me a job that changed my life (I don't think I'll ever find one quite so fun).

Thanks to Richard Hurst for being the first person to

encourage me to write, for his steadfast support and advice and for introducing me to punk rock when I was sixteen.

Thank you to Ed Cripps and Jack Ford who make me want to be funnier, just so I can make them laugh.

Thank you to Jackie Annesley and Laura Atkinson for giving me my column in the *Sunday Times* Style, for editing and guiding me with patience and care, and for teaching me so much about how to tell a story.

Thank you to the spectacular women who have not only lived through all these stories of the last decade with me, but who have allowed me to share them. Particular thanks to Farly Kleiner, Lauren Bensted, AJ Smith, India Masters, Sarah Spencer Ashworth, Lacey Pond-Jones, Sabrina Bell, Sophie Wilkinson, Helen Nianias, Belle Dudley, Alex King-Lyles, Octavia Bright, Peach Everard, Millie Jones, Emma Percy, Laura Scott, Jess Blunden, Pandora Sykes, Hannah Mackay, Sarah Hicks, Noo Kirby and Jess Wyndham.

Thank you to the Kleiner family, for allowing me to write about and dedicate the book to Florence – whose humility, integrity and passion will forever embolden and inspire me with every word I write.

Thank you to my family – Mum, Dad and Ben – who have always told me that anything is possible. Who have always encouraged me to tell a story honestly, safe in the knowledge that I will never be judged by them. How exceptionally lucky I am to have you – I love you so very much.

And, finally, thank you to Farly, without whose unwavering cheering and championing I would not have written this book. You are – you always will be – my favourite love story.